MODERN GERMAN PHILOSOPHY

MODERN GERMAN PHILOSOPHY

Rüdiger Bubner

Translated by Eric Matthews

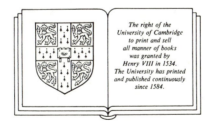

The right of the
University of Cambridge
to print and sell
all manner of books
was granted by
Henry VIII in 1534.
The University has printed
and published continuously
since 1584.

Cambridge University Press

CAMBRIDGE

NEW YORK   NEW ROCHELLE

MELBOURNE   SYDNEY

Published by the Press Syndicate of the University of Cambridge
The Pitt Building, Trumpington Street, Cambridge CB2 1RP
32 East 57th Street, New York, NY 10022, USA
10 Stamford Road, Oakleigh, Melbourne 3166, Australia

First published 1981
Reprinted 1984, 1988

Printed in the United States of America

Library of Congress catalog card number: 81-3901

British Library Cataloguing in Publication Data
Bubner, Rüdiger
Modern German philosophy.
1. Philosophy, German – 20th century
I. Title
193 B3180
ISBN 0 521 22908 1 hard covers
ISBN 0 521 29711 7 paperback

Contents

Translator's note

Except where otherwise indicated, all quotations from German-language works have been specially translated for the present volume. This is so even when other translations exist and are referred to in the text or footnotes.

The general aim of the translation has been to combine accuracy with as natural an English style as possible. In the case of quotations from, and discussions of, the work of Heidegger, however, this aim has proved impossible to achieve. Heidegger's thought is essentially untranslatable, and the more naturally an English version reads, the more misleading it is likely to be. Most of the key terms are explained by Professor Bubner in context, but it may be helpful to indicate here which German expressions correspond to the English words I have chosen. The word Dasein has been left in German, since there is no short English equivalent which would not be seriously misleading. The word *Sein* has been translated as 'Being', while *Seiende* has been rendered as 'a being'. *Existenz*, *existieren*, etc. have been translated as 'existence', 'exist', etc. I have chosen to translate *das Offenbare* and *Offenbarmachen* or *Offenbaren* as 'the manifest' and 'manifestation' respectively. The word *Sorge* has been translated as 'care'. 'Destiny' is the translation of *Geschick*, while *zuschicken* has been translated as 'to transmit'. Finally in this connexion it might be mentioned that, in the sections on Gadamer, the phrase 'the continuing influence of the past' is my paraphrase of Gadamer's word *Wirkungsgeschichte*.

I am extremely grateful to Professor Bubner for reading my translation and for making a number of very helpful criticisms and other comments.

Preface

John Stuart Mill makes the following remark in his *Autobiography* about the *System of Logic*: 'The German or a priori view of human knowledge . . . is likely for some time longer (though it may be hoped in a diminishing degree) to predominate among those who occupy themselves with such enquiries, both here and on the continent.' That was more than a hundred years ago. Since then, the dominance of German philosophy in the Anglo-Saxon world has long passed its peak, and Mill's hopes have been fulfilled to a far greater extent than he might have expected. There is much less familiarity, even of a fairly superficial kind, with philosophical developments on the continent than there used to be. It is common to come across ignorance combined with the old prejudice that German thinkers lose themselves in a priori speculation and prefer dark musings to clear statement.

The change just sketched began around the turn of the century and coincided with the renewal of British philosophy in this century. Bertrand Russell and G. E. Moore rejected once for all the metaphysical neo-Hegelianism of their teachers Bradley and McTaggart, in order to restore the ancestral traditions of empiricism to their rightful place. At the same time, two thinkers, Gottlob Frege and Ludwig Wittgenstein, who in their own country had suffered the fate of misunderstood prophets, were elevated to the rank of authorities in Britain and America. To be sure, this paradoxical situation has since changed; for, by a circuitous route through the analytic school, Frege and Wittgenstein, like the émigré members of the Vienna Circle up to and including Popper, have returned to the German-speaking world and are taken seriously as stimulants to the present debate.

In recent decades, philosophy in Germany has undergone an obvious and rapid transformation. The phenomenological school, dominant since the first half of the century and still active, with its offshoots in the philosophies of existence and in hermeneutics, has had to come to terms with the increased receptivity to philosophy from the Anglo-Saxon countries, which has also effectively revived the concern with theory of science, in abeyance since the twenties. In addition, there has been a revival of certain classical nineteenth-century theories, especially the dialectical philosophy of Hegel, together with that of his followers, the Young Hegelians and Marx. It is striking and philosophically suggestive that the various currents do not simply run alongside one another, so that continuity, receptivity and renaissance remain independent. Rather, there has developed out of the elements thus crudely described a climate of intense debate, full of the exchange of ideas and controversy. Contemporary German philosophy is therefore much less homogeneous than the Anglo-American scene; nevertheless, for all the diversity of positions and programmes, a clearly discernible connecting thread runs through it. To depict this scene is an appealing task, although not altogether an easy one. What is required is to characterize the ways in which everything is connected without ignoring the diversity. The different tendencies must be given their due, while a general view of the different currents should not be neglected. With this in mind, the title 'Modern philosophy' must be understood in a wide sense. Essentially, it refers to the phase of philosophy from the Second World War to the present, although from time to time there is also a reference back to the twenties and thirties. Since things are naturally in a state of flux, no claim can be made to historical objectivity or finality of judgment. Besides, in any strict sense, that is probably simply an ideal, to be striven for but never attained.

Anyway, it is obvious that no account of the present can be given with the detachment and calm of the historian concerned with distant and now completed epochs. To a certain extent the author's subjective viewpoint still prevails. He cannot leave out of account his own participation in current research and debate. The presentation will have to leave several judgments open, and occasionally theses will also be subject to rapid revision in the future. That may indeed even assist the liveliness of the general picture.

A methodological conclusion follows, however, from this special situation of an account of contemporary philosophy. The book will take the form of an essay, working through outline sketches, foreshortening and perspective. In the circumstances it would certainly be impossible to produce a work of minute analysis, encyclopaedic comprehensiveness and definitive validity. To be precise, there will be an Introduction, to give a general orientation, followed by a number of essays on the three main currents. The currents which I distinguish are: *phenomenology and hermeneutics*; *linguistic philosophy and theory of science*; and *dialectic and the philosophy of practice*.

Introduction:
On the historicity of philosophy

The fact that philosophical thought has a *history* should surprise us more than it does. At the end of a long philosophical tradition it seems so obvious that it is easy to overlook what a philosophical puzzle is involved in this simple statement. From a historical point of view there seems nothing out of the ordinary in it, for here philosophy is anyway looked on as part of the history of humanity. In this regard, it plays a more or less subsidiary part in the general picture of an epoch composed of many other historical facts, if it is not made totally dependent, by a radical critique of ideology, on the social and economic changes which proceed autonomously and support the superstructure of thought. For philosophy itself, however, its own historicity must retain an element of the scandalous. Does not philosophy have to do with truth, and is not historical relativity inconsistent with the whole idea of truth? Does not philosophy make a fundamental claim to rationality, and is not rationality, properly understood, necessarily always one and the same? Is there not a profound error contained in the notion of the historical development of reason, since at least that reason which allows us to articulate the very notion has a validity which transcends history? Or is all possible knowledge of the conditioned character of alleged expressions of reason in their historical context itself conditioned in its turn? Is there any way out of this regress? These questions deserve a moment's consideration.

The observation that philosophy is subject to historical change has always acted as a *challenge to thought* to put an end to this situation, so fatal because so harmful to reason. Let me explain this by some classical examples. The short survey of the history of philosophy by which Aristotle in his time introduced the themes of his *Metaphysics* does not imply merely that the correctness of his own formulation is confirmed by its agreement with others. It implies above all the proof of the inadequacy of previous philosophy. Where conceptions are still changing, the questions have not really been solved. Reason thus has a definite task to fulfil, one in which it can succeed only by relying on its own powers. It would have completely misconstrued its task if, instead of the rational understanding which is required, it were to fall back once more into historical relativity. Metaphysics derives from this its solemn character as conclusive truth which puts an end to all uncertainty.

With similar intentions, Kant's attempt to lay *new critical foundations* for philosophy arises from the scandal of unclarity in method and indeterminateness in outcome which are inappropriate to a science of reason. Metaphysics, for all its wealth of tradition, must allow itself to be assessed by its actual condition. It is for Kant a historical fact, though one which is profoundly inconsistent with the idea of reason, that on all important questions the argument goes to and fro and opinions change. Kant's programme of a definitive philosophy grounded on reason, which for all future time 'will be able to be regarded as a science', expresses the hope that an end can be made once and for all of the historical character of philosophy as the precarious sequence of alternating conceptions.

Even Hegel, who took the history of philosophy with more philosophical seriousness than his predecessors, started from the conviction that this act of historical reflection is necessary in order to bring about the final triumph of reason. He is indeed the *father of all history of philosophy* in the strict sense, since he does not simply collect together the superseded theories in a purely doxographic manner or misuse them as an opportunity for the polemical devaluation of predecessors and the justification of his own theses by comparison. In the intensive period of system-building after Kant he had made the discovery that new theories continually appear asserting their absoluteness and that allegedly conclusive solutions of all cosmic problems supersede one another all too quickly. For him, therefore, the clarification of the contradictory relationship between the undeniable Idea of reason, that philosophy is a unity, and the notoriously conditioned character of its historical manifestations is a primary philosophical problem. On its solution depends the possibility of a comprehensive system of the kind satisfied in a more than merely illusory way by the traditional expectation that philosophy could provide real and lastingly satisfactory answers. Once confidence in Hegel's project of a speculative system of knowledge of all-embracing validity had been lost, interest was confined to his reflections on the history of philosophy. Thus Hegel the founder of historicism was able to outlive Hegel the last of the systematizers.

If we pursue this line of thought just one step further, we shall see that the nineteenth century in fact capitulated before the philosophical paradox of the historicity of thought. It is useful for our undertaking to be aware of these nineteenth-century developments. Since they to some extent still shape the preconditions of contemporary thinking, a preliminary clarification may help to lead our steps in the right direction. After the stratospheric flights of German Idealism in the systems of Fichte, Schelling and Hegel, there began a process of evasion of the puzzle of historicity which took two main directions. In one direction there developed an awareness of the fruitful progress of the *positive sciences*. The slogan of the 'downfall of Idealism' came into vogue. Compared with the daily increasing and indubitable knowledge achieved by scientific enquiry, philosophical speculation seemed to be a forlorn hope. If it was not to break down completely, it had to take its bearings by this paradigm. In Germany at least this attitude was associated with the cry, 'Back to Kant!' The idea was to return to a solid philosophy, scientifically orientated and cured from the illusions of historicism. Even as early as 1831, a year which had a doubly symbolic value as the year of Hegel's death and as the fiftieth anniversary of the appearance of Kant's major work, the *Critique of Pure Reason*, a minor figure like Friedrich Eduard Beneke, for example, lamented the perversity of the post-Kantian visionaries, who had lost contact with the scientific approach and had thus initiated a peculiar development in Germany which contrasted with the sober, progressive thought of France or England.

Such notes were later to be sounded more generally. The neo-Kantian school, which dominated the academic world until well into the twentieth century, expressed the general philosophical credo in calling for the primary recognition of the 'fact of science'. From that time on, philosophy has claimed legitimacy for itself largely as the *theory of science*. In that respect, it has disregarded the problem of its own history. The certainty of a rationality superior to, and forever withdrawn from, historical change, such as appears to be embodied in the sciences, in their knowledge, methods and standards, has led to a disregard of the fact that even science is an institution with a history and cannot be withdrawn from the historical process. Only lately has the reminder that scientific knowledge has its own specific historicity shaken the positivistic edifice of dogma in the theory of science. Phenomenological hermeneutics and the historicist later phases of the Popperian school have together contributed to this recognition in contemporary philosophy.

The theory of science was one reaction to the collapse of the pretensions of systematic philosophy; alongside it, there developed in the course of the nineteenth century another method of evading the problem of the historicity of philosophy. Strangely enough, this was so-called '*historicism*'. At first sight, the name might seem to promise the opposite – a philosophy utterly taken up with the role of the historical. Jacob Burckhardt actually spoke of the special 'aptitude of the nineteenth century for historical studies', once the extravagant claims made for projects *à la* Hegel to reveal the purposive workings of reason in world history had been disproved by real developments. Nevertheless, historicism involves an element of immunization against the historically conditioned character of reason.

If everything is historical, then the specific shape given by time to one theory as against another is a matter of indifference. Since the point of departure is always the way in which all thought is conditioned by and rooted in its own age, this does not represent any further problem. In the 'imaginary museum' of the history of philosophy are collected all past doctrines, right up to those of our immediate contemporaries. They do not interfere with each other, but they also have no further relationship with one another. All of them, as historical phenomena, have an equal, relative claim. Thus their multiplicity does not in the end involve any inconsistency with the unity of reason. The problem of historicity is in this way given a sceptical solution. As a result of such levelling, however, all philosophical force is lost. Not for nothing did the outsider, Nietzsche, hold up a mirror to his age, explaining historicism as a lifeless sign of weakness, which was a plain indication of modern decadence in contrast to the philosophical originality of the 'unhistorical' Greeks.

Our reflections have arrived at the end of the nineteenth century. It is there, of course, that the general thesis of the historicity of philosophy comes to have a particularly close bearing on our theme. The *nineteenth century*, as the nearest past period, still exerts a subterranean influence on the philosophy of our own century, even up to the present day. I am not referring simply to such obvious matters as influences and the continuity of particular schools. I mean rather that the hardest thing of all is to look at what is immediately behind one. The most recent past has an unnoticed effect, precisely because it is regarded as being, in a particularly emphatic way, over and done with. When the separation is greater, everything seems more or less equally distant, whereas self-assurance about contemporary concerns requires one to seek to dismiss what came immediately before as something superseded and obsolete, without really getting free of it.

Thus, the feeling of the superiority of an uncluttered new beginning held total sway in philosophy in the first half of our century, until awareness slowly dawned of what was relative in its supposed originality. There can be no doubt that even the philosophy of the *present day* is indebted to the past in ways which are difficult to reckon and hardly to be paid off. I am certainly not claiming that contemporary thought should be seen as a mere reflection of traditional positions. There can be no question of that, since the vitality and spontaneity of philosophical thought is in principle inexhaustible. It would be equally mistaken to think that the present is in contact only with the immediate past. Philosophical knowledge is long-lived, and the fact of greater or lesser renaissances constantly makes it clear how much capacity for new life can lie, in certain respects, even in theories from the distant past. It is not just contemporaneity which guarantees actuality. It is easy to find philosophical positions in the contemporary world which are in truth much deader than many of those classical views which are regarded as obsolete. In every age of philosophy, therefore, a real effort is needed to get clear what it has to say that is new and genuine, and what represents rather a traditional truth in a different form, an old war on fronts which have moved elsewhere or the straightforward continuation of work already accomplished.

I fear these last remarks may in some ears sound pretentious or even trivial. All that I want to say is this: a meaningful account of *contemporary philosophy* must take note of the formal nature of temporal demarcation. Concentration on the contingent date at which a book is written or read has little value. In the calendar sense there is no present in philosophy. What counts as a relevant philosophical theme today and will continue intellectually to excite the living for some time more becomes clear only in the larger context. It is thus always related to the philosophical past. This relationship may be overt or concealed and may reach back a greater or lesser time. Nevertheless, to act as if philosophical questions fell from heaven would be consciously to close one's eyes to such relationships. *Our* questions cannot be described without further ado as *the* questions of philosophy or the only important questions which it is possible to raise. They should not be taken as lucky achievements of untroubled reason at the end of a turbulent history of philosophical blind alleys and pseudo-problems. The formulation and solution of philosophical problems can never be completely detached from historical circumstances and the force of tradition.

Of course, we must be convinced of the *importance* of a problem in itself if we are to make the effort of understanding it. What we regard as philosophically important, and what we do not, does not depend on its having a certain place in a historical context, but on our recognition of it as a problem. On the other hand, what at any given time we see as a problem and what we do not is by no means a matter for our free decision or something which is obvious to reason alone. Historical conditions lead to the selection and modification of problems, determining the form in which they are conceived and the modes of preference and evaluation. None of this is incompatible with philosophical reason, but equally it is not a direct consequence of its activity and so represents a limitation. The always present, and to that extent not immediately detectable, limitations on the activity of reason in the questions which occupy it (as compared with those which might occupy it) are an expression of the *historicity of philosophy*. This comes to light only concretely and so can be discussed only by means of concrete instances. The historicity of contemporary philosophy finds its expression in the shape of its problems. In the range of problems which are recognized as actual, contemporary philosophy defines itself as against tradition and at the same time puts itself into a relationship to it.

What is meant may be illustrated in a very fundamental way by the structure of a *problem*. By the harmless-sounding word 'problem', which adorns so many book titles and with which everyone is so familiar in the colloquial speech of everyday life, we mean something latently philosophical. In our understanding of the word 'problem', there is still present a last echo of what, in the naive terminology of antiquity, was called 'wonder' (*thaumazein*) and regarded as the beginning of philosophical reflection. Problems tend to emerge unexpectedly. One comes up against them especially where one does not anticipate them. They hinder one's progress along the path of habits which one takes for granted. The attitude of wonder in the face of problems corresponds to the reaction described by Wittgenstein in the words 'I do not know my way about.'

Since it is characteristic of problems in the real sense that they emerge unforeseen, all those tasks or difficulties to be dealt with which we customarily call 'problems', although we know full well when they emerge, what form they take and how they can be dealt with, ought not properly speaking to be called 'problems' at all. In such cases, one should speak rather of inducements to make use of long-available and well-tried knowledge. There are indeed methods, techniques and procedures which have been developed and are learned for disposing of such previously assessable 'problems', whether in everyday life or in the sciences. Fundamental problems, on the other hand, when first encountered, leave one at a loss. Problems which emerge suddenly and are genuinely difficult to solve really reveal, that is, how inadequate is the knowledge which has so far been at one's disposal and has in practice been capable of bearing the load. Where I can make no progress along any familiar path, where no expedient is of any help, because I simply do not know my way about, I make the *discovery that my knowledge is insufficient*.

Problems do not arise in a vacuum, but appear first against a certain background, which must be given. It is crucial to see that problems take on the character of problems only in comparison with what has so far been unproblematic. It is the possession of a little knowledge which first makes it possible to understand that not enough is known. The *presupposition* of a certain state of knowledge, the limitations of which are made visible by the emergence of a problem, constantly proves to be a *historical fact*. Where problems compel us to reflect on the deficiencies of our apparently satisfactory knowledge, the immediate given character of that knowledge returns. A further step has been taken. Problems stimulate the effort of thought about the state of knowledge at any given time, which in this regard already belongs to the past.

Knowledge which is recognized as limited is interpreted as in need of extension or improvement. In it there arises the direct challenge to go beyond it; for inadequacy of knowledge implies the *obligation to know more*. It is only in this way that problems may be overcome. The situation of perplexity which arises as a result of defective knowledge must be removed by a situation in which this troublesome deficiency has been eliminated, so that the knowledge presently at one's disposal becomes once more reliable. The *solution* of problems, therefore, presupposes reflection on their genesis. When one knows why one ran up against problems, one knows more precisely where the deficiency lay. By locating and delimiting the difficulties, one has not yet eliminated the deficiency, but one does already possess an essential guide in one's quest. While attention is concentrated on what is new, from a wider standpoint a continuity in knowledge is to be found running through the phase of the emergence of problems.

The knowledge already available as the background, the experience of breakdown in the face of emerging problems, the resulting awareness of the limitations of the knowledge already available, the quest for solutions along the lines of a complete elimination of the problems, either by making up the deficiencies in knowledge or by reinstating the original situation of adequate knowledge – the different stages of thought about problems can perhaps be analysed in this way. The historicity of philosophy is reflected in this model.

In what follows, I shall attempt to apply this model to the principal problems which presently engage the attention of philosophers who have a certain tradition in common. It is those problems which I understand best, because I share that tradition. Thus, contemporary German philosophy will be presented as a complex of problems around which the discussion has come to centre. This is the concrete form taken in our day by that connecting path between tradition and the open horizon, along which philosophical thought always moves.

1

Phenomenology and hermeneutics

Husserl's beginning

In many fields of intellectual life, of culture and of politics, the twentieth century began with an enthusiastic sense of new beginnings. The preceding age bore the stigma of weakness and decline. The desire was felt to get as far away from it as possible in order to return once more to the sources. This was no less true of philosophy than of the arts and social organization. The nineteenth century was felt to have been philosophically unfruitful. Once the classical period of philosophy in Germany was over, the field had been dominated by epigoni and original thought had largely been replaced by the vanity of professorial idols and scholastic academic disputes. Only a few outsiders such as Kierkegaard, Marx or Nietzsche pursued the quest for truth in the radical spirit which had always been the glory of philosophy, since it is only urgent and substantial questions which excite the world outside the class of professional scholars. To this must be added the embarrassment caused to philosophy by the advances of the special sciences and their success among the general public. Philosophy was faced increasingly with a crisis over its own legitimacy. What did pure thought still have specially to say? Have not most philosophical themes already become subjects for scientific enquiry and will not the same fate soon overtake the remainder? Scientific rigour and clarity of method surely deserve to be given preference in all judgments, so that philosophy seems to be a relic of prescientific thought and threatens to decline slowly to the position of a cultural reservation for the traditional educational élite. Between the expansion of science and *belles lettres* there seemed to be no room left for serious philosophical work.

It is necessary to bear this situation in mind if one is to understand the enthusiasm with which, around the turn of the century, the momentous phenomenological movement began: the influence of this movement can still be clearly traced right up to the present day. I shall therefore briefly outline the beginnings of the programme in Husserl and its further development by Heidegger, in order to elucidate the background to the current activity in phenomenology and hermeneutics. Essential features of phenomenological philosophy can be explained by the revolutionary situation of that time and have in the meantime been subjected to criticism. No one would wish to say that philosophy could continue unchanged along the path proposed by Husserl. The great movement of a new philosophical consciousness which he set in motion under the banner of phenomenology very early lost its unity of direction. Martin Heidegger, Husserl's most gifted disciple, who at first seemed to be the one to take up the torch, soon went along his own highly independent path. It was above all under the influence of Heidegger's objections that Husserl was led in old age to think of a revision of his original conception. Phenomenology has given rise in different countries to schools in which a variety of influences intersect. However, Husserl's initial impetus would seem nowadays to survive only in a few aspects, perhaps in that maxim which is well worth taking to heart, that philosophy should get away from all abstractions and constructions and return 'to the things themselves'.[1] Perhaps there are here and there even in disciplines such as sociology and psychology more faithful disciples of Husserl than in philosophy. How far phenomenological doctrine, in modified forms – in particular in the form of hermeneutics, is responsible for the contemporary philosophical debates will become evident only in the context of its development. Let us begin at the beginning!

It was to *Husserl* that the task fell of re-establishing the peculiar

---

[1] '. . . we can absolutely not rest content with "mere words", i.e. with a merely symbolic understanding of words . . . we must go back to the "things themselves". We desire to render self-evident in fully-fledged intuitions that what is here given in actually performed abstractions is what the word-meanings in our expression of the law really and truly stand for' (Husserl, *Logical Investigations*; from the translation by J. N. Findlay, London, 1970, Vol. I, p. 252).

claims of philosophy against scientific imperialism. To this end he had to demonstrate two things. First, it was necessary definitively to indicate the limits to the conquest of previously philosophical territory by the special empirical sciences. Secondly, philosophy had to be freed from the appearance of frivolity and arbitrariness – of being nothing more than a Weltanschauung – and must be proved to be at least the equal, if not the superior, of scientific rationality. The first step was taken by Husserl in his trail-blazing undertaking, the *Logical Investigations*, which appeared in three volumes from 1900 onwards and went through many further editions.[2] This first major work of Husserl probably also offers most points of contact with those interests which are distinctive of present-day philosophy,[3] although the terminology needs a certain amount of translation. Most importantly, language, which has come to occupy an absolutely central place in the philosophical development of our own time, played for Husserl a merely subordinate role in comparison with the primary analysis of the phenomena of consciousness.[4]

Husserl projected nothing less than a '*new foundation for pure logic and epistemology*', which, as the Foreword says, had to be defended against the aggressive psychologism of an empirical scientific explanation of intellectual operations (Prolegomena, Vol. i). Since psychology had long before begun to treat the activities of consciousness as objective facts, to be studied by the methods of scientific investigation, it was necessary to demonstrate the pure and a priori nature of logic and epistemology, which were still the foundations even of the sciences and their procedures. Scientific psychology could not explain what thinking is, since its activity depends on the formal principles and logical rules which determine all thought. At the same time, a similar intention inspired *Gottlob Frege*, who, incidentally, had subjected Husserl's early pre-phenomenological work, *The Philosophy of Arithmetic* (1891) to rigorous criticism on account of its residual psychologistic elements.[5] Frege too wanted to reserve the

---

[2] See above, n. 1, for details of translation.
[3] Cf. J. Mohanty, *Husserl's Theory of Meaning*, The Hague, 1962.
[4] See below, Ch. 2, 'Phenomenology and linguistic analysis' (pp. 92–7).
[5] *Zeitschrift für Philosophie und philosophische Kritik*, 103, 1894 (translated in *Mind*, 81, 1972). See also D. Føllesdal, *Frege und Husserl, Ein Beitrag zur Beleuchtung der Entstehung der phänomenologischen Philosophie*, Oslo,

logical sense of expressions for autonomous analysis and to resist the pretensions of psychology to competence. He even went so far, in a late work, as to postulate a quasi-Platonic 'third world' of thoughts, alongside the physical and mental worlds.[6] Frege and Husserl were interested in the purity of logic, this interest leading the one into semantics, the other into the phenomenological method. We shall observe further below, taking the contemporary example of Ernst Tugendhat's works,[7] how Husserl's logic and epistemology can be presented in a Fregean perspective.[8]

Husserl let the second step follow the first. The demonstration of a realm of objects which could not be surrendered to scientific enquiry made possible the *rehabilitation* of philosophy in the face of the standards of science. Philosophy is not unscientific or extra-scientific, but satisfies precisely the highest standards of knowledge. 'Philosophy as a rigorous science' – this was the militant-sounding title of a treatise of 1911.[9] The true realization of the programme was presented by Husserl in his *Ideas for a Pure Phenomenology and Phenomenological Philosophy* (Vol. I, 1913).[10] There it is stated right at the beginning: 'Pure Phenomenology, to which we are here seeking the way, whose unique position in regard to all other sciences we wish to make clear, and to set forth as the most fundamental region of philosophy, is an essentially new science, which in virtue of its own governing peculiarity lies far removed from our ordinary thinking, and has not until our own day therefore shown an impulse to develop. It calls itself a science of "phenomena".'

The claim seeks to fulfil an ancient hope of European phil-

1958; the few letters between Frege and Husserl have been translated in Gabriel et al. (eds.), *Frege, Philosophical and Mathematical Correspondence*, Oxford, 1980.

6 'Der Gedanke' (*Logische Untersuchungen* I), 1918 (translated in Geach (ed.), *Logical Investigations*, Oxford, 1977); see also K. Ajdukiewicz, 'Sprache und Sinn', *Erkenntnis*, 4, 1934 (translated in Ajdukiewicz, *The Scientific World-Perspective and other Essays*, Dordrecht, 1978).

7 *Vorlesungen zur Einführung in die sprachanalytische Philosophie*, Frankfurt, 1976; see also G. Ryle, 'Phenomenology and linguistic analysis', *Neue Hefte für Philosophie*, 1, 1971 (Göttingen).

8 Bar-Hillel had already sought to see Husserl as an unskilful precursor of Carnap ('Husserl's conception of a purely logical grammar', *Philosophy and Phenomenological Research*, 17, 1956).

9 Translated in Q. Lauer (ed.), *Phenomenology and the Crisis of Philosophy*, New York, 1965.

10 Translated by W. R. Boyce Gibson, London, 1931, p. 41.

osophy, which had never been entirely realized and now at last seemed on its way to being achieved. It extends from Descartes' *Meditations on First Philosophy* (*Meditationes de prima philosophia*) right up to Kant's reconstruction on the basis of a transcendental critique, Fichte's *Theory of Science* and all the other repeated attempts to establish a philosophical theory on solid foundations with a scientific status. Husserl clearly understood himself as belonging to this line.

Phenomenological method

What, however, is a 'science of phenomena'? In the argument with psychology Husserl starts with *conscious experiences*, which, to be sure, he does not treat like an object of science, that is, a real datum in the world which merely bears the special mark of the mental. Rather, it is all a matter of a peculiar concentration on phenomena. The concept of phenomenology is thus to be understood principally in the sense of a *method*. After all those presuppositions of existence which are regarded in the natural attitude of our consciousness as self-evident have been artificially excluded, the pure contents of what is present in consciousness are to be described. To refer to the methodological disregard of the interpretations of conscious experiences in our everyday life in the world, Husserl introduced two complicated terms, the relation of which to each other does not seem to be completely clear: the '*epoché*' recalls the sceptics' suspension of judgment and the '*reduction*' aims at the pure content of experiences, free of subjective modifications. But do not the disregard of all immediate presuppositions about the objective world and the withdrawal into subjective consciousness lead into a cul-de-sac?

The concentration on the pure content of what we discover in our consciousness through introspection is not empty, because from the outset consciousness is conceived of as consciousness *of something*. The elementary structure of consciousness is so constituted that there is no such thing as a consciousness without a content, of which the consciousness is a consciousness. Consciousness fundamentally refers beyond itself. Husserl makes use of a concept taken from scholastic philosophy, which was transmitted to him by his teacher Brentano: he calls the elementary structure of consciousness *intentionality*. The intentionality of consciousness, or its directedness on to something other than itself, is one of Husserl's most fruitful insights. It is not in any way a new notion, as the origin of its name in itself shows, but in fact it denotes an important part of all our experience. A theory of consciousness which concentrated on the pure inwardness of a reflective awareness of the ego would go astray, since it would disregard the specific nature of consciousness, which is not only to be an inner awareness but also to be filled with content. Husserl even spoke of 'transcendence in immanence', suggesting by that that a gaze directed on to consciousness, free from contingent assumptions and subjective intuitions, would not shrink into nothing, but would rather be related to contents of all kinds.

The projected dismissal of psychology is successful, if it makes sense to interpret phenomena no longer as the appearance of an object for a subject, but to prepare them methodically in such a way that they present themselves for analysis in a pure form. Our immediate conception of the world must therefore first be 'bracketed' – that is, we must in philosophical reflection disregard what as naive human beings we take as real. In no way does this act abrogate once for all the initial certainty of our dealings with the objective world, or construct a new world in the manner of a wrong-headed Idealism out of consciousness itself. In imitation of Platonic terminology, Husserl defines the task of philosophy rather as the path from *doxa* to *eidos*, from unfounded opinion to the essence of the matter. The phenomenological change of attitude is thus nothing more than a procedural device which is to reveal to us at a stroke 'the things themselves'.

The words 'to the things themselves' have done much to contribute to the persuasive power of phenomenology. At the end of an intricate methodical analysis, in which natural certainties have been systematically renounced, the whole substantial content is nevertheless to stand; an undiminished grasp on reality in its essential structure is the aim. Instead of having to deal with painstakingly demarcated processes of inner life or mental images, for which the real content has first to be found, one has to do with the full authenticity of things. The old and largely insoluble problems of modern epistemology, the interaction of subject and object and the justification of our conception of the external world as genuine knowledge, are eliminated. In view of the plausibility of the phenomenological procedure, they turn out to be chimeras and pseudo-problems. They are, that is, based on the artificial distinction of subject and object and cannot overcome this dualist ontology. Phenomenology on the other hand founds everything on *immediate evidence and intuition*. Once the initial step has been taken of rejecting, along with the Cartesian sceptic, the unexamined acceptance of what exists, what remains of consciousness is more than the fact of thinking itself. There remains a content that can be phenomenologically analysed. To this end, Husserl introduced the symptomatically extended formula, '*ego cogito: cogita*'. By itself, this act of philosophical self-reflection, in which all false dogmas are avoided, makes accessible the totality of what is real, without the questionable detour of a proof of the existence of God *à la* Descartes or a Transcendental Deduction *à la* Kant. If they are but seen correctly, the pure phenomena of consciousness already contain the essence of things.

Obviously, the argument depends entirely on equating the *purity* of the phenomena with real factual content. If one resolutely reduces the subjectively changing facets of the stream of consciousness to what is essential, one obtains direct access to all thinkable contents, both sensory and intellectual. That is, 'there is' nothing but what can be, in some way or other, a 'phenomenon'. Phenomenology operates, frankly, with a form of 'ontological commitment'. Over and above the possibility of being the particular something of which a consciousness happens to be the consciousness, entities cannot be further taken into account. Everything is a potential phenomenon, provided that is understood to refer to the intentional directedness on to some object and not the psychological occurrence. The step from psychological fact to phenomenological essence, however, is taken by means of the process of purification.

The *purity* of phenomena can be attained thanks to a method which Husserl calls, somewhat tautologically, 'ideation through variation'. *Ideation*, that is, the process of purification and elevation to the *eidos*, does not come about as a result of any mysterious faculty of intellectual intuition, but is founded on a basis of immediate perception. On the basis of experiences which have actually been had, further analogous experiences can be excogitated through free imagination, so that an extension beyond the contingent in the direction of a complete account of all aspects can be achieved. The phenomenological investigator is required, by relativizing the subjectively present view of a thing, to invent alternatives for as long as necessary until what is intended stands before his gaze in full 'self-givenness'. For example, the investigator must, as it were, go round in thought a table which is seen in such-and-such a position and in such-and-such lighting conditions, in order to perceive it completely in all its aspects.

This sounds innocuous, but it contains nevertheless one of the fundamental difficulties of phenomenology. Self-givenness can be demonstrated only by the fact that it would be superfluous to continue. The transition from satisfied imagination to the evidence of the thing is certainly hard to determine. The process of playing through further possibilities, unfettered by any particular impression, until the whole is constructed in imagination is certainly possible in most cases – indeed it constantly occurs, even in pre-philosophical activity. It is a constant feature of our perception that we anticipate a *Gestalt* in its fullness and spontaneously fill in the details. Yet who would say that in so doing we are immediately perceiving an *eidos*, a pure essence in the sense of something a priori? This doubt remains.

Perhaps it is a matter of a mere suggestion that it is thought possible to trust completely in intuition, especially where there is any question of the *universal*. For Husserl, there is, as far as the demand for intuitive evidence is concerned, no difference of principle between the concrete and the universal contents of the unified set of phenomena. Between the particular table here in front of me with its particularities of form, colour, state of preservation etc. and the 'table in itself' there is no unbridgeable chasm in the sense of the Platonic *chorismos*. That is rather the illusion of the old ontology. The phenomenological method is meant to show that the particular *hic et nunc* of the subjective concrete perception and the objective essence of a thing merely mark the extremes on a continuous scale of degrees of evidence.

Comparable problems, moreover, were later to face the champions of so-called 'phenomenalism', though in other respects they had little in common with the phenomenologists. There was a dispute within the positivist theory of science of the Vienna Circle over the question when and why it was possible to infer the existence of the corresponding object from the sum of sense-data. The fundamental ideal of the unity of science forbade any separation of the subjective appearance from the objective facts. The subject–object dualism to which he nevertheless adhered finally compelled Carnap to accept an 'isomorphism', for which no further foundation could be found, between the phenomenal language of the protocol sentences and the thing-language of physicalism.[11] Leaving aside the circumstance that this solution is formulated in terms of the logic of language, one can recognize the analogy with Husserl's problem of a justification for interpreting appearances as things.

Modern philosophy, of which phenomenology has all along understood itself to be the completion,[12] reaches its fulfilment in the attempt *to eliminate the fundamental problems of the philosophy of subjectivity by using its own resources.* Therein lies the result, but also the limit, of the Husserlian enterprise. Phenomenology hopes to avoid the traditional cleavage between subject and object and the connected separation of the empirical and transcendental egos, in so far as it thinks through the subjective philosophical approach to its conclusion with sufficient radicalism. This explains the link with Descartes' model of meditative reflection – a meditation in which reflection at no time abandons the level of the individual's concrete experience. Contact must be continuously maintained with real conscious experiences, such as psychology also deals with, in order that philosophy should not float in a gaseous realm of mere projections. A sophisticated methodological twist makes immediate self-consciousness into philosophical knowledge. The suspension of the natural belief in the world leads to the reduction to pure phenomena, while their purity guarantees the a priori essence. In this way Husserl takes over the encumbrances of all theories of truth as evidence. That is the main objection that must be made.

This conception stands and falls with the *immediacy of intuition.* Only if essences are as accessible to intuition as the appearances of things is a transition possible from phenomenon to *eidos* without discursive mediation. What is fully intuited is precisely the thing in its self-givenness and the completeness of the exhibition comes about on the basis of simple perception when the latter is de-

[11] *Der logische Aufbau der Welt* (1928) e.g. §§ 63ff., 175ff. (translated by R. George, Berkeley, 1969); 'Die physikalische Sprache als Universalsprache der Wissenschaft', *Erkenntnis*, 2, 1931 (translated in Max Black (ed.), *The Unity of Science*, London, 1934).
[12] E.g. Husserl, *Ideas*, Vol. I, § 62.

veloped through the free play of imagination (ideation through variation). The elementary dogma of intuition has typically bound Husserlian phenomenology to perception, whereas areas of experience such as language and action, which were to become relevant in the course of the later development of philosophy, were quite improperly neglected.

The foundation of the whole of phenomenology on the immediacy of intuition also makes it harder to understand Husserl's assertion that he is the true heir to Kantian *transcendental philosophy*. Certainly it is easy to see that the tension between sense-perception and understanding, which Kant took over from his predecessors and proceeded systematically to increase still further, has been modified. Kant's dictum that intuitions without concepts are blind, while concepts without intuitions are empty, comes fully into its own and is applied critically to its own author's theory of knowledge. The peculiar structure of a transcendental reflection, which consciously directs itself to the conditions of knowledge, is however hardly consistent with the simple programme of ideation through variation to the point at which essences become self-given.

Kant's transcendental turn fits in exactly with the assumption of an unknowable thing in itself, which is never itself given to us. It is only because a metaphysical knowledge of essences is denied to us that it is possible to discover the conditions of the possibility of that knowledge of appearances which remains to us. The structural determination of the necessary conditions of knowledge and the judgment that it is impossible to overcome them are for Kant systematically connected. The transcendental process of making the conditions of knowledge conscious is nothing but the admission of the limitations of our knowledge. In approaching the limits, we nevertheless remain on this side of them. Since Husserl's doctrine of essences is intended expressly to move beyond the old limits of epistemology, reflected in the distinctions between sense-experience and understanding, or sensibility and intuition, or immediacy and mediation, he cannot claim without qualification to be continuing the line of thought of transcendental philosophy.[13]

In truth, Husserl did not create a school as a transcendental

[13] On this point there is a detailed study by J. Kern, *Husserl und Kant*, The Hague, 1964.

philosopher, but won adherents with his initial confession of faith in a concrete method of philosophy. He is supposed to have said that one should not forget, in polishing one's knives, to use them for cutting – otherwise the blade will be ground away before one gets down to business. If one can trust such remarks, philosophy seems, in contrast to a notorious tradition, to be no longer content with its own words, definitions and constructions, but to come a good way towards meeting ordinary common sense. The concrete facts of real experience are the common ground on which everyday understanding and philosophical reflection are to meet one another. Every reader of Husserl knows, however, what an abstract categorial apparatus, what a clatter of terminology, what a pedantic mania for distinctions he encounters on every page, both of the works published in his lifetime and of the other works which have since become available.[14] The philosophy of the concrete is itself extremely abstract. This deep conflict between claims and their realization proved impossible for Husserl to resolve. The inheritance of phenomenology has thus consisted for a long time in a certain attitude to the business of philosophizing, not in the completion of Husserl's system.[15]

Heidegger's transformation of phenomenology

The profound lack of concreteness in Husserlian phenomenology became evident, at the latest, when *Heidegger* made his fresh start. It then became obvious what degree of concreteness phenomenology was capable of. The appearance of *Sein und Zeit* in 1927 attracted the attention of the entire philosophical world and also of a wide non-professional public. With Heidegger, the real moment for the appearance of a philosophy of existence had arrived. Of course, the fascination did not arise in a vacuum. Politically, the ferment was at work in the aftermath of the First World War and during the brief life of the Weimar Republic. Expectations of something new were great.

The humanities above all found themselves in a state of crisis. Expressionist literature had created an emphatically expressive language which made the cool precision of the academic style

---

[14] The works are published in the series *Husserliana*, The Hague, 1950–.

[15] See the collection of essays edited by Elliston and McCormick under the title *Husserl*, Notre Dame, 1977.

look merely tedious. The intellectual climate had been prepared through the Kierkegaard renaissance, the movement of renewal within Protestant theology (Barth, Bultmann) and the general boredom with the dominant philosophy of the neo-Kantian school. To be sure, there are also others who might be named as fathers of the philosophy of existence, most notably Karl Jaspers, whose continuing relations with Heidegger were always precarious[16] and whose noble stance in the thirties was distinctly different from Heidegger's short-lived but fatally mistaken attempt to create an alliance in educational policy with the powers-that-be. Nevertheless, Jaspers became more the writer of the educated middle class than a philosopher who, like Heidegger, determined the further development of thought.

Since this is not the place for a historical presentation of Heidegger, and since also it could not possibly be my purpose to evaluate all aspects of his work,[17] I shall confine myself to a single point, which certainly marks the special significance of Heidegger for contemporary philosophy. I shall concern myself solely with the *development of phenomenology into hermeneutics*, and even on that little more than a hint is possible.

Heidegger was scandalized by the abstractness and profound lack of concreteness of classical phenomenology. He was convinced that this weakness was connected with the lack of radicalism in the way in which the questions had been posed: the result was failure to overcome in a consequential manner certain long-naturalized prejudices of the philosophical tradition. Thus, Husserl clung firmly, and without real change, to the subject–object schema, even when, under the heading of the *epoché*, he cancelled the assumption of a real subject and a real object in order to retain intentionality, with its position between the two poles. With this artificial outcome of a cumbersome methodological contrivance the whole conception of phenomenology hung in the balance. It was without any basis or foundation. Heidegger's aim therefore was to 'found' phenomenological analysis. This impelled him

[16] Cf. his *Notizen zu M. Heidegger* (ed. Saner), Munich, 1978.
[17] One of the best works is that of O. Pöggeler: *Der Denkweg M. Heideggers*, Pfullingen, 1963; see also the collection of essays entitled *Heidegger and Modern Philosophy* (ed. M. Murray), New Haven, 1978. In the series of books on German philosophy to be published by Cambridge University Press, that of H. Schnädelbach in particular will discuss various aspects of Heidegger's philosophy.

towards the renewal of *ontology*, which was to take as its theme
the Being of the world which had been posited as 'doxic' in
Husserl's conception, as well as the Being of that which undertakes such positing. It is not enough to reduce Being merely to the
naive positings of a consciousness which has not yet been phenomenologically instructed. The meaning of Being must be
understood in a wider and more fundamental sense. Heidegger's
turn towards ontology, to be sure, also unquestionably has other
sources. Aristotle's exposition of the ontological problem[18] in the
medium of everyday language and at a level above the objectiva-
tions of the special sciences was probably one of his models.

In the debate with Husserl, at all events, Heidegger formulated
his question in the following way:

> What is the mode of Being of a being, in which 'world'
> constitutes itself? That is the central problem of *Being
> and Time* – that is, a fundamental ontology of Dasein. It
> is worth showing that the mode of Being of human
> Dasein is totally different from that of all other beings
> and that it contains precisely within itself, as that which
> it is, the possibility of the transcendental constitution.
> The transcendental constitution is a central possibility of
> the existence of the factual self. This, the concrete
> human being, is, as such, as a being, never a 'fact
> existing in the world', since the human being is never
> merely present, but exists.[19]

Heidegger's newly introduced concept of *existence* has nothing
to do with the traditional ontological enquiry into 'what there is',
but concerns the specifically human mode of existence (Dasein) in
its concrete and factual fulfilment. The existing Dasein is, however, to be understood as the ultimate source of the question of
Being in general, in so far as this question refers to the beings in
the world, the positive objects and states of affairs. It is in the
horizon of human Dasein that the existence of the other beings
becomes a problem. It is only because there is Dasein that the
question of Being arises. Heidegger defines Dasein as 'a being for

[18] *Metaphysics*, IV, 2.
[19] Remarks on Husserl's article on 'Phenomenology' for the *Encyclopaedia
Britannica*, in a letter from Heidegger dated 22.10.1927 (in *Husserliana*,
Vol. IX, The Hague, 1962, p. 601).

which in its Being this Being itself is at stake'.[20] The philosophical theme of ontology must therefore properly be founded on this fundamental basis, instead of being given an autonomous role as a traditional branch within the structure of theoretical philosophy. Although the ontological question is a completely general enquiry about Being, the definition of existence in Heidegger's sense contains from the outset yet another difference between the specific Being of the Dasein and the Being of those beings which the Dasein positively encounters. An echo of the subject–object relationship is still detectable. Heidegger, to be sure, would reply that the structure of existence indicates an absolute foundation in the things of the world and that here lies the common basis for the Being of Dasein and of the world. Dasein means Being-in-the-world and nothing more. The phenomenological concept of intentionality is thus deepened in an existentialist fashion.[21]

Heidegger explains the close relation of *Being and Time* to the thought of his teacher Husserl still in terms of the categories of *transcendental philosophy*. It was only later that it became completely clear to him that the project of transcendental philosophy is itself a relic of the past, which must be superseded if the doctrine of existence is thought through to its conclusion. Without wishing to underrate the difficulties of an acceptable definition of the 'transcendental', in Kant and in its various mutations in his successors,[22] one can nevertheless say that a transcendental philosophical reflection, in the sense of an enquiry into conditions of possibility (*quid juris*), operates with two considerations. One, the ground of whose possibility is sought, is given, and another,

---

[20] *Sein und Zeit* (1927), 8th edition, Tübingen, 1957, p. 12 (translated by J. Macquarrie and E. Robinson, *Being and Time*, New York/London, 1962).

[21] Particularly instructive in this connexion is the lecture which has since become available on 'Die Grundprobleme der Phänomenologie' ('The fundamental problems of phenomenology'), which Heidegger delivered at the end of his period of teaching at Marburg in 1927, the year in which *Sein und Zeit* appeared. Although Heidegger here presents himself more clearly than in his book as a loyal follower of the tradition of Husserl, the 'Introduction' in particular contains a radical reinterpretation of phenomenology in the direction of ontology. The lecture, which is published as part of the *Gesamtausgabe* (Frankfurt, 1975), can usefully be read as a sort of commentary on the problems discussed in *Sein und Zeit* (English translation by A. Hofstadter, *Basic Problems of Phenomenology*, forthcoming 1981).

[22] Cf. my study 'Kant, transcendental argument and the problem of deduction', *Review of Metaphysics*, 28, 1975.

which satisfactorily supplies this ground in the framework of a theory, is specified by philosophical reflection. This reflection itself introduces, in the form of an enquiry into the ground for the given starting-point, a separation between these two sides which belong together. It is the task of transcendental reflection to show how they belong together.

This two-pronged transcendental strategy, however, which in Kant is embodied in the separation of the empirical and transcendental egos is quite unsuitable for an analysis of Dasein, properly understood. Dasein as an existent and Dasein as transcendental ground of the constitution of the world are not two different things, but one and the same. Therefore, it would be to misunderstand the essential thesis to treat transcendental reflection as a level of philosophical theory over and above the concrete conduct of life. The methodological *mise en scène* of the phenomenological reflection appears, compared with the factual concreteness of the Dasein, as so much superfluous superstructure, with which a philosophy concerned to interpret the concrete bars all access to its real tasks. Phenomenology in Husserl's style is not concrete enough! It must be replaced by a *hermeneutics of the Dasein*, which follows the lines of the initial reconstruction of philosophy, but which achieves this goal not merely approximately but finally.

That, at all events, was Heidegger's view at the time he wrote *Being and Time*. The later, much-discussed 'turn' in his philosophy was the outcome of drawing the ultimate consequences from the insight that transcendental philosophy had failed to pose the problem in adequate terms. The misunderstanding of a separate reflection on the conditions of constitution of a world was reconsidered. It is not we, as philosophers, who should discuss the question of Being with Dasein; rather, the whole mode of reflection should be, so to speak, 'reversed' and Being itself should be made responsible for bringing itself to expression in Dasein. The result is a quasi-mythical form of 'reminiscence' of Being, which Heidegger's later philosophy makes intelligible in such an ambiguous and difficult style. However, we have not yet reached that point. For the moment, the transformation of the concept of phenomenology into that of hermeneutics of the Dasein must be explained in more detail. The important section 7 of *Being and Time* is instructive in this regard.

The transition to hermeneutics

> When we pose the important question of the meaning of
> Being, our enquiry is face to face with the fundamental
> question of philosophy in general. The way in which
> this question is to be considered is *phenomenologically*. In
> adopting this approach, this treatise does not subscribe
> either to a 'point of view' or to a 'tendency', since
> phenomenology is neither of these two things and can
> never become so as long as it understands itself. The
> expression 'phenomenology' refers primarily to a
> concept of method. It connotes, not the substantive
> What of the object of philosophical enquiry, but its
> How. The more genuinely a concept of method operates
> and the more comprehensively it determines the general
> character of a science as embodied in its principles, the
> more naturally is it rooted in dealings with the things
> themselves and the further is it removed from what we
> call a 'technical knack', of which there are many
> examples even in the theoretical disciplines. The title
> 'phenomenology' expresses a maxim which can thus be
> formulated as 'To the things themselves!'[23]

Heidegger then analyses the central term into the two compo-
nents 'phenomenon' and 'logos', so that he can practise on them
the kind of exhaustive, indeed violent, etymology which he is
also fond of in other cases. This practice of his has attracted a good
deal of criticism, and it has to be admitted that several of Heidegger's interpretations are largely the imposition of his own
thoughts on to expressions which are historically far removed
from them. In and for itself, such elucidation in terms of the
history of a concept is always useful when we are dealing with an
idiom as burdened by past theories and as much marked by dead
languages such as Latin and Greek as is that of philosophy.
Certainly, it should not, under the cloak of philological fidelity to
the archaic meanings of words, lead to projections which anticipate what is strictly speaking to be proved, so that historical
authors suddenly become the chief witnesses for assertions by the
interpreter which are still in need of justification.

---

[23] *Sein und Zeit*, pp. 27f.

As opposed to the generally accepted interpretation of the word 'phenomenon' as 'appearance', Heidegger finds an underlying meaning, the original significance of the Greek word *phainomenon*: that which shows forth itself in itself, or the manifest. 'Logos', on the other hand, means not merely 'judgment' but 'manifestation' (*deloun*)[24] or that which lets itself be seen. Logos is consequently the reaction which corresponds to the phenomenon: the manifestation of what shows itself forth. Thus understood, phenomenology as it were submits to the things themselves: that which seeks to show forth itself from itself is unveiled and brought to visibility. Whether the etymological derivation thus attempted is tenable may be disregarded. At all events, it prepares the ground for the elucidation which guides it from the outset.

> The methodological meaning of the phenomenological description is *interpretation*. The logos of the phenomenology of the Dasein has the character of *hermeneuein*, through which the understanding of Being appertaining to the Dasein itself is informed of the essential meaning of Being and the fundamental structures of its own Being. Phenomenology of the Dasein is *hermeneutics* in the original meaning of the word, according to which it denotes the business of interpretation.[25]

Thus hermeneutics recovers the 'philosophically primary' sense of an 'analytic of the existentiality of existence'. The meaning of hermeneutics which is familiar to philosophers, theologians or jurists, according to which it is the art of interpreting classical, sacred or legal texts, consequently seems derivative in relation to the primary sense.

In fact, Heidegger took up the name applied in antiquity to a canon of rules, which had led a marginal existence in those disciplines which dealt with texts, and modified it to suit his own purposes. An intermediary role in this was played by *Wilhelm Dilthey*, who had extended the ancient form of hermeneutics, which, as an '*ars interpretandi*' had occupied a somewhat indeterminate position between a technique and an art, making it into a

---

[24] E.g. Aristotle, *Metaphysics*, IV, 1003b24.
[25] *Sein und Zeit*, pp. 37ff.

methodology of the historical sciences of man.[26] Dilthey's contribution belongs to the dispute between the natural and human sciences which flared up in the course of the nineteenth century. At the root of the dispute was the recognition of the paradigm of the methodical pursuit of knowledge which had been defined, throughout the whole of the modern period, by the exact natural sciences. Once the Idealist systems, especially the Hegelian, had lost credibility, the philosophical theories of history, society and mind became aware of their deficiencies, and it became necessary to find a methodology which could pass muster. This had to take account of the peculiarities of cultural objects and nevertheless to be able to compete as a respectable procedure with the methods of the natural sciences. Dilthey sought help in this situation by reviving the half-forgotten notion of hermeneutics.

The interpretative treatment of texts was taken as a model for the *understanding* of historical reality as a whole.[27] The objective documents of the past, the vestiges, monuments, sources and works which reflect the life of a past historical period in solidified objects, were to be interpretatively revivified. Hermeneutic interpretation is thus an act in which we make living contact with a life which has become historical, and in which we who come later recognize ourselves. In understanding, the cycle of life, which redeems even the past from its solidification into a mere object, comes full circle. To overcome the objectifying relationship to history through active participation by the understanding subject seemed to Dilthey to be the ideal to be aimed for. In this point he saw the decisive difference between the interpretative sciences of historical and cultural life and the objectifying sciences of nature, though the former were not on that account any less 'scientific'. The celebrated distinction of 'explanation' and 'understanding' was here given its classical formulation.[28]

[26] *Die Entstehung der Hermeneutik* (1900), in Dilthey, *Gesammelte Schriften*, Vol. v, Göttingen, 1957 (partially translated in Connerton (ed.), *Critical Sociology*, Harmondsworth, 1976).

[27] See Dilthey, *Selected Writings* (ed. Rickman), Cambridge, 1976, Pts iii and iv.

[28] Cf. R. Makkreel, *Dilthey, Philosopher of the Human Studies*, Princeton, 1975, esp. Pts i and iii; also the interesting re-evaluation in G. H. von Wright, *Explanation and Understanding*, Ithaca, 1971. K. O. Apel, in *Die Erklären–Verstehen-Kontroverse in transzendentalpragmatischer Sicht*, Frankfurt, 1979, is in agreement with von Wright.

Dilthey's efforts to defend the human and cultural sciences made use of a vague concept of an all-embracing 'life', which was not further elucidated, since it was always in the background. From a systematic point of view, this corresponds to Hegel's theory of Spirit, although Dilthey took great pains to get away from Hegelian metaphysics in order to appeal throughout to the pragmatic reality of everyone's direct experience.[29] Collingwood was later to defend a very similar emphasis on the role of history for philosophical knowledge.[30] As far as Dilthey is concerned, he took it for granted that Hegel's philosophy of history served the ends of a metaphysic which had been completely superseded. The reality of history had to be taken out of the dimension of speculative Idealism and made a matter of the concrete understanding of each actual individual. 'Life' seemed to be the right word for a history which was not opposed to scientific enquiry. Nevertheless, even Dilthey's all-embracing and generally accessible concept of life remains rather vague.

Heidegger clearly saw the ambivalence of Dilthey's conception and his total reinterpretation of hermeneutics was implicitly a polemic against it. Hermeneutics is neither an obsolete canon of rules, nor a method alongside others. On the contrary, it turns out to be an original attitude towards the peculiar structure of the Dasein. From this offspring of whatever we call truth[31] all methodical training to acquire knowledge is derived. The essential character of human existence – to constitute a world and to understand Being – forces philosophy directly towards hermeneutics. Interpretation, as the form in which Dasein is fulfilled, finds its authentic counterpart in a rightly understood 'phenomenology', that is, in the making manifest of that which shows

---

[29] In his important essay on the 'Construction of the historical world in the human sciences', Dilthey notes, à propos his debate with Hegel, 'In that the place of Hegel's universal Reason is taken by life in its totality, experience, understanding, the historical continuity of life, the power of the irrational in it, there arises the problem of how a science of history is possible. For Hegel, the problem did not exist' (Gesammelte Schriften, Vol. VII, Göttingen, 1958², p. 151).

[30] R. G. Collingwood, An Autobiography (1939), chs. 7–10 (new edition, Oxford, 1978, with a Foreword by Stephen Toulmin).

[31] See the penetrating study Der Wahrheitsbegriff bei Husserl und Heidegger by E. Tugendhat, Berlin, 1967.

itself in itself. In this way phenomenology for the first time comes really to do justice to its theme and leaves behind all invented philosophical constructions. That characterizes Heidegger's position.

In exceedingly minute and detailed analyses, which initiated the philosophy of existence, *Being and Time* defends the thesis that everything turns on the hermeneutics of existence. Heidegger deploys all his creative skill with language in order to arrive at new insights in opposition to the clichés of technical terminology and the pallid jargon of everyday language. His idiosyncratic style has been the chief obstacle to the understanding of Heidegger in other countries. His extremely unusual neologisms have certainly been compared, not unjustly, with the ruthless use of language by Aristotle, whose vigorous coinages, such as *to ti ēn einai*, must also have had a harsh resonance in the sensitive ears of the Athenians.

Thus Heidegger calls the fundamental condition of Dasein which he seeks to elaborate '*Being-in-the-world*' and means by that a life-relationship to the concrete environment at any given time which is underivative and is prior to all distinctions of subject and object. Being-in-the-world is the manner in which Dasein actualizes itself. It holds out before itself the horizon of an already projected world which makes possible simple dealings with things. Everything which we encounter appears in a context of meaning, in which it possesses relevance for our action and is unproblematically accessible. Since the world-project is a mode in which Dasein actualizes itself, and the Being of the Dasein is at stake in its existence, the fulfilment of Dasein is characterized by 'care'.

The use of this expression emphasizes that Dasein anticipatorily dwells on the world of things and facts which are relevant for it. The world-project therefore always reaches forward, that is, it happens in the dimension of time which is open to the future. In existing, the human being is governed by what lies ahead in the open space of his Dasein-possibility, and is at the same time fettered by the past in the sense of the contingent conditions of his factual existence at any given time. Temporal duration belongs to the original essential characteristics of existence. In the last analysis, the temporally existing Dasein is to be treated as historical. The ground was prepared for these analyses of the fundamental structure of existence by the essentially systematic interests of Heidegger's philosophy, which aimed to combine the ancient *ontological enquiry into Being with a theory of time.*

I shall first pause to consider this allusion to systematic goals. Future historians of philosophy will certainly measure Heidegger's position in relation to European thought by this original connexion between ontology and the philosophy of history.[32] The *Collected Works* which have been appearing for some years[33] will help to elevate Heidegger definitely to the Pantheon. The study of Heidegger's philosophy – its early phase as a philosophy of existence and a transcendental philosophy, its later expressions, and the unity of the two – kept the German academic world productively occupied in the forties and fifties. Not only did the philosophers produce some shrewd and not-so-shrewd interpretations and, unfortunately, a number of second-hand imitations, but there was also a fashion for adaptations in several neighbouring disciplines. The need felt in the period after the Second World War for a secure return to the great masters did give Heidegger the status of a central figure. In the Latin countries, Heidegger's popularity continued still longer,[34] whereas Anglo-Saxon philosophy remained resistant to the 'Teutonism' of the existential message.[35]

In the sixties, the vacuity of the mindless cult of Heidegger became intolerable: the Marxist-inspired critique of ideology in particular gave the idol's statue a vigorous shaking.[36] To be fair, it should be added that no philosopher can be made answerable for the defects of his followers. Moreover, every school tends to stagnate – this is true of Marxism and also of analytic philosophy. Since Heidegger is not really our theme, perhaps we may be permitted a leap at this point. It will take us to the point at which

[32] Cf. W. Marx, *Heidegger und die Tradition*, Stuttgart, 1961 (English translation by Kisiel and Greene, Evanston, 1971).

[33] Frankfurt, 1975– .

[34] It may even be surmised that the structuralist school which has been dominant since the sixties represents, at least in France, a reaction against the long post-war prevalence of existentialism. Seen from this point of view, Althusser is indirectly replying to Sartre!

[35] Cf. the early review of *Being and Time* by Gilbert Ryle (*Mind*, 38, 1929), with its mixture of understanding and distaste.

[36] Specially influential was Adorno's *Jargon der Eigentlichkeit, zur deutschen Ideologie*, Frankfurt, 1964 (translated by K. Tarnow and F. Will, *Jargon of Authenticity*, London, 1973).

Heidegger's criticisms of Husserlian phenomenology received a new and pertinent answer.

Crisis and life-world

The document is the great treatise *The Crisis of European Sciences and Transcendental Phenomenology*, on which *Husserl* worked unremittingly in the last years of his life up to his death in 1938. Because of political difficulties, only parts of it could appear abroad, so that it was the definitive edition,[37] published as part of the collected works in 1954, which first emphatically corrected the received interpretation of phenomenology. Since then the debate among interpreters has concerned the question whether Husserl's later work indicates a deviation from his own beginnings or the last presentation, secured against all misunderstandings, of his unchanging authentic intentions. This seems to me to be merely a question for the orthodox, and of secondary importance, whereas it is impossible to overlook the fact that in this last treatise Husserl really gave his reply to his pupil and challenger Heidegger.[38]

The theme of a *crisis of modern science* embodies a widespread concern of a current of contemporary thought which has grown sceptical of the positivist optimism about progress. Philosophy must unlearn its blind confidence in this model by which it was once so dazzled. Husserl noted as early as 1935, remembering his own early optimistic slogans: 'Philosophy as science, as serious, rigorous, indeed apodictically rigorous science, is a dream from which we have now awoken.'[39] Ethical demands must instead be made on the sciences, which have resolutely distanced themselves from the life and interests of human beings. The connexion of scientific activity with the prior pragmatic sphere of life must be consciously established. A comprehensive first section of the treatise is taken up with studies in the history of science, on Galileo, Descartes, rationalism and empiricism. The aim of this

[37] *Husserliana*, Vol. VI, The Hague, 1954 (English translation, Evanston, 1970).

[38] E.g. the notes on *The Crisis of European Sciences* (Husserliana, Vol. VI); cf. also the retrospective essay by H. G. Gadamer, 'Die phänomenologische Bewegung', *Philosophische Rundschau*, 11, 1963 (translated in *Philosophical Hermeneutics* (ed. Linge), Berkeley, 1976).

[39] *Crisis of European Sciences* (Husserliana, Vol. VI), p. 508.

reminder of the historical development of the modern ideal of science is to elucidate its origins and deformation in the course of history.

All these problems are thoroughly discussed by Husserl, but this is not where his originality lies. He shares this view with many of the cultural critics of the inter-war period. When he develops the concept of the 'life-world' as the real foundation of science, he does not appeal merely to these historical observations. He replies to Heidegger's hermeneutics of the Dasein, in order to show that what is there analysed can be perfectly well fitted into the framework of phenomenology – that indeed that is where, rightly understood, it properly belongs. The extension of transcendental phenomenology into the area of the life-world thus establishes a continuity in Husserl's philosophy in face of the existentialist attacks.

Husserl's main insight is expressed in the following thesis: the _life-world_ is the forgotten foundation of meaning for science.[40] In the concept of a 'life-world', Husserl found a readily understandable term for those everyday constituents of reality which everyone has confidence in, and with which we are already dealing before we pursue theories or even engage in philosophical reflection. The life-world embraces all those orientations which have come to be taken for granted and have been practised from an early stage. In our practical life, both of the simplest and the most complex kind, we move in a world which is familiar through custom, marked by situations, interpreted in the light of interests and experienced in active contact. Philosophical theories have always disregarded or glossed over this sphere in which we are unproblematically and totally at home. The realm of the most everyday things was not a theme which seemed worthy of serious reflection. What more was there to be discovered here, where everything was familiar to the point of boredom and had been worn by now into a routine of behaviour?

In fact, Husserl's interest in the life-world too was not for its own sake. Sociologists and psychologists may see a field for research in it. Philosophy is much more concerned with the fact that the sciences which consciously mark themselves off from the homely knowledge of everyday life in order to achieve a

40 Ibid., pp. 48ff. (§ 9, h).

more precise and complete cognition of reality nevertheless rest on foundations in the life-world. Without a prior orientation in the life-world no science would be possible. The *antithesis* which the general opinion has long believed to exist between life and science is merely apparent. Science does not emerge from nothing; it owes its more exacting standards of knowledge to no higher inspiration of reason and it does not deal with a second reality alongside that in which we have long felt confidence. The specific activity of science is rooted in the life-world, since without the knowledge there available from our dealings with reality the specialization and methodological perfection of knowledge could not even arise.

The American *pragmatists*, of whom Husserl obviously hardly knew,[41] had already long before referred to the connexion between enquiry and practical needs. Enquiry is to be understood, in the title of one of Dewey's books, as 'The Quest for Certainty'. The exigencies of the provision for life and of an uninterrupted flow of activity necessitate a precision and certainty which are not afforded by common experience. Where problems emerge which obstruct our progress, where there are doubts which cannot be set at rest, but which interfere with the practically necessary confidence in the course of events, there first arises something like scientific enquiry. The autonomous and highly complex institution which science has now become in economically and technically advanced societies ought not to deceive itself about these origins. Through reflection on the practical origins of science, the pragmatists, as is well known, obtained a corrective against a theory of knowledge which had been carried away into speculative heights. At the same time, there developed from this the pedagogic ideal that learning should be closely bound up with concrete practical effects.

Husserl's philosophical enquiries proceeded, to be sure, in a different direction. He saw in the process of the increasing autonomy of science a historical development which, with a certain inner necessity, allowed the foundation of meaning in the life-world to fall into *neglect*, until the European sciences, at first so triumphal in their advance, fell into a crisis which urgently required philosophical clarification. Fully developed science has

---

[41] With the possible exception of William James' *Principles of Psychology*.

paid the price for the suppression of the prior life-world. This connected set of problems, which gradually unfolds historically, makes a fresh effort of reason necessary, of a kind which phenomenological reflection alone seems competent to make. Whereas the lessons of pragmatism are essentially meant to tie theory down to practice, Husserl's doctrine of the life-world ultimately serves the purpose of a pure philosophical theory which, because of its comprehensive foundation, also includes even the forgotten aspect of practice.[42]

From the point of view of method,[43] Husserl proceeds by taking as his starting-point the observation of crisis, expressed both in the great debate over the foundations of physics and mathematics around the beginning of the twentieth century and in the evident 'loss of human significance' of science. The crisis first made us aware on what unquestioned 'presuppositions' the validity of science rests. The presuppositions which characterize the scientific world-picture first came to be understood in the historical retrospect which disclosed the genesis of the ideal of a mathematicized science in the modern world. The disclosure of these dogmatic presuppositions in the course of historical examination made it possible to see the universal life-world as originally given.

It represents the ultimate framework[44] on the basis of which it is possible to explain what constitutes science. This immediately makes it possible to interpret the interest in enquiry which specializes in pure theory as a particular form of practical conduct. Thus it is the life-world which produces that confidence with straightforward techniques and procedures which, as in the case of induction for example, are simply exploited and improved by developed science. Above all, however, the life-world brings about an initial acquaintance with objects, given in concrete intuition, which are made by enquiry, by means of mathematical idealization, into objects for exact investigation.

Experience in the life-world thus corresponds to Husserl's old

---

[42] To this extent Jürgen Habermas was right, in his inaugural lecture at Frankfurt in 1965, to describe Husserl's analysis of the life-world as connected with the traditional ideal of '*theoria*' ('Erkenntnis und Interesse', translated in the Appendix to *Knowledge and Human Interests* (2nd edition), London, 1978).

[43] *Crisis of European Sciences*, cf. esp. §§ 9, 1; 15.

[44] Ibid., e.g., §§ 28; 34, d, e, f.

conviction of the priority of intuition as the source of immediate self-evidence; but he no longer directly constructs on that particular basis a pure theory with claims to strictly scientific status. Like Heidegger, he thinks in terms of a historically developing alternation between disclosure and concealment;[45] the fact that objectifying science derives from the original openness of the world means at the same time that these origins are inevitably disguised. The more the sciences come to occupy the foreground, the more inevitable it is that their origins in the life-world, without which they would not exist, should come to be forgotten.

Unsolved problems

Heidegger's philosophy sought to respond to the alternation which he recognized between disclosure of the world and concealment of its ground (which in his language corresponds to the 'ontological difference' of Being and beings) by adopting the strategy of 'ad-vertence'. If a pre-objective context of meaning is necessary in order for beings to encounter us, then the whole situation, beginning with the primary origination of meaning, must be brought to reflection. Otherwise, this presupposition would be unduly neglected in favour of the apparently unproblematic presence of the objects in the light of scientific methods. Husserl does not follow this route into ontology. He holds fast to the model of *transcendental philosophy*. This leads him, however, into considerable difficulties, of which the largely uncritical secondary literature on Husserl's later thought has hardly taken sufficient account.

Husserl writes:

> I use the word 'transcendental' in a very broad sense for the original motif which, through Descartes, is the source of meaning in all modern philosophies and which seeks, so to speak, to come to itself in all of them and to achieve the genuine and pure form of problems and systematic operation. It is the motif of enquiry into the ultimate source of all cognitive formations – of the

---

[45] On the characteristically vague conception of history which developed in the later work of Husserl and which contrasts with the initial intentions of methodical phenomenology, cf. P. Ricoeur, 'Husserl et le sens de l'histoire', *Revue de Métaphysique et de Morale*, 54, 1949.

self-reflection of the knower on himself and his cognitive life, in which all the scientific structures which hold good for him come into being in a purposeful way, are preserved as acquisitions and have been and are freely at his disposal.[46]

The radical meditative reflection of the concrete ego, in accordance with Descartes' model, is supposed to lead to the knower and equally to his cognitive life as the source of all sciences and their results. The connexion of subject and object remains unclear. Certainly the ego can be appealed to only as a living ego. But its 'cognitive life', that is, its activity as a knowing subject, coincides with that as little as do all the contents and structures which are the objects of its scientific knowledge. There is equally little coincidence between the activity of knowing and naive conduct within the familiar life-world. It is the intimate connexion between the concrete ego and its life-world that is at stake here.

Obviously, Husserl's concern is to abolish the traditional dualism of subject and world (in Cartesian terminology, *res cogitans* and *res extensa*) and at the same time to reconcile the corresponding difference of the transcendental and empirical egos. On this point, the claims of transcendental philosophy must logically run aground. The identity of the reflecting ego and of the theme of that reflection is a fundamental condition of all transcendental arguments, from Descartes' *'ego cogito me cogitare'* to Kant's 'The "I think" must be able to accompany all my representations.' In that transcendental reflection refers to itself, it does not at the same time refer also without distinction to the relations to the world of the knower and the one who naively lives in the world. It must therefore first be shown in a general way, by definite step-by-step argument, why reference back to self-consciousness expresses something about its relation to the external world. The kind of simple meditation in which a concrete consciousness retreats into itself in the way that the Cartesian *ego cogito* does is, taken by itself, of no value at all for this task.

Quite different arguments are necessary, based precisely on the self-reflexive character of consciousness, but of such a kind that they can lead outside pure *inwardness*. To this end, Descartes

[46] *Crisis of European Sciences,* § 26.

employed an argument for the existence of God, which in virtue of the presence of the idea of God in consciousness rebuilt the bridge to the external world by means of that metaphysical entity whose absolute idea necessarily includes existence and excludes deception. Kant appealed, for the same purpose, to the controversial procedure of the Deduction from a supreme principle of synthesis, in order to establish the legitimacy of the relation of the subject, who knows himself, to the world of objects which he also knows. Husserl's hope of avoiding these ancient and troublesome complications by calling traditional solutions misunderstandings and replacing them with ingenious simplifications did not lead to the desired result. Husserl over-simplifies the problem of transcendental philosophy, in so far as the connexion within the life-world of subject and object remains groundless.

In a certain respect, moreover, Husserl clearly has to face this problem, in that he allows the life-world to be constituted *anonymously*.[47] The life-world is in an essentially indeterminate way an intersubjective phenomenon. It supports the practice of all of us and is everyone's horizon of understanding; for it is collectively constituted by groups and societies at different times. In it are preserved the influences of tradition and past generations, which naturally cannot any longer be referred to clearly defined subjects. The absolutely comprehensive validity of the life-world makes it necessary that the work of constituting it should be anonymous. Anyone may enter the framework of the life-world, since no one has exclusively created it. The character of subjectivity of the community which sustains the life-world must thus remain indeterminate.

To attribute responsibility to an ego, an ego-group or a society or race which has formed a conscious identity would destroy the underivative and original character of the life-world. There would then be, before the life-world in which we find ourselves, a still more original principle to which the life-world could be reduced. Husserl, indeed, tends to postulate this towards the end of his treatise, but gets entangled in insoluble paradoxes. The anonymity of the life-world cannot be achieved if one has in view an ultimate point of collective subjectivity. The act of transcendental reflection comes up against it, but strictly in a void. Since

---

[47] Ibid., §§ 49, 54.

one cannot say who constituted the life-world, one cannot single
out who is transcendentally reflecting it.

Another problem which belongs to the unclarified remnants of
the old phenomenological conception may, however, be more
easily elucidated. A special puzzle[48] was formerly presented by the
step from the naive attitude of natural life in the assumptions of
doxa to the phenomenological *epoché*, which inhibits all positing
of meaning, and to the reduction, which regards what is intentionally meant purely in terms of its eidetic content. The naive life
in the world has no motive for phenomenological reflection.
The latter itself however, once entered upon, cannot retrospectively give meaningful reasons why it has been entered upon,
since for that it would have to suspend itself again. What then
supplies the *impetus* to raise the phenomenological question? In
fact, Husserl knew of no answer to the question why and how one
comes into philosophy. Anyway, the practice of referring constantly to models from Descartes to Kant exists only among
professional philosophers. Phenomenology, however, which is
fond of emphasizing the concrete rooting of its activity in practical life, ought not to appeal to the Schools.

Heidegger was well aware of the problem and sought a motive
for reflection prior to all reflection on the basis of *existential
experiences*. He had in mind the anticipation of death achieved in
rare and deeply felt moments in life – death as the total and
irreversible falling-away of the world in which one has unconsciously lived. The existential confrontation with the 'nothing'
abruptly brings the world as a whole and as such to consciousness. The Dasein is dramatically wrenched from the worn
mechanisms of everyday life, to which the world and things seem
entirely a matter of course, and brought to the understanding
of his existence. Kierkegaard's theology of individuality was
evidently the midwife for this unusual form of philosophical
protreptics. The solemnity of the encounter with the nothing,
which found confirmation in real historical catastrophes, was not
the least contribution to the attraction of existentialism beyond
the narrow circle of philosophers. In this way for a time a wider

---

[48] This had already been noticed by Husserl's pupil E. Fink in a defence
of his teacher ('Die phänomenologische Philosophie E. Husserls in der
gegenwärtigen Kritik', *Kant-Studien*, 38, 1933, esp. pp. 346ff.; now in
Fink, *Phänomenologische Studien*, The Hague, 1966).

public was reached by means of the literature and drama of the post-war era (Camus, Sartre, Beckett). But what does phenomenology have to offer instead?

The later Husserl's reply to the question about the motive for philosophical reflection is, by contrast, not at all existential but rather *historical*. The historical experience of the crisis of science produces the connexion, which at first remained open, between a pre-philosophical naivety and the entry of philosophical methods in the sense of phenomenology. On the one hand, the certainty of the original life-world no longer remains untouched by the crisis of science. The loss of meaning and the lack of direction of the scientific enterprise, on the other hand, inevitably call to mind the forgotten foundations in the life-world. The historical process encourages philosophical reflection. The later Husserl's answer to the question, how and why human beings in the contemporary world come to philosophize, was subsequently taken up by Gadamer's hermeneutics.

Consequences in social science and logic

The fruitfulness of the concept of a life-world for other disciplines is very plain. The methodology of the *social sciences* has particularly benefited from it. At this point we should mention the name of an outsider, who was at first at odds with the professional sociologists, but has promoted the application of Husserl's phenomenology in the investigation of social phenomena with increasing success up to the present day. The credit is due to *Alfred Schütz*, who, in addition to carrying on his profession as a banker in Vienna, familiarized himself in a more or less self-taught way with the phenomenological mode of thought and first attracted attention in 1932 with his book *Der sinnhafte Aufbau der sozialen Welt, Eine Einleitung in die verstehende Soziologie*. Although at that time Husserl's *Crisis* had not yet been published, Schütz, with great sympathetic imagination, showed that phenomenological methods were applicable to the social field. He was later able without transition to operate with the mature Husserl's concept of the life-world.[49] Because of the amazing continuity of Schütz' thought, it seems permissible to concentrate our gaze exclusively

---

[49] *Collected Papers*, Vols. I–III, The Hague, 1962–6; A. Schütz and T. Luckmann, *Strukturen der Lebenswelt*, Frankfurt, 1975.

on the earlier book, especially since its influence began to be fully felt only after the war.

The title of Schütz' first work is obviously formulated in reaction to Carnap's *Der logische Aufbau der Welt*, which was considered as the principal work of the positivism of the Vienna Circle and showed an exaggerated emphasis on the natural sciences. The conception of the problem, however, originated from *Max Weber's* project of an interpretative sociology[50] whose problematical foundation in a category of 'action' Schütz hoped to improve by using phenomenological methods. In the years of his emigration in America, Schütz began a debate with Talcott Parsons, another disciple of Weber, who had further developed Weber's approach in the direction of the functionalist systems-theory and so had become the founder of a school of sociologists which was dominant for a long time. The occasion was a review of Parsons' first pioneering work *The Structure of Social Action* (1937) by Schütz, who objected to the positivistic elements in it. The voluminous correspondence which followed is a document of mutual misunderstanding.[51]

Only towards the end of his life did Schütz' influence grow, thanks to his activity as a teacher at the New School for Social Research in New York, from which his disciples spread the new message of a phenomenologically enriched social science.[52] Under the monstrous title of 'Ethnomethodology',[53] Schütz' influence had in the meantime returned to the Continent.

Schütz bases himself primarily on Weber's classical definition of action as behaviour 'when and to the extent that the agent or agents see it as *subjectively meaningful*'. It is with this that Weber begins the 'Doctrine of Sociological Categories' which at the start of his great work *Economy and Society* lays down the most general conceptual classifications under which a science of the social stands. Sociology needs a methodological framework in which

[50] Cf. the translation of relevant writings of Weber, *Methodology of the Social Sciences*, Glencoe, 1949; more recently, W. G. Runciman (ed.), *Weber, Selections in Translation*, Cambridge, 1978.

[51] *The Schütz–Parsons Correspondence* (ed. R. Grathoff), Evanston, n.d. (German translation by W. Sprondel, Frankfurt, 1977).

[52] P. Berger and T. Luckmann, *The Social Construction of Knowledge, A Treatise in the Sociology of Knowledge*, New York, 1966; T. Luckmann (ed.), *Phenomenology and Sociology*, New York, 1978.

[53] Cf. H. Garfinkel, *Studies in Ethnomethodology*, New York, 1967.

are set out its objects and procedures. Since the science has to do with social reality, and this specific reality is constructed out of actions, theoretical knowledge must be adjusted to this specific state of affairs. If actions are seen as subjectively meaningful, it is important to understand the meaning in order to give a scientific explanation of the action. In this way sociology is established as an 'interpretative' science. Weber owes both the concept of meaning and that of understanding to the neo-Kantian controversy between natural and cultural sciences. In a widely influential book, Heinrich Rickert had drawn the 'limits of concept-formation in natural science'[54] precisely at the point where individual events are not subsumed under general laws but grasped in their unmistakable individuality and particularity. Rickert called this the understanding of meaning and Weber followed him in a not entirely precise manner.

One must see the origins of this concept of meaning in a debate about methodology, which generally hinged on the question of law-formation *versus* individuating representation (nomothetic – idiographic), in order fully to evaluate Schütz' objection. Schütz emphatically insists on the *social* origin of meaning, which does not belong as an epistemological category in an abstract debate about method but arises from the common life-world. Schütz criticizes Weber on the grounds that the association by an agent of a subjective meaning with his behaviour, of which Weber speaks, must remain obscure since the investigation is concentrated on the isolated individual. The conclusion to be drawn, however, is that all action is always embedded already in the prior social life-world. The life-world is not the sum of the agents' individual meanings, but is stratified at many levels and complexly structured out of the collective achievements of the establishment of meaning.

Within the social environment we move with great assurance in the framework of everyday understanding. The conscious consideration of a subjective meaning of action, which Weber took for granted, first originates from a specific act of attention of phenomenological reflection within the practical life which is constantly moving forward. The social establishment of meaning thus forms the basis of action, from which the subject first distills his

---

[54] *Die Grenzen der naturwissenschaftlichen Begriffsbildung* (1902); for Weber, see Preface to the 3rd edition, 1921, p. xix.

'meaning' through alteration of the natural attitude of immediate understanding in a special act of reflection. In fact, in Schütz' hands, in the example of Weber's definition of action, Husserl's phenomenology shows its usefulness for social science. In a similar fashion, Peter Winch later made fruitful use of Wittgenstein's conception of the language-game in application to Weber's definition.[55]

Still another example of an outsider may be mentioned. *Hans Lipps*, one of the oldest of Husserl's pupils, who was killed in the Second World War, unlike Schütz failed to cause much stir with his *Untersuchungen zu einer hermeneutischen Logik*.[56] In it can be seen the beginnings, despite a somewhat old-fashioned-sounding terminology, of a potential contribution to the contemporary discussion of *speech-acts*. Following the work of J. L. Austin, who after all occasionally described his project as 'linguistic phenomenology',[57] Lipps' earlier clumsy attempts can thus be brought up to date. The common starting-point is the interpretation of logic, which was traditionally conceived as the investigation of the forms of propositions, in the context of actions.

Lipps' book begins with a quotation from Aristotle, which, in the manner of Heidegger's attempts to look behind the traditional surface meaning, is to be given greater depth.

> ἔστι δέ λόγος ἅπας μὲν σημαντικός.' Trendelenburg translates this as, 'All speech has the function of naming.' The proper meaning of *semainein* is not correctly conveyed by this translation. For it means: to indicate something to someone, in the sense that it can mean even 'to give him an order'. Signs in general have the function of getting someone to recognize something.

Lipps is right to have misgivings about the traditional conception of the 'semantic' function of language as a matter of purely constative assertion.

In fact Aristotle in the passage quoted[58] places *semainein*, in the sense of 'getting-to-recognize', in a wider framework, which

[55] *The Idea of a Social Science*, London, 1958.
[56] Frankfurt (1938). An edition of Lipps' works has since appeared (Frankfurt, 1976–).
[57] 'A plea for excuses', in *Philosophical Papers*, Oxford, 1961, p. 130.
[58] *De interpretatione*, 17a1.

stretches beyond apophantic assertions. The referring function of language rests on a consensus which is ultimately social in origin. It also covers utterances such as requests, which have no truth-content in the way that assertions have. To be sure, Aristotle limits his enquiry to the logic of assertoric propositions, since the other linguistic phenomena belong rather to rhetoric or poetics. At the historical beginnings of propositional logic, therefore, can be found an awareness of the wide-reaching meaning of 'to indicate' or 'to get to recognize', which includes intersubjective action-situations of various kinds, but this awareness was to be reduced, with the development of the Schools, to the one-dimensionality of truth-bearing assertions.

Lipps attaches to these observations about Aristotle his own reflections on the embedding of logic in the understanding-dimension of existence. *Hermeneutics*, as the original setting-forth of the world for an existing Dasein, provides the foil for this theory of logic. Judgments which admit of determination as true or false should be referred back to meaningful acts in the inter-subjective context. They belong, that is to say, to situations which first show themselves in the light of practical orientations of the Dasein as situations in their particularity. Besides, speech-acts are always basically directed towards a partner in discourse, to whom something is signified, even when they look like neutral statements of fact. Formal logic in the customary sense, therefore, represents an artificial product of abstraction, in which the con-text of intersubjective encounter and the situation marked by action and decision are played down.

Lipps can be reckoned as one of the first to attempt, in the name of a *philosophical* conception of logic, to put an end to this ancient practice of reducing it to technical formulae. The insights on which he stumbled in the process are no longer generally suf-ficient for the refined distinctions of more recent speech-act theory. The tendency which he initiated was, however, more promising in its results than the phenomenological grounding of formal logic which his teacher Husserl had had in mind. In his *Formale und transzendentale Logik* (1929)[59] and even in his post-humously published *Erfahrung und Urteil*,[60] Husserl takes the

[59] Translated by D. Cairns, The Hague, 1969.
[60] Edited by L. Landgrebe, Hamburg, 1948 (translated by Churchill and Ameriks, London, 1973).

structures of judgment acknowledged by classical logic as much for granted as Kant had in his project of transcendental grounding. Whereas Kant develops the table of judgments without further ado into a table of categories,[61] Husserl attributes the forms of judgment merely to the appropriate phenomenological intuitions.

In contrast, Lipps, starting from classical phenomenology, struggles towards a radical change in point of view – the interpretation of judging and concluding as an *action*. Analytic philosophy too, after all, has long been accustomed to moving away from the purely logical concept of an ideal language and regarding language-games, with Wittgenstein, as a 'form of life'. In the case of Lipps, the Heideggerian analysis of existence enabled him to open his eyes to a broader classification of the logical. 'The so-called "divisions" of philosophy such as logic and epistemology always establish themselves on the borders of other areas. Philosophy is not to be divided up into such compartments. It enquires into the human being; only the fields of work are different.'[62] The association of language and form of life, or in other words the overcoming of the deep-rooted divisions between the logical and the pragmatic, belong to the heritage of hermeneutics.

In recent decades, *hermeneutics* has become more and more of a key-word in philosophical discussions of the most varied kind. It seems as if hermeneutics creates cross-connexions between problems of different origin. In linguistics and sociology, in history and literary studies, in theology, jurisprudence and aesthetics, and finally in the general theory of science, hermeneutic perspectives have been successfully brought to bear. In this way, the traditional philosophical *claim to universality* is renewed under another name and in the face of an altered situation in science. Sceptics have suggested that hermeneutics is so successful only because its theme is so indefinite and its mode of procedure unduly flexible. Let us consider in more detail the legitimacy of the claims or the justification for scepticism.

It has already been mentioned that the newer philosophical hermeneutics takes up an older, half-forgotten discipline belonging to those subjects which have to do with meaningful texts. The hermeneutic '*ars interpretandi*' always comes into operation in cases

---

[61] *Critique of Pure Reason*, A67ff., 79f.
[62] *Untersuchungen zu einer hermeneutischen Logik*, Frankfurt, 1968², p. 52.

where, as for instance in theology, jurisprudence or the philological study of classical authors, it is a matter of interpreting a text of special value or standing in a manner that is adequate and intelligible enough for the needs of the time. A presupposition of a technique of interpretation which is skilfully performed and learnable and transmissible as a discipline is always the value of and the need for interpreting certain texts. When the question is to know what a text which has either become historically alien or remote because of its supratemporal validity really has to say to us in a definite historical situation, it is worth making the effort to produce specific interpretations which have been improved to the condition of an art. Hermeneutics thus rests on the *pre-eminence of texts which are valuable and which continue to be influential over a historical distance.*

The idea of an insurmountable pre-eminence in every knowledge-situation of the tradition of which we form part, and the conviction of the exemplary status of an interpretation trained on texts have been championed with great emphasis by *Hans-Georg Gadamer.* His hermeneutics thus has inscribed on its banners the theses of the historicity and the linguistic character of all understanding. Historical-linguistic understanding has come to be widely recognized as a model of theoretical knowledge and practical interaction. Before we go into this in more detail, it would be appropriate to look again at the preliminary phase of Gadamer's hermeneutics in the late philosophy of his teacher Heidegger.

Heidegger's late philosophy

One of the first documents of *Heidegger's late philosophy* was the debate with the subjectivist and humanist character which the earlier philosophy of existence had taken on immediately after the war in the countries influenced by French culture. It was suggested that, as in Sartre,[63] the analysis of existence should be interpreted as a philosophy which moves the individual human being and his freedom unqualifiedly into the centre of consideration. Nevertheless, that was a misunderstanding of the intentions of *Being and Time,* whose author had spoken out against all forms of anthropology and other empirical accounts of the essence of

[63] *L'Existentialisme est un humanisme* (1946) (translated by Philip Mairet, London, 1948).

human beings. With the help of the analysis of Dasein, the ground was to be prepared for a new ontology. The existing text of *Being and Time* was initially entitled the 'First Half' of a whole work, though the 'Second Half' has never appeared.[64] That a misunderstanding of the intentions of the philosophy of existence in the manner of Sartrean humanism was nevertheless possible reveals in retrospect a difficulty in the exposition of the problem of *Being and Time*, which Heidegger sought to correct in his 'Letter on Humanism'.

Certainly, the catch-word 'humanism' is merely a pretext and the name of Sartre occurs only incidentally. In reality, Heidegger's 'Letter on Humanism' of 1947 is an attempt to surpass himself philosophically. The philosophy of existence ultimately becomes a philosophy of Being. The interpretative character of existence in the world, which in *Being and Time* furnished the basis for a deeper grounding of the subject-object relationship, now appears to the contrary as a relation in which Being itself first of all reveals itself to the human being. Being is primary, not man. The true priority shows itself in the fact that Being 'transmits' itself historically to human beings and the latter must be adequate in thought to their historical 'destiny'. The place where Being and man encounter each other in this relationship is, according to Heidegger, *language*. 'Language is the house of Being. In its lodging dwells man. The thinkers and the poets are the caretakers of this lodging. Their watch is the accomplishment of the manifestation of Being, in so far as through what they say they bring it to speech and preserve it in speech.'[65]

Heidegger makes use of a metaphorical mode of expression, to which, as on occasion in Wittgenstein,[66] philosophical language

---

64 Cf. however the late lecture 'Zeit und Sein' (in *Zur Sache des Denkens*, Tübingen, 1969; English translation, New York, 1972).

65 *Platons Lehre von der Wahrheit; mit einem Brief über den Humanismus*, Bern, 1954, p. 53 (translated in *Basic Writings*, London, 1975).

66 Incidentally, Wittgenstein's remarks in the Vienna Circle about Heidegger are worth reading: 'To be sure, I can imagine what Heidegger means by being and anxiety. Man feels the urge to run up against the limits of language. Think for example of the astonishment that anything at all exists. This astonishment cannot be expressed in the form of a question, and there is also no answer whatsoever. Anything we might say is a priori bound to be nonsense. Nevertheless we do run up against the limits of language . . .' (*Waismann-Gespräche*, ed. McGuinness, Frankfurt, 1967–8; the translation quoted is from Schulte and McGuinness, *Ludwig Wittgenstein and the Vienna Circle*,

always resorts when the states of affairs to be described cannot be fitted into well-worn terminology and the expressive possibilities of routine jargon. Heidegger's aim is to call in question the regimentation of speech by traditional logic which has, since the time of Plato and Aristotle, gone hand in hand with the dominance of classical metaphysics. For this reason he must of necessity have recourse to modes of expression which at first sight have little in common with the official language of philosophy.

He is of the opinion that the *metaphysics* which has shaped Western thought up to the time when modern science and technology began to extend their influence is a historical phenomenon in philosophy, not by any means the final unshakable truth. Already, in such an early writer as Plato,[67] the principle of metaphysics denotes a loss of substance as compared with the unspoiled nature of pre-Socratic thought. It is a disguise and a narrowing of the primary manifestation of Being when philosophy begins to enquire into the principle of the definition of the Something, as is shown by the Platonic theory of Ideas, with its question about the *eidos*. It is the Fall of philosophy to reduce the truth of Being to the essence of beings. With this step, Western metaphysics and consequently logic too took a fateful path. The traditional theory of Being as the doctrine of the most general and highest determinations of beings prepared the way for the typically modern objectification of anything and everything as objects of scientific control. The unexamined tendency of our thought towards objectivism thus has a historical background. The beginnings of ancient metaphysics already contained the unacknowledged withdrawal of Being, the blindness in the face of the true question of Being.

The philosophy which is interested in the full dimensions of the question of Being must draw a radical consequence from this. It must reckon, in the highest sphere of philosophical conceptformation, which according to the traditional conception of metaphysics lies beyond historical change, with a species of *historicity* which does not arise in our categories of thought, but

Oxford, 1979, p. 68). In general, cf. K. O. Apel, 'Wittgenstein und Heidegger' in *Transformation der Philosophie*, Vol. I, Frankfurt, 1973 (English translation, London, 1980).
67 Heidegger, *Platons Lehre*.

embraces even the principal forms of thought itself. In order to characterize the dependence of philosophical thought on such conditions which are prior to it and escape its clutches, and to distinguish it from profane history, Heidegger chooses the emphatic expression 'destiny'. Certainly, the question remains to be answered where the place for possible insight into these dependencies which originally control and confuse thought is to be sought. Heidegger's answer is: in *language*, to the extent that, in spite of the modes of speech which have been practised since ancient times in philosophy and science and the corresponding logical regimentation, it is flexible enough to create expressions even for those insights which can be gained only in opposition to the domination of terminology and formal rules.

A language which is open in this way goes beyond the boundaries of the various specialisms. The philosophy which seeks to do justice, in spite of the dominant scientism and systematic metaphysics, to the true task of thought approaches poetry – indeed it consciously toys with the possibility of transforming itself into *art*. In this an essential trait of Heidegger's late philosophy may be recognized. The emphatic pre-eminence of Being in the forefront of his philosophical approach to his theme, which comes to expression in the historicity of metaphysics, throws philosophy back behind the traditional, but inadequate, forms of understanding. Reliance can be placed only on the undamaged powers of language as such, which constantly come to fresh expression in poetry also. On this line lie the interpretations of the poems of Hölderlin or Rilke, behind which the philosopher Heidegger likes to retreat. One may understand the object in view even if the gain in knowledge sought for is not always as revolutionary as Heidegger thinks, and if occasionally the standards of philology and aesthetic sense of style are neglected.

Heidegger's later recourse to art seeks to find a home for the true philosophical question of Being, which the philosophers however since the archaic Greeks have neglected to pursue. In the essay 'Der Ursprung des Kunstwerks' ('The source of the work of art')[68] art is placed on an equal footing alongside philosophy as a way of accomplishing the 'disclosure of Being as a whole, truth'. 'All art, as a means of allowing to come to pass the advent of the

---

[68] *Holzwege*, Frankfurt, 1950, e.g. pp. 44, 59 (translated in *Basic Writings*).

truth of Being as such, is essentially poetry. The essence of art, on which the work of art and the artist chiefly rest, is the self-accomplishing of truth.' It is not a question to be considered here in any way whether such a massive recruitment of art to support a concept of truth of *philosophical* origin is legitimate: I do believe that the difficult problems of aesthetics cannot be solved in this way, but only circumvented. For our purpose, of an approach to the main themes of the late philosophy of Heidegger, it is however sufficient to see how directly art is enlisted in the service of philosophy.

There is moreover a prominent precedent in the history of philosophy for the attempt to project philosophical questions first of all into art, in order then to make use of the artistic experience to instruct philosophy about its own proper tasks. *Schelling's* theory of the work of art as an 'organon of philosophy'[69] proceeded in exactly this way. In the context of Schelling's system of the absolute identity of subjectivity and objectivity, philosophy was charged with the task of conceiving a distinctionless unity. The distinctionless identity of the determinations which were still distinct for the understanding did not allow of further determination in its turn, since every determination required the introduction of a fresh distinction. Philosophy thus had at its disposal no further conceptual means of conceiving that which precedes all determination and all concepts. In this necessity to impose on philosophy a task of thought which could not even in principle be tackled by employing the usual means of thought, Schelling called to mind the intuition of the work of art. Every work of art seems to present a distinctionless unity of subjectivity and objectivity or of form and matter, immediately and beyond all processes of thought. Philosophy does not have recourse to art for the purposes of autonomous aesthetic concept-formation, but rather to assist with the internal systematic problems of philosophy. Here therefore there is a *metabasis eis allo genos* or transition to another kind which the Aristotelian-sounding title of an 'organon' conceals in a merely instrumental fashion. Heidegger's attempt to reflect philosophy in art is more cautious than Schelling's systematic take-over of art, but ultimately follows a similar strategy.

<hr/>

[69] *System des transzendentalen Idealismus* (1800) (translated by P. Heath, Charlottesville, 1978).

Gadamer's hermeneutics

It is to H.G. *Gadamer* that we are indebted for the great integration achieved by hermeneutics, which is at present enlivening philosophical debate and has even been influential in many fields outside philosophy. His book *Wahrheit und Methode*[70] essentially builds on the insights of the later Heidegger, but translates his sometimes cryptic allusions into rather more accessible philosophical language and definitely gives added strength to the conception with its historical, philological and aesthetic studies. In its wealth of material, the book reflects the breadth of a vision which comes from a truly humanistic scholarship. That this has little to do with empty book-learning is shown by the fascination exerted on the modern special sciences by the creatively assimilated material. The modern disciplines, self-conscious and convinced of their progress as they are, sometimes find it difficult to approach the philosophical foundations of Gadamer's hermeneutics, but they seize with alacrity on the illumination to be found in the prismatic breakdown of the fundamental ideas into concrete individual aspects. Not the least part of the fruitfulness of hermeneutics lies in its ability to shed light on the current state of knowledge in various subjects.[71] In this way, philosophy again establishes contact of a knowledge-advancing kind with the sciences, which have long been separated from it in a way which is certainly not to the advantage of either side.

The philosophical tradition of hermeneutics in the widest sense, which Gadamer has intentionally revived, is naturally favourable to contact with all the *human sciences*. The whole range of directions of enquiry in the 'humanities' is no longer subject to judgments passed on it from the abstract height of a theory of science orientated to formal logic, but is regarded first from the point of view of its own specific interests. Something similar is true of the specific requirements of jurisprudence, the social sciences and even theology. Hermeneutics makes contact, on a new level of thematization, with the methodological distinction,

[70] Tübingen, 1960 (translated as *Truth and Method*, New York, 1975). See also Linge (ed.), *Philosophical Hermeneutics*.

[71] E.g. H. R. Jauss, *Literaturgeschichte als Provokation*, Frankfurt, 1970; J. Rüsen, *Für eine erneuerte Historik*, Stuttgart, 1976; C. Taylor, 'Interpretation and the sciences of man', *Review of Metaphysics*, 25, 1971.

first defined in the nineteenth century and since simply extended, between the natural and the human sciences,[72] and shows that unexamined presuppositions underlie the dualism, that these presuppositions arise out of the tradition and hence that they can be undermined also by reflection on the tradition.

The necessary objectification and preliminary narrowing of vision on which *all methodical* work is based is common to all disciplines. As long as the dispute about 'explanation' and 'understanding' or the nomothetical method of formulating laws versus the idiographic method of shaping the individual and particular is in the foreground, it diverts attention from the fact that in both cases an original experience of reality is methodically restricted. Whatever the objects and interests in knowledge of the sciences may be at any given time, to the extent that they are methodical the sciences arbitrarily and in accordance with preconceived rules mark out domains from the totality of our relations with the world, in order to subject them to the specific instruments of perfected knowledge.

The dominant role of the different cognitive interests has moreover concealed the fact that understanding and explaining frequently or always intermesh. The gross dualism of methods is an illusion willingly sustained by both sides in the polemics. The human and cultural sciences, whose predominant orientation is towards understanding, can certainly draw attention to their use of explanatory procedures, without which even they could not get by (e.g. in philological criticism of texts and sources). After all, they were long at a disadvantage in comparison with the respectable natural sciences and sought recognition through assimilation to the kinds of explanation given in the natural sciences. On the other side, however, the front seemed firmly closed until the recent doubt raised in the liberal positions of Popper and Kuhn about positivism. In the meantime, historical understanding had been conceded a not insignificant status even in the natural sciences alongside strict explanation on the basis of general lawlike hypotheses.[73]

Of course, it would be to underrate the philosophical aims of

---

[72] Cf. also the late version of neo-Kantianism in E. Cassirer, *Zur Logik der Kulturwissenschaften*, Göteborg, 1942 (English translation, New Haven, 1961).

[73] See Popper on hermeneutics, *Objective Knowledge*, London, 1972 (e.g.

hermeneutics, if one were to regard it merely as a new contribution to the old dispute over methodology. Hermeneutics rather follows Heidegger's analyses of existence and Husserl's doctrine of the life-world, in that it shows how derivative and secondary is all methodical knowledge in the form of scientific specialization. One method ought not to be played off against another, nor should any dogmatic methodological point of view be presented as superior to another. Equally, however, it is not a wholesale repudiation of all methodically conducted knowledge, or a recommendation in its place of an irrational and intuitionist alternative. Some have tried to construe the title of Gadamer's main work as if it read 'Truth and *not* method'. This excessive subtlety does not accord with the purpose of hermeneutics, although Gadamer does at times tend towards a position critical of science, the formulation of which might encourage such a misunderstanding.

The antithesis of truth and method is not meant to be exclusive, as if the methodical procedures of all sciences were to be denied on principle all claims to truth, whereas in totally unmethodical discourse there lay an allegedly higher truth, which was more felt than known. It is rather a matter of explicating the *reciprocal relations between methodical science* and an *original truth* which transcends the methodical. The specialist and rule-governed concentration on definite expectations of knowledge in the sciences presupposes a prior horizon of general experience of the world which cannot be replaced by anything, even by a 'unity of science' of however perfect a kind. The original relation in which we as human beings are orientated in a quite elementary way to the world, or in which the world is accessible to us, will, for the purposes of augmented and more precise knowledge which the sciences in all their expressions serve, be brought into focus in accordance with the specific optics of the method. The priority of the open world-horizon and the particular limitations of the methodical point of view stand in close relationship.

'The hermeneutics which is here developed is not a methodology of the human sciences, but the quest for an understanding of what the human sciences are in truth beyond their methodical

pp. 183ff.). On this point, see Ch. 2 below. Cf. also H. Putnam's recent *Meaning and the Moral Sciences*, London, 1978, Lectures 5 and 6.

self-consciousness and what connects them with the whole of our experience of the world.'[74]

> But the function of the hermeneutic reflection does not exhaust itself in what it signifies for science.
> Characteristic of all modern sciences is a deep-rooted alienation, which they demand of the natural consciousness and which already in the initial stage of modern science attained to reflective consciousness through the concept of method. Hermeneutic reflection cannot seek to change anything in it. But in that it makes transparent the pre-understanding which guides science at any time it can expose new dimensions of the question and thereby indirectly serve methodical work. It can however, beyond that, bring to consciousness what the methodology of science pays for its own advances, what glossings-over and abstractions it demands, through which it leaves behind in perplexity the natural consciousness, which, however, as the consumer of the inventions and information acquired through science, constantly follows them.[75]

This critical *reflection on the methodological dogmatism* with which the expanding sciences have consistently overwhelmed modern consciousness up to the present time represents one of the main achievements of hermeneutics. It is all the more compelling, in that it does not end in romantic cultural pessimism, in cheap contempt for science or Rousseauesque utopianism. Most critics of the modern world, whether in the conservative or in the progressive camp, tend to slide into such equally unsatisfactory solutions. Hermeneutics does not only concede a relative legitimacy to science, it also contributes to its grounding. The grounding, to be sure, does not result from a standpoint which is due to the institution of science itself.

Official theory of science generally identifies itself straightforwardly with the dominant conviction in science of its universal

---

[74] *Wahrheit und Methode*, Introduction, p. xv (cf. epilogue to the 3rd edition, 1972).

[75] 'Rhetorik, Hermeneutik und Ideologiekritik, metakritische Erörterungen zu *Wahrheit und Methode*', in Apel et al., *Hermeneutik und Ideologiekritik*, Frankfurt, 1971, p. 79.

competence and hence produces only immanent elucidations, which become ideological when they are taken for foundations. Even the logic of knowledge of transcendental philosophy in the Kantian style proceeds from an undoubted fact of science, in order to furnish it *ex post die* with appropriate premises and formal conditions. Philosophical reflection can therefore no longer break free from the dominant position of science. Hermeneutics, by contrast, seeks to look behind the paradigm of specialized and methodically regulated cognition, which is established by tradition but which is nevertheless a historical product, in order to relativize its pretended autonomy. In that it helps to overcome those presuppositions which have become congealed into a second nature, it smooths the way for scientific activity to be carried on on its true grounds. That undoubtedly represents an independent act of philosophical reflection in elucidating the genesis and structure of scientific knowledge, as well as a contribution to its legitimation.

Linguistic understanding or practice

Anyone who has followed the self-interpretation of hermeneutics thus far must however be able to answer the question, what are the science-transcending sources of this peculiar hermeneutic understanding? The point of this question, strictly taken, is the meaning of 'truth' in the context of hermeneutics. Undoubtedly, Gadamer, imitating Heidegger, advocated an exaggerated *concept of truth*, with which he contrasts, equally provocatively, scientistic positivism and its methodological doctrines. He proceeds in two stages: first the question of truth is expounded in its entire compass in the undistorted experience of art, and then a broad concept of the linguistic is sketched, into which is fitted the whole socio-historical existence of humanity in its artistic, scientific and institutional manifestations. The recovery of a concept of truth by means of *art* is achieved through the refutation of the subjectivist reductionism of recent aesthetics. In wide-ranging discussions of ancient theories of art as compared with those of the moderns, and with the aid of preliminary studies in conceptual history, Gadamer further develops Heidegger's hints about the truth which is achieved in art. In terms of the history of philosophy, he repeats the step taken by Hegel's substantive aesthetics, which had attributed art to the whole fullness of spiritual substance and sought to go beyond the limitation to enquiry into merely subjective receptivity to be found in Kant's *Critique of Judgment*.

It is instructive in this connexion that one vigorously disputed thesis of Hegel's aesthetics is not taken up, although it is certainly among the consequences of elevating art to the level of Hegel's 'Spirit'. That is, Hegel attributes art, after first revaluing it in the name of philosophy, to a past form of Spirit, since the more complete and final realization of Spirit in the form of philosophy follows it with historical and logical necessity.[76] This definitive step in the unfolding of Spirit is, as it were, revoked by Gadamer: philosophy does not supersede art, it must turn back and learn from it. Gadamer's essential argument consists in unmasking as a *proton pseudos* the separation of the subjective enjoyment of art. 'The experience of art should not be forced into the isolation of the aesthetic consciousness. This negative insight signifies positively that art is knowledge and the experience of the work of art participates in this knowledge.'[77] The full reality of art shows itself as a *game*, in the course of which subject and work fuse together in such a way that they seem to surrender to it their own being-for-themselves: the work is unthinkable without the recipient, and the receiving subject, in the face of the work, does not remain in detached independence. Without doubt, tragedy furnishes the classical example of this unity of the game, becoming perceptible in the duration of a production and taking hold on the living subject. Tragedy is, according to the conceptions of antiquity, the manifestation of a truth which concerns everyone and for that reason takes hold of and moves the spectator.

By this model, then, Gadamer measures all understanding. Not that every process of understanding rises to the level of the aesthetic. But the perplexity of the subject and his being laid hold of by a process in which truth is manifested serve as a standard of genuinely successful and not abstractly restricted understanding. The most general medium of such understanding Gadamer sees in the irreducibly *linguistic* character of our relation to the world and to human beings. All objective states of affairs and all intersubjective relations with individuals, with society and with the history of the human race are comprised in this. Every human mode of

---

[76] Hegel, *On Art, Religion, Philosophy* (ed. Gray), New York, 1970, pp. 32ff.
[77] *Wahrheit und Methode*, p. 92.

behaviour, to the extent that it is meaningful, has a linguistic foundation. Linguisticity is however always associated with understanding, since the meaning communicated in language becomes tangible only in this way. Thus, hermeneutics, as a *philosophical theory of understanding*, is as it were the new '*prima philosophia*'. It opens our eyes to 'a universal ontological structure, that is, the fundamental condition of everything to which understanding can in general direct itself. *Being that can be understood is language*.'[78]

The philological and aesthetic intuitions of the older hermeneutics, consequently, merely point the way to an experience, on the universality and originality of which the whole of philosophy in its totality ought to be based. Understanding in this primary sense underlies all acts of understanding concerning works and texts, including those texts which happen to articulate scientific theories. Even in relations with other subjects, individual or collective, understanding is always present. It is important to assimilate texts and subjects, which in the perspective of understanding surrender their ontological independence. Understanding in the most general medium, language, conforms to the model of *dialogue*, which in appropriate formalizations is the same as the most varied forms of communication with different kinds of 'partner'.

> Philosophical hermeneutics lays claim to universality. It bases this claim on the fact that understanding and interpretation do not mean primarily and originally a methodically trained approach to texts, but are the form in which human social life is achieved – that life which is in its ultimate formalization a language-community. From this language-community nothing is excluded. No experience of the world whatsoever, neither the specialization of modern science and its increasingly esoteric activities, nor material work and its forms of organization, nor the political institutions of domination and administration which maintain the ordering of society, lies outside this universal medium of practical reason (and unreason).[79]

[78] Ibid., p. 450.
[79] Reply to the contributors to the collection *Hermeneutik und Ideologiekritik*, p. 289.

From this premise it follows, furthermore, that hermeneutics must be transferred to the realm of *practical philosophy*.[80] This already seemed legitimate to Gadamer, since he had formed his broad concept of understanding not least on the model of Aristotle's *phronesis*.[81] The practical competence of hermeneutics, which allowed understanding to extend to include successful and practically valid formation of a consensus, has earned hermeneutics much praise, but also criticism from sociologists, social psychologists and political scientists. *Habermas* in particular has taken up the connexion of hermeneutic understanding with living social practice,[82] in order to move from understanding to consent or from dialogue to reciprocal recognition of the partners as subjects.

It seems to me, however, that this step ought not to be taken without further preconditions and that hermeneutics should not suggest that there is ultimately no difference between theory and practice.[83] I do not wish to assert that Gadamer and Habermas intentionally blur distinctions; they do however succumb to a certain extent to the illusion of thinking that the hermeneutic act of bringing into consciousness is already an act in the practical conduct of life. The necessary distinction may be illustrated by the example of Aristotle.

Aristotle is rightly regarded as the founder of the philosophy of the practical in the true sense, since he grasped in the course of his criticism of Plato that the knowledge of the good alone does not promote the doing of the good. Where it is a matter of practical questions, clarification of practice is required. The '*philosophia practica*' cannot get by without the foundation of a concept of action, which forms the primary basis for the specific character of

---

[80] See also Gadamer's essay 'Hermeneutik als praktische Philosophie', in M. Riedel (ed.), *Rehabilitierung der praktischen Philosophie*, Freiburg, 1972.

[81] *Wahrheit und Methode*, Pt II, Ch. 2b: 'Die hermeneutische Aktualität des Aristoteles'.

[82] *Erkenntnis und Interesse*, Pt II, Ch. 8, Frankfurt, 1968 (translated by J. Shapiro, *Knowledge and Human Interests*, London, 1972); 'Zur Logik der Sozialwissenschaften', *Philosophische Rundschau*, Beiheft 1967, esp. p. 168; 'Vorbereitende Bemerkungen zu einer Theorie der Kommunikative Kompetenz' (translated in H. P. Dreitzel (ed.), *Recent Sociology* 2, London, 1970).

[83] Cf. my essay *Theorie und Praxis – eine nachhegelsche Abstraktion*, Frankfurt, 1971.

this kind of philosophical enquiry. The characteristic structure of performance (*energeia*) of the Aristotelian concept of action,[84] which rules out any technical guidance derived from freely available theoretical knowledge, defines the role of practical reason as *phronesis* or prudence. It is only under the presupposition of a *concept of action*, of practice conceived of as the concrete realization of the good at any time, that understanding of a social situation acquires the practical meaning which several authors attribute to hermeneutics. Without these presuppositions, certainly, hermeneutics remains an understanding developed for dealing with texts and historical documents from which no practical conclusions are to be drawn. Hermeneutics, as Gadamer outlines it, does not have such a concept of action. The adaptation of hermeneutics by Habermas in the direction of a so-called 'universal pragmatics' is no better in that respect. It even conceals with this deficiency another deficiency, namely the lack of any grounding for the practical relevance of the critique of ideology.[85]

The limits of a possible practical extension of understanding are shown by an old concept of hermeneutics which Gadamer takes over. He speaks, following a tradition of theological hermeneutics, of '*applicatio*', where it is a matter of successful understanding of a text.[86] When a text or a work are genuinely understood, this does not remain a merely intellectual act without further consequences: rather it is a matter of the active transformation of what is said in an application. One can, so to speak, 'do' something with what one has indeed understood. Active understanding produces a definite effect in the surrounding sphere of practical life. This observation is certainly to the point, but nothing conclusive follows from it for the problem of the practical in the true sense. To the extent that the text does not expressly contain imperatives for action, as perhaps it does in the exceptional case of legal texts, the 'application' may take a wide variety of conceivable forms. Understood texts or successful dialogues may influence my later actions in the most varied ways. I may proceed to action, I may alter my life, become a better human being, or merely permit some marginal modifications to my conduct to follow.

---

[84] *Ethica Nicomachea*, I. 1; VI. 5, 11. [85] On this see below, Ch. 3.
[86] *Wahrheit und Methode*, p. 290.

Nevertheless, even when no immediate consequences are re-cognizable in action, no one will have the right to conclude that what is to be understood has not been understood. For practice is not an infallible criterion of understanding. For this reason, we must content ourselves with the assertion that understanding in the sense of the hermeneutic application extends into practical situations in a manner that is *never specifiable with final determinateness*. From this it follows that understanding and action remain two spheres which can never be perfectly combined by hermeneutic reflection alone, although it is capable of studying the various intermediate forms. We shall encounter this problem again in connexion with philosophy of language and the philosophy of practice.

The continuing influence of the past

One of the central problems of hermeneutics is *history*. From the very beginnings of hermeneutical activity understanding has been shown to be a special accomplishment, which is not achieved always as a matter of course, but must be purposefully pursued, and presupposes the unfamiliarity of what is to be understood. Unfamiliarity, however, which does not imply total indifference, is the unintelligibility of what is in itself intelligible, the interruption of a communication which is otherwise in principle guaranteed. The hermeneutic overcoming of unfamiliarity results therefore in the assimilation of what really belongs to one or in the bridging over of the distance which separates the interpreter and what is to be interpreted. The normal case of unfamiliarity on the basis of community ought to be temporal distance. Persons become unfamiliar to each other in the course of time, works recede into historical distance, texts from other epochs have an alienating effect and stand in need of mediation. The same is true of manifestations of earlier stages of civilization, even if the distance to 'primitive' societies is experienced in temporal synchrony.[87]

The point of departure, of course, is that one already stands in a history when one becomes aware of the unfamiliarity of a content

[87] Cf. on a comparable problem the essays of P. Winch ('Understanding a primitive society'), A. MacIntyre, E. Gellner and others in B. Wilson (ed.), *Rationality*, Oxford/New York, 1971.

which requires interpretation. Hermeneutics introduces the category of 'continuously influential history' for this phenomenon. It can appeal in this to R. G. *Collingwood*'s idea of 're-enactment'.[88] History is not to be treated from the outside or from above in an artificial objectification. History is always experienced by us, as it were, from the inside, in so far as we stand in it and become conscious of this unalterable fact of standing in a continually elapsing history. The experience of history normally implies the experience that one cannot detach oneself from this history since it is one's own. The dependence on something which already existed before I was conscious of it and which there is no prospect of escaping, since my being has already been marked by that which preceded, was characterized in Heidegger's analysis of existence as historicity. Gadamer recalls this when he conceives of interpretation as a process by means of which the past continues to exert its influence. He connects interpretation in this way very closely with the past.[89]

'Understanding is itself not to be thought of so much as an act of the subjectivity, but as an insertion into a process of tradition, in which past and present constantly adjust themselves.'[90] In understanding we are already part of history and subject to its continuity, which discloses itself more clearly to our eyes through hermeneutic activity. Since it is the background of the continuing influence of the past which in general enables us to make progress in understanding, our hermeneutically acquired insights remain also constantly limited and circumscribed. Hermeneutic philosophy has never been able to transcend the *limitations* on its own possibilities of knowledge. The thesis of the continuing influence of the past thus contains on the one hand a sort of relativistic philosophy of history which dismisses all higher-level syntheses *sub specie aeternitatis*, and on the other an attitude towards the epistemological status of hermeneutics itself. Gadamer elucidates both with the aid of a reference to Hegel.[91]

---

88 *Wahrheit und Methode*, pp. 352ff.; cf. Collingwood, *Autobiography*, chs. 5, 7, 8, 10. Gadamer's term is *Wirkungsgeschichte*.

89 The essentially future-orientated interpretation of *Being and Time* (cf. section 74) had already given way in Heidegger's late philosophy to the scepticism of the 'destiny of Being'.

90 *Wahrheit und Methode*, pp. 274f.

91 See also the collection of essays, *Hegel's Dialectic* (translated by C. Smith), New Haven, 1976.

To be historical means never to rise to self-knowledge. All self-knowledge arises from historical givenness, which we with Hegel call 'substance', since it is the bearer of all subjective intention and behaviour and thus also prescribes and delimits all possibilities of understanding a tradition in its historical otherness. The task of philosophical hermeneutics may actually be characterized by this: it has to go back along the path of Hegel's *Phenomenology of Spirit* inasmuch as in all subjectivity there is revealed the substantiality which determines it.[92]

In fact Hegel's philosophy of the historical Spirit can be regarded as one of the systematic vanishing-points of hermeneutic reflection, in so far as here the problem of history is brought together with the epistemological status of philosophy.

Dilthey's project of a 'Critique of Historical Reason' had already based itself on the paradigm of Hegel. To be sure, the follower expressed considerable doubts about the speculative reliance on a metaphysics of absolute Spirit.[93] Dilthey objects to Hegel that 'The historical understanding is sacrificed to the metaphysical scheme'.[94] Hermeneutics ought therefore to limit itself unequivocally to the historical forms of expression of the living spirit, which are immediately understandable to a concrete subject through re-enactment, and not to permit any passing over into transcendent realms. In this repudiation of speculative Idealism lay Dilthey's tribute to the scientific atmosphere of his time. For Heidegger too, Hegel was all his life the secret reference point, the great opponent whom it was worthwhile to reject and with whom, for all that, a debate was unavoidable. Even the young Heidegger's first published work ended with the following astonishing sentences: 'The philosophy of the living spirit . . . is confronted with the great task of a debate on fundamental principles with *Hegel* and his system of a historical world-view, the most powerful in fullness and depth, in wealth of experience and in conceptual articulation, which, as a historical world-view, has taken up into itself all previous fundamental problems of

[92] *Wahrheit und Methode*, pp. 285ff.
[93] *Gesammelte Schriften*, Vol. VII, pp. 148ff.
[94] Ibid., pp. 285f.

philosophy.'[95] In fairness it should be added that the first step towards this debate was taken in a profoundly unsatisfactory manner in a polemical section on Hegel's concept of time in *Being and Time*.[96]

The more or less latent dispute with Hegel in Heidegger's philosophy[97] was explicitly taken further by Gadamer. In the passage quoted above, the movement of the *Phenomenology of Spirit* is very cogently expounded in reverse. *Hegel* had demanded that philosophy should, in historical elaboration and assimilation of the historical forms of the Spirit, take care that the substance become subject.[98] No given content should be simply accepted by philosophy – the Spirit must rather recognize itself in everything and comprehend itself with full consciousness. Gadamer reads the summons to the active autonomizing of Spirit through reflection on the historical constituents of a tradition, in opposition to Hegel's intention, as the affirmation that all conscious reflection, in which the Spirit comes to itself, stands inevitably in a context of historical tradition, which can never be reflectively analysed and completely replaced by the inherent powers of the self-knowing Spirit. The passage of reflection through all relevant forms of a Spirit which is historically given and not yet fully in possession of itself, which Hegel's *Phenomenology* undertakes, serves the systematic purpose of transcending finite history in the absolute Spirit. As its name suggests, phenomenology is concerned with Spirit as it merely appears in the horizon of history. The investigation of the historically appearing Spirit is however by no means an end in itself. Rather, there stands at the end of the study of the phenomenological 'appearances' of Spirit the absolute knowledge which permits the construction, without historical limitation, of a speculative logic and metaphysics. To be sure, Hegel's system does not relapse to the level of a historically blind School metaphysics, since the constitutive preliminary work of a phenomenology overthrows all dogmas in the historical forms in

[95] *Die Kategorien- und Bedeutungslehre des Duns Scotus*, Tübingen, 1916, p. 241 (italicization in original).

[96] Section 82.

[97] See also Heidegger's late essay on 'Hegel and the Greeks' in Henrich et al. (eds.), *Gegenwart der Griechen in neueren Denken, Festschrift für Gadamer*, Tübingen, 1960.

[98] *Phänomenologie des Geistes* (ed. Lasson and Hoffmeister), Hamburg, 1952, Preface, p. 19 (translated by A. V. Miller, London, 1977).

which Spirit appears. Nevertheless, history is regarded as a barrier to be passed beyond, which arises at the end of a long and profoundly decisive tradition of thought before the total freedom of the autonomous activity of Spirit.[99]

May one however, without further ado, read Hegel's *Phenomenology* backwards in the manner of Gadamer's hermeneutics? This question has remained controversial in the subsequent debate right up to the present. Two objections above all have been raised. First, the historical dimension in which hermeneutic reflection takes place seems not to be as limited as Gadamer has claimed. The assimilation of those conditions of its own appearance in history which at first elude consciousness is an act in which consciousness necessarily advances towards the transcendence of these conditions and final autonomy. However much the initial standing-in-history is emphasized, there yet lies in it also the starting-point for the complete theoretical overcoming of history. Hermeneutic reflection can by no means continue to stand in its original conditions. Its activity inevitably contributes to a widening of the horizon of knowledge, so that the ultimate scope for hermeneutics consists in a *general philosophy of history* and not merely in the claimed interpretation of a situation here and now. Hermeneutics, according to this objection, is in reality a disguised Hegelianism.[100]

The other objection arises from the standpoint of the *critique of ideology*. Habermas has found fault with the regression on principle to tradition and the dominant function of the historical past. He has accused the hermeneutic exposure of the pre-understanding which guides all conscious thought, even the sciences, of a covert preference for conservatism.[101] It is true that Gadamer follows absolutely the line of a critique of the Enlightenment and the hopes which were placed in it for immediate change when he says that the movement of reflection and thus also the activity of enlightenment involved in it always proceed

---

[99] On Hegel's conception cf. my 'Problemgeschichte und systematischer Sinn der Phänomenologie Hegels', in *Dialektik und Wissenschaft*[2], Frankfurt, 1974.

[100] W. Pannenberg was one of the first to put forward, in a very plausible version, this now frequently heard argument ('Hermeneutik und Universalgeschichte', *Zeitschrift für Theologie und Kirche*, 60, 1963).

[101] Cf. his contribution in the collection edited by Apel et al., *Hermeneutik und Ideologiekritik*.

from presuppositions of which it is not fully aware. If critical reflection is directed towards historical data and political prejudices, then it does not in the same act direct itself to the conditions of its own activity. Rather it is itself subject in this case to *b* certain prejudices, which must be raised in a fresh step to become the object of explicit reflection. But does this go on ad infinitum? If no genuine advance were possible on this road, then an ultimate residue of the burden of tradition could never be shaken off. It is this defeatist consequence which Habermas disputes.

Both objections relate fundamentally to the degree of *knowledge* in the hermeneutic reflection or else to its theoretical self-evaluation. The first objection insinuates that hermeneutics can in *(1)* the last resort work only if a total comprehension of history is premised, without of course admitting this. The second objection *(2)* rests on the suspicion of conservative ideology, which always justifies the past without real foundation. Both objections seem to me to be not entirely sound, though that does not mean that the essential question has been answered. The objections are not aimed in the right direction, but the question of the true knowledge-content of hermeneutics, which is implicit in them, is still open.

First, it is not correct that it would be possible to make historical conditions explicit only on the level of a comprehensive theory of universal history, or even that there is any inherent tendency in that direction. The philosophical theory of universal history is a product of the end of history or, strictly speaking, is already transhistorical. Only someone who in thought is evidently no longer located in history could freely speak of history in its totality. The Hegelian philosophy of history is thus also part of the Encyclopaedic system which is to be developed on the level of absolute knowledge, while the *Phenomenology* prepares the way for this perspective by reflecting within history.

To be sure, this preliminary activity of phenomenological reflection on the conditioned nature of the historical forms of Spirit depends on the internal ordering in which the forms follow one another with necessity and contrary to the actual chronology of history. As long, however, as thought moves in the sphere of phenomenology itself, whether it be forwards in the Hegelian style to absolute knowledge or in the reverse direction because of a hermeneutically inspired renunciation of such a goal, for so long are absolute and universal-historical premises not required. It is thus possible to defend Gadamer against the reproach of disguised Hegelianism by referring to the never completed infinity of a hermeneutical reflection which is constantly recommenced on historical conditions which are always newly given or changing. Where we take seriously the historicity of thought, we must reckon with its conditioned character. The theological origins of universal history are thereby overcome. There is no way out of the realm of history, no redemption from our bondage to it.

This same insight can easily be used in reply to the reproach of subservience to tradition and lack of an enlightened attitude. No act of reflection on historical conditions is performed free of such conditions. Critical activity directed towards one well-defined historical state of affairs presupposes the obscuring of another. Of course, the process of reflection for its part can be continued endlessly, so that further and further domains are illuminated, but it never finally leads out of history. In a certain sense, an independent position would have to be adopted if there is to be a priori certainty about the progressive implications of reflection. In carrying out reflection as such one is never sure of this, since one has only insufficient information about the goal of the historical process while it is going on. What is more, historical experience shows that along with enlightenment there can also be a return of obscurantism, that supposed progress in reality may be reaction. Those members of the Frankfurt School who advocate a critique of ideology, Horkheimer and Adorno, have called this surprising and disillusioning finding the 'Dialectic of Enlightenment'.[102] Consequently, it remains the case that we must take account of the relativity of the process of enlightenment. But that is done even by hermeneutics.

Truth?

For all that, what remains after these attacks, even if hermeneutics can parry the objections brought against it, is the unclarity about epistemological status which was the real occasion of the controversies. What kind of 'truth' is especially revealed to her-

---

[102] On this see below, Ch. 3.

meneutic thought and is it the only truth?[103] Perhaps we shall make more progress on this point if we bear in mind that hermeneutics allows the reflection which it requires in all individual cases to be valid also in its full conclusiveness in relation to itself. The understanding of the historically conditioned character of world-pictures and social orientations affords practical enlightenment in concrete situations. To recall the unthinking preunderstanding or the implicitly used background knowledge in all processes of scientific enquiry breaks down the dogmatic belief in the ultimate superiority of method. Hermeneutic reflection thus demonstrates case by case and ad hoc the finite nature of our knowledge at any time.

It does not demonstrate this absolutely, in general and once for all, since for that a standpoint free of all limitations would have to be adopted. Hermeneutics does not operate with a suprahistorical universal knowledge, under which individual cases have merely to be subsumed. It is not an a priori theory. But also it does not exhaust itself in the contingent series of reflections on changing facts, without drawing conclusions of a higher epistemological level from them. It formulates a *theory of the historicity and finite nature of all theory*. Consequently it says in general terms that theoretical generality must be measured against the concrete.

How is the paradox to be resolved? The insights of hermeneutics are to be acquired and verified only in concrete terms – generally expressed, they seem rather empty. In that hermeneutics explicitly connects its own possibility of knowledge as a philosophical theory with concretization, it applies to itself what its doctrine says applies to all other cases. Hermeneutic philosophy does not float above the clouds, but accepts its own relation to the fundamental relativity of knowing. Anyone who is not satisfied by this should be clear in his own mind what he is demanding: an a priori theory which establishes its own validity in the face of the historical change in knowledge and science, without itself being touched by such change.

One can play down the question of the epistemological status of philosophical theories by simply pursuing what everyone is

---

[103] Cf. Richard Rorty's sympathetic remarks on hermeneutics (*Philosophy and the Mirror of Nature*, Princeton, 1979). I doubt, however, if his term 'edifying hermeneutics' is adequate, since it is more than a successor to classical '*Bildung*'.

pursuing, whether it be linguistic analysis or logic or theory of science. One then shares with everyone else the conviction of the importance of this pursuit, which even seems well founded, as long as this conviction is everyone's conviction. Nevertheless, one in this way takes over a historical point of view, whose historical character is not perceptible for the moment, because there are no alternatives, but comes to be seen without fail whenever it is relativized by the past or the future. A sophisticated way of evading the problem of history in regard to the epistemological status of philosophical theories is represented by the postulation of a 'third world', in which, according to Popper, the development of human knowledge is preserved in crystalline structures and free from the dross of history. In this way, of course, one resists historicism at the price of a world of Platonic Ideas, which can be established, not on the basis of a metaphysical certainty, but only by means of the reconstruction of the history of thought.

The only one who would be finally secure against the danger of the subversion of the knowledge-claims of a theory by history would be someone who was capable of deriving wisdom from sources which bubbled forth independently of historical experience. Such an isolated philosophy, beyond the self-understanding of its epoch and the available knowledge of the time, would of course have little of interest and probably not even anything new to say. It would continue to play its self-contained games within the traditional canon of themes of a *philosophia perennis*. At all events, hermeneutic reflection can teach us that even the idea of a *philosophia perennis*, contrary to its title, is a historical phenomenon and merely a product of tradition. The suprahistorical philosophy proves to be a historical illusion!

2

Philosophy of language and theory of science

Language as a philosophical focus

It has justifiably been said that the philosophy of our century, in contrast to that of all previous periods, is united by a common interest in language. The topic of language unites the various schools, from phenomenology and hermeneutics to analytical philosophy and theory of science. This does not mean that language is regarded as the principal or indeed the only object of philosophical reflection. Such a narrow view is taken in only a few groups who are gradually transforming philosophy into linguistics. It may be predicted that this is an ephemeral phenomenon; for all over-subtle or extreme reductionist theories enjoy acclaim only for a time, until calm inspection reveals their narrowness. A philosophy which sought to do nothing but investigate language would surrender its claim to be regarded as of enduring value. It would, that is, from the outset limit to a single domain its remarkable capacity to recognize and treat of problems which arise in life and the sciences. Philosophy has never before been a matter for '*terribles simplificateurs*'.

Thus, if one takes into account the whole development of the century, the omnipresence of the theme of language is to be seen, not in the imminent replacement of philosophy by philosophy of language, but in the fact that all the questions of philosophy, even those inherited from the past, are discussed in more or less obviously linguistic terms. That applies to epistemology and theory of science as well as to ethics and social philosophy, to aesthetics as a theory of symbolic communication and history as a hermeneutic context of tradition. Seen in this way, the common theme of language provides a basis on which not only a variety of specialist debates but also the separately proceeding traditions of the more recent developments in philosophy may be set in relation to one another with some prospect of success.[1]

It remains one of the ironies of the history of philosophy that important German contributions to the articulation of this general topic of contemporary philosophy first found an echo abroad and that this amplification by echo was necessary for them to receive any attention in their own homeland. Thus, Frege, the scarcely known Professor of Mathematics who never obtained a regular Chair, achieved fame above all through Bertrand Russell and his successors. Until fairly recently, Frege was read much more in English translation than in the original. Wittgenstein, whose deep roots in the cultural milieu of Vienna have only gradually come to be recognized,[2] taught in Cambridge from the twenties onward. Although he wrote predominantly in German up until the end, there is a tendency to regard him as the archetypal English philosopher. His exotic connexions were completely naturalized.

For all that, the preliminary work done by phenomenology and hermeneutics makes it easy for Germans to make contact with the forms of philosophy of language developed with lasting effect in America and England since the early sixties. Anything significant which happened since then in philosophy of language from the German-speaking world represents an amalgam of what is native and what comes from outside. The later Wittgenstein's concept of a language-game naturally fell on fertile soil in the hermeneutic school, while further original contributions on the lines laid down by Frege have been made above all by Ernst Tugendhat. In what follows, I shall consider two outstanding examples: the theory of a hermeneutic–pragmatic communication community (Apel, Habermas) and formal semantics (Tugendhat).

The adaptation of the language-game

Let us begin with the first-named theory, whose genesis and aims

---

[1] Cf. Apel, *Analytic Philosophy of Language and the Geisteswissenschaften* (translated by H. Holstelilie), Dordrecht, 1967.
[2] See Janik and Toulmin, *Wittgenstein's Vienna*, New York, 1973.

require a somewhat detailed presentation, if the necessary critical remarks are really to hit their target. The theory of the *communication community* or of the *ideal dialogue* has been advocated, amongst others, chiefly by Karl-Otto Apel and Jürgen Habermas, though with different emphases. Since Habermas' philosophical ideas are more appropriately to be treated under the heading of 'Dialectic' in the next section, I shall mostly confine myself here to an account of Apel, though I am conscious of a certain artificiality about separating them. Some allowance should also be made for an occasional variation in the formulation of the programme: its outlines have been clearly enough discernible for some time, making it possible to speak of a programme, but its gradual realization is still to be treated as a kind of 'work in progress'.

Wittgenstein's philosophical efforts were always directed towards the clarification of the logic of language. Originally he believed, as the *Tractatus Logico-philosophicus* makes clear, that this required an exact ideal language, which would strip away without remainder the 'disguises' with which everyday language conceals thought.[3] The positivists of the Vienna Circle, to whom Wittgenstein's first work was almost a Bible, derived from the concept of an ideal language the demand for a physicalistic unified science. This would include the corpus of all sentences which were meaningful by scientific standards, which helped to establish philosophy as the 'handmaiden of the sciences' in the sense of being the logic of science. While the Vienna positivists still held on to this attractive idea, Wittgenstein had long been concerned to abandon the old ideal. He had recognized that the dogma of the one logically exact language which would include all scientific truth itself stood in the way of the real intention of clarifying the logic of language.

In a number of phases, which can now be observed in the posthumously published works, Wittgenstein lighted upon the notion of the language-game which the *Philosophical Investigations* has made popular. In this way, the picture of the two Wittgensteins, for so long fashionable in the literature, is untenable. The later philosophy pursues further the initial intentions, admittedly in the form of a self-criticism of the earlier philosophy, to the

[3] *Tractatus*, 4.002ff., 4.112.

extent that it represents a misleading attempt at a solution which impedes genuine elucidation of the logic of language.[4]

The job is to be better done by means of the conception of a philosophy of language which connects language with practice in a more flexible way. Logical enquiry must always take into account the contextual conditions of the current *language-game*, in which we successfully move and come to an understanding with each other. 'Here the term "language-*game*" is meant to bring into prominence the fact that the *speaking* of language is part of an activity, or of a form of life'.[5]

This suggestive definition leaves a lot open and so may be used for several purposes. It remains unclear how the 'part' which the speaking of language is said to be is related to a whole, which other parts are possibly relevant, whether these parts are themselves activities, or whether activity is the whole, and finally whether activity and form of life are identical. Be that as it may, the fruitfulness of the concept of a language-game cannot be divorced from its conscious lack of precision. The hermeneutic conception of intersubjective understanding in the 'life-world' found here some welcome support.

A direct part of the looser treatment of language as a multiplicity of possible games, in which language is used in accordance with current pragmatic conditions, is the thesis that the games have a merely family resemblance to each other. By alluding to analogies which disclose themselves only to concrete intuition, Wittgenstein rejects the demand that he should state what is essential to the language-game; for that is just a reappearance of the old misleading demand for the one ideal language, valid for all discourse and all purposes, on which the *Tractatus* had, in the eyes of its self-critical author, run aground.[6]

It is precisely on this point of a methodical moderation in philosophy which limits itself to sensitive descriptions of actual practice rather than prescription that the theory of the communication community, which had gladly welcomed the concept of the language-game, turns its back on Wittgenstein. Philosophy

---

[4] On the corrected image of Wittgenstein, cf. A. Kenny, *Wittgenstein*, London, 1973; also some remarks by the present writer ('Die Einheit in Wittgensteins Wandlungen', *Philosophische Rundschau*, 15, 1968).

[5] *Philosophical Investigations*, section 23 (from the translation by G. E. M. Anscombe, Oxford, 1953).

[6] Ibid., sections 65ff.

should not be a matter of carefully tracing the manifold and remarkable forms of intersubjectively reliable ways of coming to an
understanding in functioning language-games, but of the specification of the *ideal language-game*, which represents the transcendental condition of the possibility of all actual language-games.
Dissatisfaction with Wittgenstein's stoical maxim that philosophy should leave everything as it is, since in the end it merely
creates unnecessary problems for itself through criticism,[7] goes
hand in hand with the refusal to rely on the hermeneutic confidence that in all contested cases it must be possible somehow or
other to come to an understanding. The discussion of hermeneutics had indeed shown that its claims to universality were
grounded essentially on the fact of the hermeneutic experience as
the occasionally complete and constantly successful assimilation
of what is unfamiliar, but not on an independently specifiable and
intrinsically compelling principle of reason. To the critics, the
reference to the actual practice of the art of interpretation had
appeared mere empiricism, which did not satisfy the philosophical demand for foundations in the strict sense. From dissatisfaction with simple recourse to actual understanding emerged the
thesis of the ideal communication community, which admittedly
in a peculiar way vacillates between the status of a postulate of
reason and recourse to given facts.

Apel writes in a typical passage:[8]

> In order to translate into our terms the dividends to be
> derived for the philosophy of language from the notion
> of a language-game, it seems to me necessary to think
> with Wittgenstein against Wittgenstein and beyond
> Wittgenstein. Thus, for instance, it is not sufficient to
> replace, as Wittgenstein does, the referential model of
> language, and with it the idea of a 'meaning' as a kind of

---

[7] E.g. Ibid., sections 124ff., 133.

[8] 'Der transzendentalhermeneutische Begriff der Sprache', in
Transformation der Philosophie Vol. II, Frankfurt, 1973, pp. 346ff.
(partially translated, London, 1980); cf. also Apel's paper in C. H.
Heidrich (ed.), *Semantics and Communication*, Amsterdam, 1974, and
'The a priori of communication and the foundation of the humanities',
Man and World, 5, 1972. Peter Winch makes sympathetic, though
critical, comments on Apel's conception of the philosophy of language
in S. C. Brown (ed.), *Philosophical Disputes in the Social Sciences*,
Hassocks, 1979.

object, which (in its original form) fits only proper
names, by the demand for a 'description' of the manifold
functions and rules of use of language – necessary
though precisely such a pragmatic widening of horizons
proves to be in view of the one-sidedly logical and
epistemological orientation of Western philosophy of
language . . . Wittgenstein's insight that all meaningfully
thinkable (i.e. checkable) observance of rules is in
principle *public*, and hence dependent on language-games,
includes the further requirement that the describer of the
language-game *participate* in it in a manner which is still
to be explained. If he were to observe it merely from the
outside, he could by no means be certain that the rules
which he presupposes in his description are identical
with those which are in fact followed in the sense of the
language-game.

Connected with this, however, is the fact that the
philosopher does not empirically observe and describe
human language-games (and so the 'forms of life' in
which they are interwoven) *only* as objectively occurring
facts, but always also as something which he himself can
practise, *reflected upon* from the point of view of *critical*
and *normative* discourse. Without this assumption,
Wittgenstein's programme of therapy through the
critique of language, his talk of the use of language in
philosophy as 'meaningless' or 'idling', is completely
unintelligible. In short, the philosopher as critic of
language must be clear that in the business of describing
language-games he is himself laying claim to a specific
language-game, which is reflexively and critically related
to all merely possible language-games. Consequently,
the philosopher always assumes that he is capable in
principle of participating in all language-games, or of
entering into *communication* with the corresponding
language-communities. In this way, however, a
postulate is assumed which seems to contradict
Wittgenstein's thesis that the indefinitely many and
varied 'language-games' which he has in mind must have
nothing further *in common* than a certain 'family
resemblance', and thus have no essential feature present

in them all. In reality, the *common* element of all
'language-games' lies, in my opinion, in the fact that,
when *one* language is learned, and so when successful
socialization into *one* 'form of life' interwoven with that
use of language takes place, something like *the*
language-game, i.e. *the* human form of life, is also
learned: that is, the *competence* is acquired to reflect on
one's own language or form of life and to *communicate*
with all other language-games. . .

Only the *ideal* (in the normative sense) *language-game*
of an *ideal communication community* (can) be regarded as a
postulated control-instance of human rule-following in
general. This ideal language-game is indeed anticipated
as a *real possibility* of the language-game in which he
participates, that is, is presupposed as a *condition of the
possibility and validity of his action* as a meaningful action,
by everyone who follows a rule – implicitly by anyone
who, for instance, acts *meaningfully* in accordance with
its requirements, explicitly by anyone who engages in
argument.

The aim of the reflection is the universal capacity of every
competent speaker to participate in every concrete language-
game. To be able to talk means to be able in principle to talk to
anyone about anything. The philosopher who makes this demand
should not be content with the empirical description of all possible language-games and the factual demonstration of constantly
repeated success in entering into determinate communication
with others. He should in so doing have in mind a *norm* which
serves for the critique of certain language-games which do not
satisfy the norm. This norm consists in the ideal of a communication community, which is not only to be thought of as all-
embracing but also provides the guarantee of 'meaningful' action,
especially in the case of argumentation. The norm of an ideal
communication community, however, does not result only from
the analysis of language-games themselves, nor even from
reflection on the presuppositions of functioning intersubjective
intercourse by means of language, but represents in its turn a
philosophical postulate. The complexity of the position which Apel
takes arises from the fact that in this case several things are mixed

up together which seem to be capable of shedding mutual light on each other.

What is transcendental pragmatics?

It is probably clear that the appeal to Wittgenstein as a way of introducing the pragmatic dimension has a predominantly strategic character. Other kinds of support are brought in as required. Searle's theory of speech-acts or the three-way division of semiotics according to Charles Morris, who besides the logical ordering of symbols in syntax and the dimension of reference in semantics takes into account also the use of signs in pragmatics, are frequently introduced by way of confirmation and built into a new version of the pragmatist model of a community of enquirers (Peirce[9] and others). However, from none of the above-mentioned sketches of the philosophy of language is it possible to read off the a priori pre-eminence of the pragmatic aspect of linguistic action; rather, taking seriously the pragmatic aspects helps to correct the one-sidedness of a purely logical analysis in the traditional manner. Apel on the other hand places unlimited transcendental hopes on taking the pragmatic aspect seriously. The whole question is thus that of producing a convincing connexion between *pragmatics* and *transcendentality*.

This connexion, however, simply cannot be produced on the basis of the two elements taken on their own. The undeniable and important insight into the pragmatic aspect of language, which is actively used and intersubjectively employed, does not in itself permit any inferences at all to transcendental states of affairs. One cannot say that the role which language plays in the communication community has the status of a transcendental condition of the possibility of something. Of course we must use language in order to be able to come to an understanding with each other. But there is the risk here of circularity in one's justificatory arguments. As long as the achievement of understanding amongst human beings is left to the use of language (and cannot be replaced by the intelligible relations in which beings of pure reason like angels may stand to each other), language is a necessary institution for the purposes of intersubjective understanding. This simple truism cannot therefore be what is intended.

[9] Cf. Apel, *Der Denkweg von C. S. Peirce*, Frankfurt, 1975.

In fact, associated with the model of the transcendental-pragmatic communication community there is a clearly *normative* element. What is to be insisted upon is not that we employ language in talking to each other, but that we should observe a certain kind of language-use when we associate in a certain manner with each other as human beings. Instead of merely describing the variety of possible language-games, in order to recognize the existing family-resemblances of all language-games to each other, *one* language-game is to be picked out which everyone ought to play and against which all other forms of language-use are to be measured. The one language-game to be played by everyone is ascertained by attending to the clear exigencies of *rationality*.

Everyone who speaks intelligibly and meaningfully has to observe entirely determinate rules in speaking. These rules, however, govern not only the use of words and sentence-construction, but also the relationship with the partner in discourse who is presupposed in every speech-transaction. The pragmatic dimension of speaking extends beyond linguistic requirements to the standards of treatment of the partner as a partner. The recognition of the other as a rational and equal alter ego extends to all possible partners in reciprocal discourse without exception. The universal recognition of all human beings as having equal rights which is obviously involved here seems to arise on the basis of a more exact analysis of the language-game. By this means ancient difficulties in the foundations of a rational ethics would be very realistically resolved at a stroke. Nevertheless, appearances are deceptive.

Apel starts from an entirely determinate language-game which he explains as the typical one and as binding. He has in mind primarily the rational mode of language-use which is called *argumentation*. In fact someone who engages in argument, rather than for instance in flattery, threatening, lying or filibustering, proceeds on the basis of a consensus about rational standards, to which he is himself as much subject as anyone else. A scientific debate or a scholarly dispute in a seminar proceeds rationally when certain norms of argumentation such as clarity, intelligibility, willingness to listen and to admit alternatives, etc., are adhered to by all participants. The peculiar form of language-use is apparent in this case in that the aim in view is recognized to be rationality rather than egoism or a common endeavour to deal with some matter of importance to all rather than the rhetorical effect of the individual. The norm of rationality must therefore be recognized and accepted if the participants in a particular language-game are to be able to follow it.

From the commendable decision to conduct discourse in a rational manner however it can certainly not be inferred that every dialogue and, still more generally, every language-game must be explicitly rational, so that the rule of language indicated in one case supplies criteria for evaluating all other cases of human speech. On the contrary, it is precisely the rational case which is probably the exception. Institutionalized language-games such as questioning, advising or commanding (Wittgenstein's favourite example) pursue quite different goals, that is to say, from the improvement of knowledge or the advancement of a common task. Frivolous small talk, polite conversation, ceremonies of all kinds and not least the wide domain of *rhetoric*, in which the aim is to win over and convince someone of something at any price – all these belong among the language-games in daily use. It is not true that in these cases the basis is always a mutually recognized equality of roles, nor do the clear principles of rationality always apply. What justification is there then for elevating into a universal norm a model of rational discussion between partners who mutually recognize each other which was first developed at a high level of culture?

The answer given is that we must work with 'counterfactual conditions', knowing full well that normally speech does not conform to the ideal. We cannot help inventing *ideal conditions* if we are to take ourselves seriously as partners in discourse, that is, to preserve our human dignity in preserving that of all others. This answer cannot be satisfactory, since it already presupposes the very thing which is being questioned. Once we accept rationality as a norm, it follows that we behave in accordance with this norm, even if the otherwise practised forms of intercourse do not always corroborate the norm. The rules which must be followed by anyone who wishes to carry on a rational dialogue are certainly binding and valid without exception. The question, however, was what compels us to decide to undertake a rational dialogue.

If the reply to this is that it is reason itself which creates the obligation, in so far as we, as rational beings, cannot abstract from it, then there is a gap in the argument; for then it is not a matter of transcendental reflection or a conclusion drawn immanently from the constitutive conditions of discourse. Rather, it is the specification of a self-evident and compelling principle of reason which is premised in the dialogue. This move is, however, inadmissible. The professed intention, of course, is to translate into the terms of linguistic philosophy the classical transcendental philosophy of the Kantian type, which is ultimately based on rational self-evidence, even if it be in the form of the practically binding moral law. Nevertheless, it has now become clear that the bridge from pragmatics to transcendental validity, which at first sight could not be built without further support, is supported by a normative element which has to be introduced from outside. What is in dispute is not whether the norm of rational dialogue (and so a dialogue conceived of as taking place in ideal, counterfactual conditions) is desirable: it is! The point at issue is only whether this norm results of itself from the analysis of the language-game in terms of transcendental pragmatics: and that is not so!

Practical hypotheses for argumentation

In an instructive passage, *Habermas*, who is rightly much more cautious than Apel about repeating postulates of transcendental philosophy, acknowledges the dilemma just referred to in the form of an allusion to Kant. He writes:[10]

> The ideal speech-situation would be most properly compared with a transcendental illusion, except that this illusion, instead of being due to an inadmissible transfer (as in the use of the categories of the understanding outside experience), would also be a constitutive condition of possible discourse. The anticipation of the ideal speech-situation has for all possible communication the significance of a constitutive illusion, which at the same time is the appearance of a form of life. We cannot know a priori whether that appearance is a mere

[10] 'Vorbereitende Bermerkungen zu einer Theorie der kommunikativen Kompetenz', in Habermas and Luhmann, *Theorie der Gesellschaft oder Sozialtechnologie*, Frankfurt, 1971, p. 141 (translated in H. P. Dreitzel (ed.), *Recent Sociology 2*, London, 1970).

delusion (subreption), stemming as usual from inevitable suppositions, or whether the empirical conditions for the actualization, be it only approximate, of the supposed form of life can practically be produced. The fundamental norms of possible discourse which are built into universal pragmatics include from these points of view a practical hypothesis. From this hypothesis, which must be developed into a theory of communicative competence and given a foundation, the critical theory of society takes its start.

A *practical hypothesis* which aims at the production of the kind of social relationships under which the ideal speech situation would be a reality and not merely a postulate is, however, something different from the transcendental condition of possibility a priori, without which we could not under any circumstances do what we do when we communicate with each other. The metaphor of a *transcendental illusion*, which Habermas borrows from Kant, goes to the heart of the matter. Kant, in the *Critique of Pure Reason*, at the beginning of the 'Transcendental Dialectic', had made use of the term 'illusion', associated as it was with deception and sophistry, in order to explain why the human mind, which is situated between the finitude of sense and the absoluteness of reason, is constantly afflicted by an 'illusion'[11] which it can never shake off despite all critical enlightenment by philosophy. The peculiar nature of a finite reason necessarily involves a tendency falsely to transgress its own limits. Although we know that we must, for the theoretical purposes of knowledge, limit our reason as understanding to the finite conditions of sense, we simply cannot avoid doing something similar to what happens, for example, in the case of optical illusions, namely, treating pure reason as constitutive even beyond the world of experience.

To transcend the world of experience leads, in a theoretical context, to the confusion which Kant calls 'Dialectic' and seeks to remove by means of his critique. To go beyond the actual situation of dialogue towards counterfactual assumptions has in Habermas, however, a practical intention, and to that end is supposed to be called for precisely in the name of a critical theory of society. The reference to Kant's 'transcendental illusion' thus

[11] *Critique of Pure Reason*, A297.

shows the double polarization, from the theoretical dialectic to a practical hypothesis and from a prohibition resulting from the critique of knowledge to a postulate inspired by the critique of ideology. I said that this unorthodox reference to Kant is in reality more suited to communication theory than the straightforward claim to reformulate the classical transcendental philosophy in terms of modern philosophy of language. Apel usually presents his programme in fact as the continuation of a reflection on the conditions of possibility of knowledge, in the course of which in important places the concept of knowledge is replaced by that of argument.

The impression is given that argumentation is the modern successor of cognition, corresponding to the advance of philosophy of language. In the context of the communication community, knowledge is presented in the form of argumentation. Anyone who argues, so we are told, could not but postulate the ideal dialogue and recognize its norms, even if he in fact does not always observe them. Thus, before I examine the legitimacy of the claim that transcendental philosophy must be reformulated as communication theory, I must look into the concept of argument. The problem of the 'transcendental illusion' will be seen in still another light.

Arguments are what, since the Socratic 'invention' of the philosophical dialogue as an intersubjectively employed means of achieving knowledge, alone count as satisfying the demand to 'give a reason' (*logon didonai*). Arguments are used therefore when justification is required. Those grounds which can be adduced to support an assertion, inasmuch as the assertion is not believed just as it stands, are called arguments. Consequently, arguments must be intelligible in the context of a determinate speech-situation and for certain purposes. A set of reasons counts as an argument when it is not further disputed or declared to be in need of further justification. Hence arguments acquire a situational and pragmatic value. In such and such a situation, and given such and such a state of knowledge, something has an appeal as an argument; though in a different speech-situation and with a different state of knowledge it would not be sufficient. Arguments must be accepted, they do not normally compel through necessity. Plausibility is required, not strict proof.

The Socratic dialogues show very clearly that the conduct of philosophical discourse between partners who work at the common clarification of some question which interests them all *never proceeds under ideal conditions*. It presupposes rather the contingent circumstances of everyday life and the assumptions made at the time by the participants. No one already knows everything, neither the so-called sages or sophists nor their critic Socrates, who emphasizes that his only advantage over them is that he is aware of his ignorance. Any of them can be mistaken and take his opinion as an argument or be convinced by a false argument. The dialogues proceed, not in a purposeful or well-ordered way, but aporetically and partly along false trails. Ideal dialogues would be ones in which no preconceptions stood in the way, no differences in knowledge would need to be compensated for, criticism and self-criticism counterbalanced each other, no one cheated or used rhetorical methods of persuasion, sufficient time was available for conclusive settlement of the issue and emotions or aggression were put aside. However, if a topic is to be discussed among completely rational partners, why do they have to enter into dialogue in ideal conditions at all? The task of the dialogue consists precisely in the *production* of rationality under conditions which still *fall short of* rationality. Ideal dialogues would lack problems and be merely playful exercises. Ultimately, if there were in fact no such deficiency in rationality, this would deprive the dialogue of all basis.

The special position of argument as the means of rationality available within non-ideal dialogue has been recognized since Aristotle's *Rhetoric* and *Topics* even from the logical point of view. The *logic of argumentation*[12] there conceived is called by Aristotle, on the model of dialogue, 'dialectical' – which is not to be confused with the modern use of the word. It aims at certain 'commonplaces' (*topoi*) which are relevant to the circumstances of the debate and which are universally recognized but not for that reason capable of satisfying all conceivable standards of rationality with respect to their validity and exactness. In this regard there is a clear difference between the logic of argumentation and scientific proof (*apodeixis*), the logical structure of which is the

---

12 A modern descendant is Stephen Toulmin (*The Uses of Argument*, Cambridge, 1958). Cf. the review by O. Bird, 'The re-discovery of the topics', in *Mind*, 70, 1961. Habermas occasionally alludes to Toulmin (cf. 'Wahrheitstheorien', in Fahrenbach (ed.), *Wirklichkeit und Reflexion*, *Festschrift für Walter Schulz*, Pfullingen, 1973).

theme of Aristotle's theory of science,[13] as found in the *Analytica posteriora*. <u>Proof</u> which is compelling under all circumstances and derived from true premises of a more fundamental and more general character corresponds to the ontology of the subject under consideration itself. <u>Argum</u>ents, by contrast, are always subject to the practical aims of the given dialogue-situation.

Only on the basis of this distinction does it become finally possible to find a clue to a very tricky problem. What if a deep *illusion of rationality*, under the guise of arguments recognized by everyone, allows purely private goals to be pursued more satisfactorily? The mere demand that one should enter into arguments and reciprocal exchange of speech between equal partners is never in itself a guarantee of genuinely rational intersubjectivity. The rhetorical topic reveals what one must represent in which situations and in which ways if one is to satisfy the demand for argumentation in the context of a controversy and nevertheless retain the upper hand. Its origins in the techniques of pleading in the law-courts are here discernible. One should not therefore allow oneself to be deceived by such declarations of readiness for argumentation into thinking that in the act itself ideal conditions are produced. The illusion of rationality, which since the time of the Greeks has borne the name of sophistry, represents rather the most stubborn problem for the theory of the ideal communication community.[14] What does the criterion which makes it possible to distinguish in discussion between the illusion of rationality and genuine rationality look like if the counterfactual assumption merely distinguishes argumentative from non-argumentative discourse? The question remains, not just unanswered, but hardly even noticed by the philosophers of language in their eagerness to give global answers to the previously distinguished questions of epistemology and ethics.

Transcendental reflection

In the course of his transformation of transcendental philosophy, Apel has not hesitated to take a step beyond which it is by

---

[13] The modern analysis of scientific explanation is but a highly sophisticated version of that proof in terms of apodictic syllogisms. Cf. E. Nagel, *The Structure of Science*, New York, 1961, ch. 3.

[14] On this see below, Ch.3.

definition impossible to go. He proposes an 'ultimate foundation of a non–deductive, but reflective kind'.[15] By the pretentious title of *ultimate foundation* is understood a foundation such that it derives from a principle which is the ultimate one in so far as it cannot reasonably require further foundation. Aristotle already used the argument that an infinite regress is ruled out, since reference back to further and further reasons must make all deduction in the sense of *apodeixis* meaningless. He inferred from this that deduction might only be carried out on the basis of first principles. There are admittedly several of these, which must moreover be weighed according to their competence in the given context in regard to what is to be founded. The relationship between the principle and what is derived from it must therefore be established case by case.

The radical thesis of an ultimate foundation clearly goes beyond this, in so far as it implies the superfluousness of any further enquiry and any relation of grounding which may be established in the particular case. The ultimate foundation terminates all reasoning once and for all. In modern systems of philosophy such a claim has been made, for instance, by Spinoza and by Fichte, who alludes to Spinoza. The '*causa sui*' is conceived of as the ultimate principle such that no abstraction can be made from its existence and such that it is certainly impossible to proceed to any further foundation because it is its own foundation. Fichte's 'absolute Ego' is to be understood in a very similar fashion. In the spontaneous, presuppositionless act of 'saying-I-to–itself' this principle originally posits itself and enables the world of the not–I to emerge at the same time as itself, so that the fact that the principle needs no foundation and its comprehensive function as a source of further deductions are mutually complementary. The examples show that to grasp such a principle amounts to perceiving the impossibility of further enquiry and the consistency of the consequent deduction at one and the same time. That is the meaning of radical ultimate foundation.

Apel is of course clear that it is impossible to establish a comparable dogma of a metaphysical kind in terms of the philosophy of language. Apel substitutes reflection for deduction and eluci-

---

15 'Das Problem der philosophischen Letztbegründung im Lichte einer transzendentalen Sprachpragmatik', in B. Kanitscheider (ed.), *Sprache und Erkenntnis, Festschrift für G. Frey*, Innsbruck, 1976.

dates the notion of an ultimate foundation in terms of the '*impossibility of going beyond it*'. This certainly involves a fundamental change in the thesis. For the argument to show that the attempt to get beyond certain assumptions through reflection is bound to fail is carried on at a purely factual level. There is no sense in a further step in reflection at that point, since the elucidation of presuppositions here runs up against its limits. But if it is a merely contingent matter that further steps would be senseless, then the work of foundation is incomplete. It would have to demonstrate that the extreme point attainable by reflection can be made responsible both for the existence and for the particular form of the facts from which the reflection began. For that reason it is far from evident that the ultimate ground has been attained at this point. For that would imply that to gain insight into it is the same as gaining insight into its uniqueness and primacy.

The contingent demonstration is based on the idleness of repeating the act of reflection and hence on the premise that it is that reflection which brings to consciousness the constitutive conditions of the language-game which is alone the ultimate meaningful act. When one sees that it would be fruitless to reflect further in the same way, while other possibilities of reflection are not open, one has the *experience* of running up against a *limit*. There is nothing in this experience, however, to show that the limit is one of principle, or that the principle is unique and not further derivable, or the principle of principles. One must rather have stylized into principles in advance those conditions on which the reflection has come aground, and that indicates an arbitrary and purely external assumption, which cannot be reached on the path of transcendental enquiry alone. Or one decides to adopt the model of a deduction[16] and then once again comes up against the problems of the Kantian position,[17] which was supposed to be

[16] Cf. S. Körner, 'On the impossibility of transcendental deductions', *Monist*, 51, 1967; E. Schaper, 'Are transcendental deductions impossible?', in L. W. Beck (ed.), *Proceedings of the IIIrd International Kant Congress*, Dordrecht, 1972; Körner, 'Über ontologische Notwendigkeit und die Begründung ontologischer Prinzipien', *Neue Hefte für philosophie*, 14, 1978 (this also contains further papers on the same topic by R. Chisholm, M. Gram, R. Rorty, H. Krings and B. Puntel).

[17] An exceedingly subtle interpretation of the Kantian doctrine is to be found in D. Henrich, *Identität und Objektivität (Abhandlung der Heidelberger Akademie der Wissenschaften)*, Heidelberg, 1976.

superseded precisely by using the tools provided by the philosophy of language.

After all this, does the reinterpretation of transcendental philosophy as a doctrine of the ideal communication community seem in general to be possible? Two weighty objections cannot be dismissed on closer consideration, despite all the elegant and wordy efforts at translation. Both are connected with the fundamental ideas of transcendental philosophy. One objection concerns the pre-givenness of a concept of *knowledge*, the other the *self-referential* structure of transcendental reflection.

The quest for the conditions of the possibility of knowledge has to begin with the *givenness* of knowledge, in order to know in general what it is of which the conditions of possibility are sought. According to Kant and the more recent theory of science, the paradigm of knowledge is to be found in the sciences; according to hermeneutics, in the historical continuity of the understanding of tradition and social institutions. However one wishes to define knowledge, philosophy must start from such a datum, in order to reveal its constitutive presuppositions. The given character of that of which the conditions of possibility are considered indicates in perfectly general terms the *direction* of the transcendental reflection.

However, on the premise of the concept of knowledge there also depends the efficiency of a reflection which must recognize as transcendental that it cannot free itself from its object. The conditions of the possibility of knowledge which are reflected upon are also at the same time the conditions of the possibility of the reflection directed towards them. Hence one may speak of '*self-referentiality*' as the central structure of any transcendental argument.[18] Only if it becomes evident that even the question of the conditions of possible knowledge, as far as concerns its own possibility as a question, stands under the same conditions into which it enquires, is the validity of the conditions exhibited demonstrated. In other words: the possibility of a transcendental reflection is connected with the possibility of the knowledge towards which the reflection is directed. Transcendental reflection itself, therefore, demonstrates, in so far as it is not entirely free-floating or does not have access to higher sources of know-

---

[18] I refer to this in my article, 'Kant, transcendental arguments and the problem of deduction', *Review of Metaphysics*, 28, 1975.

ledge, that in the conditions of our knowledge, once given, alternatives are inconceivable.

The *lack of alternatives* to the conditions of the possibility of knowledge which are available to us cannot be demonstrated a priori and independently of the act of transcendental reflection itself. For that we should have to have at our disposal a pure insight into grounds beyond the knowledge which is possible for us. But then we should have already implicitly presupposed the alternatives. The effort of transcendental reflection to get behind the knowledge which is given, however, is, since through its own activity it itself confirms the universal condition of knowledge, the touchstone of the absence of alternatives. Along this route it is possible to construct a proof, which is least burdened by further presuppositions, of the legitimacy of that knowledge which is alone in fact available to us. I grant that I am here following a particular interpretation of the fundamental structure of transcendental philosophy which I find most convincing. The interpretation may be disputed.[19] I do not need, however, by any means to broach the whole discussion about a renewal of transcendental philosophy in order to elucidate in the debate with the communication theorists at least the two objections mentioned at the outset.

Just now it was asserted that transcendental reflection operates under the premise of a concept of knowledge and only for that reason does its work in the sense of self-referentiality. Apel's transformation, however, remains characteristically *vague* with regard to *what* it is of which the conditions of possibility are to be sought. Sometimes it seems to be a matter of the conditions of the possibility of knowledge as such, sometimes of the conditions of the possibility of linguistic articulation of or critical communication about knowledge, sometimes however also of what makes possible the language-game in general, of the intersubjective form of life merely or even of a norm, to be qualified in ethical terms, for the reciprocal relations of rational beings with each other. All this is not one and the same problem, nor can the many different problems be resolved together in terms of the ultimate foundation. Above all, however, the confusion of the theoretical

[19] E.g. R. Rorty, 'Transcendental arguments, self-reference and pragmatism', in Bier, Horstman, Krüger (eds.), *Transcendental Arguments and Science*, Dordrecht, 1979; M.S. Gram, 'Do transcendental arguments have a future?', *Neue Hefte für Philosophie*, 14, 1978, p. 41.

and practical spheres can by no means be regarded as the modern reproduction of the Kantian programme of transcendental philosophy, which was based precisely on the clear separation of the understanding as transcendental condition of the possibility of knowledge and reason as the absolute motivation for action.

The second objection is directed at the *lack of a place for* the reflection called transcendental itself. The interaction community of the partners participating in the language-game forms the point of departure, at which the character of the dialogue, as something which encroaches upon the individual subjectivity, is emphatically set up as a corrective against Kant's alleged narrowing of vision to the isolated ego. The ideal norm of mutual recognition of subjects forms the vanishing-point towards which the transcendental reflection is to be orientated. The activity of transcendental reflection for its part, however, which is supposed to mediate between the given point of departure and the counterfactual assumption, does not fit at all into the assumed picture. The communication community does not reflect on itself consistently, as a kind of collective subject, with a view to the unalterable presuppositions for its existence, but a philosopher approaching from the outside points to certain normatively characterized premises on the basis of the various language-games, only loosely connected by family resemblances. This act of *external* elucidation and criticism cannot however be called 'transcendental' even in the most generous interpretation of the term. The philosopher, as privileged subject, is not by any means associated by virtue of reflection with what is reflected upon but speaks externally about it from a special meta-position. What may be said from this position may well be correct, but this insight will not have been achieved by transcendental methods, if that ambiguous and tradition-laden expression is still to retain any recognizable meaning at all. We are faced with the problem of the non-identity of the reflecter with the reflected, which earlier prevented Husserl's anonymously constituted life-world from achieving any self-elucidation which could be called transcendental. It is not the linguistic communities and forms of life which perform the act of self-reflection: for that is needed the proxy activity of the philosopher.

Ethical perspectives

If linguistic communities cannot reflect, there remain open only the following paths connecting the claim of the transcendental and the idea of ideal communication. Either one returns to the Kantian basis in subjectivity, which makes it necessary to rediscover first the transcendental subject in every empirical subject, and which thus does not coincide with linguistic communication between subjects. Or one analyses the transcendental argument in a different way, disregarding the assumptions of subjectivity and emphasizing the logical structure of the self-referentiality of transcendental reflection, as indicated above. In that case, to be sure, neither deduction nor ultimate foundation can be realized. Or else one holds fast to the premise of intersubjectivity in the linguistic medium[20] and abandons the transcendental claim.

The last way must be chosen if one wishes to consolidate the content of the programme of communication theory without superfluous embellishments from the history of philosophy. It seems to me that the brave hopes of closing the old gulf between *theory and practice* with the help of modern philosophy of language as if by a kind of magic spell have to be abandoned. In reality, it is unnecessary to support the programme by a line of argument which originates with the Kantian *aporiai* and is reinforced by the related proposals for a synthesis made by his successors from Fichte to Hegel and Marx. If one writes off the debt to this tradition, which claims to bring together in thought the ideal life of society with the principles of true knowledge, then the programme of communication theory is restricted to an enquiry into the contexts of linguistic interaction, in so far as they correspond to the criteria of rationality. Then it becomes clear that it is really a question of establishing norms of action, that is, of problems of ethics.

For Habermas, this eminently *practical* perspective has always been primary. Apel, in contrast, has successively taken the path from hermeneutics, via the pragmatics of language, to *ethics*. In the end he too believes it possible to make intelligible Kant's doctrine of the 'fact of reason' as the ultimate source, not re-

---

[20] In passing it should be mentioned that the oldest of Kant's critics already missed in his 'purism of reason' the proper evaluation of language. They had in mind however not the intersubjectivity of the dialogue but the concrete expression of thought in audible speech (J. G. Herder, *Verstand und Erfahrung, eine Metakritik zur Kritik der reinen Vernunft*, 1799; J. G. Hamann, *Metakritik über den Purismum der Vernunft*, 1784).

ducible to any further presupposition, of the moral law in the sense of an 'a priori of argumentation' already built into the rules of linguistic communication.[21]

A 'reconstruction of Kant's Categorical Imperative' presupposes, according to Apel,

> that one reflect on the difference between the universalization required by the 'intelligible ego' of the 'maxim of the intention' of each individual, in the sense of an intersubjective validity thought of in a communication-free way, and an obligation, grounded in the rules of communication, to the *social realization of intersubjectivity* through the understanding of meaning and the formation of a consensus about claims in a communication community which is in principle unlimited. The first 'principle of transsubjectivity', which ultimately presupposes a metaphysical 'fact of reason', belongs to a transcendental philosophy of the transcendental subject who is in principle non-linguistic . . . In contrast, the 'principle of transsubjectivity' which we have in mind forms the basis, without any metaphysical guarantee, for a transcendental philosophy whose 'transcendental subject' must be postulated on the grounds of a critique of meaning, but must in other respects be counterfactually anticipated and must first and foremost – 'in the long run' – be realized.[22]

Two old difficulties in Kantian ethics seem in this way to be conclusively eliminated. The *foundation of ethics* is presented as a metaphysics-free outcome of reflection on the basis of language as the medium of intersubjective understanding, which includes everyone. And the Categorical Imperative no longer exhausts itself in the mere 'ought', but is concretely realized as the active translation of the ideal anticipation in historical reality. From the beginning these two connected elements of Kantian ethics have given rise to a great deal of perplexity: the residue of metaphysics

---

21 'Das Apriori der Kommunikationsgemeinschaft und die Grundlagen der Ethik', in *Transformation der Philosophie*, Vol. II, Frankfurt, 1973, pp. 418ff.

22 'Sprechakttheorie und transzendentale Sprachpragmatik zur Frage ethischer Normen', in Apel (ed.), *Sprachpragmatik und Philosophie*, Frankfurt, 1975, pp. 126f.

in the theoretically unintelligible but practically necessary fact of reason, and the obligation which is utterly imperative, i.e. transcends the finite possibilities of human beings. Kant himself spoke here of 'the outermost limits of all practical philosophy',[23] since ethics is only conceivable by appealing to a hypothesis, which cannot be sanctioned by any empirical evidence, of a principle of freedom, while the principle of freedom itself is accessible only in the mode of ethical duty. This connexion is for Kant as impossible to dissolve as it is theoretically incomprehensible. Practical philosophy in this way runs up against an ultimate limit.

The redrafting by the philosophers of language, however, does not solve the difficulties, it merely evades them. It evades the metaphysical postulation by recognizing an a priori in given language-games, which is given with them as a condition of the possibility of all language-games. However, a condition of the possibility of something given never presents a practical problem and hence is not of ethical interest. On the other hand, the pure 'ought', in which in Kant norm and reality split apart, is evaded by reading the counterfactual anticipation unconditionally as a challenge to realize the ideal assumptions. That is, however, either circular or a *petitio principii*. Either one must understand by a counterfactual assumption a challenge to action instead of an indispensable presupposition – in which case nothing has been proved with regard to the foundations of an ethic since what is to be proved is already implicit in the premise. Or the ideal conditions are valid in the sense of being conditions to be produced rather than as critical standards – in which case again ethics is not grounded but postulated.

We shall return to the theme of a foundation of ethics in the context of a discussion of contemporary contributions to the philosophy of practice (Ch. 3). In connexion with the theses of Habermas, which are still to be discussed in detail, some emphases of our criticism of Apel may be shifted (Ch. 3). Nevertheless, the programme of an ideal communication community or of a rational dialogue projected on to the totality of society has grown in the work which Apel and Habermas have done together over many years, since their time together as students. This new tendency in the philosophy of language, in which hermeneutics

---

[23] *Fundamental Principles of the Metaphysics of Morals*, A 113ff.

and the pragmatic analysis of everyday language meet, must in later sections be tested by what it can contribute to the theory of science. That will be done in the context of the debate with the followers of Popper (so-called critical rationalism) and with the constructivism of the so-called Erlangen School. First, however, I shall take a further look at another result of the continental reception of the linguistic analysis derived from Wittgenstein and Frege.

Phenomenology and linguistic analysis

As we have seen, there are many points of contact between the phenomenological-hermeneutic tendency and analytical philosophy of language. Reference has often been made to the pragmatic turn in the later Wittgenstein, and the concept of a form of life has been taken up in order to enrich his linguistic approach with existential, ethical and historical content. In contrast to this broadly hermeneutic adaptation, there has been less of a revival of interest in properly logical questions. One of the few exceptions is *Ernst Tugendhat's* attempts to create a productive confrontation between the originally *logical* concerns of phenomenology and linguistic analysis. Tugendhat sees the relationship in the following way:

> Linguistic analysis agrees with phenomenology in its concerns, but they differ in method . . . Hermeneutics is in its philosophical concerns more extensive than linguistic analysis and phenomenology alike. In method, despite its origins in phenomenology, it is closer to linguistic analysis. Linguistic analysis can be regarded as a reduced hermeneutics, as a hermeneutics on the ground floor. It still lacks the historical dimension and a comprehensive concept of understanding. Hermeneutics, for its part, lives dangerously on the upper floor, without specially worrying about the load-bearing capacity or state of repair of the lower storey. This is what it has inherited from phenomenology or even from an older tradition . . . Linguistic analysis has never pressed so far forward, but at least it does not wish, like positivism, to demolish the structure, believing itself to

be in possession of new tools and methods which will enable it to rebuild the structure more securely.[24]

How does this confrontation thus outlined come about?

Tugendhat, as one of Heidegger's last pupils, is at the same time one of the least subservient to his master. If the lesson which can be learned from Heidegger is, as many proclaim, that the ethos of philosophy is open and relentless questioning, then Tugendhat has taken this lesson to heart and applied it not least against his teacher. He has taken seriously Heidegger's emphasis on the *concept of truth*, and for that very reason has found fault with the obscurity of Heidegger's analysis of truth as the locus of an original 'disclosure' of Being. That has brought him back, in opposition to the common opinion of the school, to the position prior to Heidegger's advance beyond Husserl.[25] The transformation of the exact method of phenomenological analysis of conscious experiences into a comprehensive hermeneutic of Dasein in the historical context is not simply reaffirmed, but painstakingly scrutinized to see what has been gained and what lost.

This scrutiny shows that, with the success of Heidegger's philosophy, the methodological exactness and the interest in logic which had been part of the foundation of phenomenology by Husserl were abandoned. Tugendhat wishes to make good this loss. It is thus with good reason that he has come to feel an affinity with linguistic analysis, to which his own views have become more and more closely related.[26] He does not, however, lapse into a new partisanship, as frequently happens with converts. He criticizes the systematic reductionism and the unquestioned assumptions which predominate in much of the literature of linguistic analysis as sharply as he does the vagueness of hermeneutics. Thus he has subjected Tarski's generally accepted definition of truth to a searching examination,[27] which demonstrates the

---

[24] 'Phänomenologie und Sprachanalyse', in Bubner, Cramer and Wiehl (eds.), *Hermeneutik und Dialektik, Festschrift für Gadamer*, Tübingen, 1970, Vol. II, pp. 3f.

[25] *Der Wahrheitsbegriff bei Husserl und Heidegger*, Berlin, 1967.

[26] In reference to Heidegger's concept of Being: 'Die sprachanalytische Kritik der Ontologie', in H.-G. Gadamer (ed.), *Das Problem der Sprache* (Akten des Heidelberger Kongresses für Philosophie), Munich, 1967.

[27] 'Tarskis semantische Definition der Wahrheit und ihre Stellung innerhalb der Geschichte des Wahrheitproblems im logischen Positivismus', *Philosophische Rundschau*, 8, 1960.

extent to which its undisputed clarity has been bought at the price of triviality, that is, by blurring the philosophical problems involved.

In the article already quoted on 'phenomenology and linguistic analysis', the confrontation begins with the conception of their task which brings together both tendencies: the understanding of the *meaning (sense) of linguistic expressions* and of the *reference to objects*. We have already mentioned earlier the common concern of both Husserl and Frege with the criticism of contemporary psychologistic interpretations of logic, which led the one to the phenomenology of intentional states of consciousness and the other to philosophical semantics. Both sought to investigate 'pure meaning' or 'sense' (because of the high degree of synonymity of these expressions in German, what Husserl called 'meaning' roughly corresponds to what Frege called 'sense' and distinguished by a terminological rule from 'meaning'). Against this common background Tugendhat argues that the breakdown of the phenomenological programme is clearly implicit in its own beginnings and the alternative is seen to lie in a semantics based on Frege.

Husserl's analysis of meaning starts basically from the model of *perception*. Intentionality is conceived of as directedness towards, or thought of, something as the phenomenological what-content of consciousness. This something, of which consciousness is consciousness, can ultimately be brought to expression in the full evidence of the *eidos*. Corresponding to the perceptual model on which the method of phenomenology is based is a logical orientation based on the naming-relation. The deep-seated nominalism which conceives of name and object on the analogy of the relation of consciousness and what-content makes it impossible for Husserl really to understand the *predicative assertion*. In every predication, something is asserted of something, and it is this synthesis which presents phenomenology with insuperable problems. It is misleading to treat the subject and predicate of a proposition as two things of a similar kind, which are both brought by phenomenological means to full eidetic self-presence. Two phenomenological essences would then stand autonomously alongside each other, but equally alongside many other comparable essences, with which they might enter into varying relations. There is however nothing in the analysis which compels us to connect just those two with each other in the way the predicative sentence by its very structure constantly connects subject and predicate. The predicative synthesis on this basis remains completely unexplained.

Tugendhat concludes from this that it is necessary to get away from the conception of a synthesis as the fundamental structure of the predicative sentence, since in it the independence of the synthesized elements is presupposed. That conception is not adequate to our normal understanding and use of sentences. Like Frege, therefore, one must start from the *sentence as an original unity*. The relation of subject and predicate can then be conceived, along the lines suggested by Strawson and more recent linguistic analysts, as the combination of a referring element, which 'stands for' the object, and an 'ascriptive expression', which contains what is asserted about the object indicated. The phenomenological notion of 'intending an object' is thus replaced by the semantics of understanding a proposition. Tugendhat explains in this connexion: 'The theory of predication which I have proposed belongs to linguistic analysis in the pregnant sense that it does not merely analyse linguistic expressions, but also has the consequence that our dealings with linguistic signs are not merely means of expression but prove to be the element of understanding itself.'[28]

Tugendhat has since developed this programme with great mastery and thoroughness in his *Vorlesungen zur Einführung in die sprachanalytische Philosophie*.[29] Tugendhat in this work quite openly acts as the advocate of the *philosophy of linguistic analysis* in general, which he introduces by means of traditional problems of philosophy in order to make it more easily understood and to demonstrate its effectiveness by confronting it with the tradition. The book plays an important role, since it creates a bridge, perhaps for the first time, between the state of the problems, as handed down in the tradition, which is the major preoccupation of continental philosophy, and the methods of linguistic analysis, which have developed in the Anglo-Saxon school in a way which has been more or less unencumbered by traditional modes of posing the questions. We need not be concerned here with a survey of the analytic discussion from Wittgenstein to Davidson,

---

[28] 'Phänomenologie und Sprachanalyse', p. 16.
[29] Frankfurt, 1976 (English translation by P. A. Gorner forthcoming).

Dummett, Grice and Searle. Tugendhat goes some way towards establishing the strategic links with Frege and Husserl which we have already observed. The result is a new formulation, based on detailed reasoning, of the *problem of truth*, with which the book is for the most part concerned.

I want to touch on only one aspect. The fundamental question of semantics, according to Tugendhat, is this: what is it to understand a sentence?[30] If the traditional analysis of the structure of predicative statements as a synthesis of elements of meaning is to be rejected, because the sentence is treated as an original semantic unity and is related to the problem of truth, then obviously everything depends on an adequate interpretation of the role of the *predicate*. The predicate does not, like the subject of the sentence, stand for an object, but characterizes it in a certain way. The result is that there is an unequal distribution of roles in the predicative sentence between a referring and a characterizing part. The characterization by the predicate consequently presupposes the identification of an object to be characterized. Truth turns out to be a correct characterization of an object in an assertion.

Tugendhat's definition of truth is as follows: 'The assertion that a is F is true if and only if the predicate F applies to the object for which the singular term a stands.'[31] This conclusion is not particularly startling, if one remembers the oldest account of truth in Plato or Aristotle, who explicated the truth of assertions in terms of the 'existence' (*hyparchein*) of what is asserted.[32] Tugendhat in general makes no secret of this borrowing. However the problem arises of what is denoted by the word 'applies'. Tugendhat falls back for its elucidation fundamentally on the correct use of the predicate, so that the understanding of the predicate and the problem of truth become well-nigh indistinguishable. The rules of verification of a sentence refer to the rules of application of predicates. But is truth to be nothing other than correct use of words? Is the wide domain of the false, of illusion, of delusion, of error to be narrowed down to a series of violations of rules of language?

The problem here is that false sentences do not tell us that they are false because the incorrect use of words does not show. These

[30] Ibid., pp. 161ff.
[31] Ibid., pp. 321ff. (from the translation by P. A. Gorner).
[32] E.g. Plato, *Symposium*, 198d4; Aristotle, *Analytica Posteriora*, 81b23

sentences look quite correct at first sight, so that it needs a special effort to find out what is wrong under the surface. How can this critical effort get under way? The intricate and protracted discussions which Tugendhat devotes to this difficulty show that he is conscious of the unsatisfactory nature of his definition, though he is unable entirely to give it up.

Two traditional themes

Tugendhat's definition of truth circles around the problem of a predicate's being 'true of' an object. A presupposition of this, however, is the identification of an object as an object. This task precedes the affirmation of the truth of statements in the sense of the application of predicates. In Kantian terminology 'object in general' indicated the return of the old theme of ontology, known as 'Being in general' or 'Being as Being'. Semantics is in a way closely connected with *ontology* and Tugendhat quite consciously draws the parallel. Heidegger's old thesis that Being in its truth discloses itself as language is still recognizable in faint outline. But instead of following the aesthetic line followed by Heidegger's essay on 'The essence of the work of art' and largely taken over by Gadamer's hermeneutics[33] Tugendhat chooses the logical direction, seeking in formal semantics a differentiated and precise answer to the ontological question of Being.[34] What the Greeks called Being as Being and modern philosophy the object as object now appears as the question what it is to understand a sentence which refers to an object in such a way that it characterizes it by means of the predicate.

The attempt to effect a thoroughgoing reconciliation between linguistic analysis and the great themes of traditional philosophy is close to Tugendhat's heart for two reasons. On the one hand the lack of historical reflection which in fact marks linguistic analysis is eliminated, and on the other the philosophy which seeks a logically clear understanding of language gains in reputation as compared with traditionalist conceptions, which would like to see in it mere technique, in which, to be sure, it may be possible to

---

[33] Cf. *Wahrheit und Methode*, Tübingen, 1960 (translated as *Truth and Method*, New York, 1975), Pt III 'Ontologische Wendung der Hermeneutik am Leitfaden der Sprache'.
[34] Ibid., pp. 53ff.

achieve a remarkable degree of precision, but which is constantly threatened by philosophical triviality.

The example of ontology may, as Tugendhat shows, be demonstrated particularly well in the case of Aristotle, since his project, which gave rise to a whole tradition, for a 'science' of ontology rests on the foundation of an analysis of the *use of language*. In Oxford, by the way, it had been known for a long time that Aristotle could be counted as the first linguistic analyst! The celebrated introduction of ontology in the fourth book of Aristotle's *Metaphysics* is based on the following argument. Since all the special sciences confine themselves to particular aspects of reality, there is a need for a new science which will go beyond all specialist limitations to concern itself with Being in general or with Being as Being. Access to this domain of objects, which is prior to all scientific methodology, can come about only by withdrawing to a universal and primary mode of our relation to the world. Language in its manifold forms and modes of use establishes this original connexion with the world.[35] It is thus important for a correct approach to the theme of ontology to appreciate the *multiplicity* of living uses of language prior to all science and philosophy and to study it without reducing the variety. What is expressed by *pollachós legetai* is the basis on which the question of Being in general can be raised. For we anyway speak already about Being, even if we do not make it our explicit theme. We say of something, that it is, or has such and such a determination, that something comes into being or passes away, stands in relation to something else, is subject to certain influences, produces something or suffers from some defect – finally, we deny something or affirm the truth of some contested fact. In all these unformalized modes of discourse there is present a reference to Being, which must be worked out as a uniform reference first by ontology, while the varying uses of language remain indisputably subordinate.

Up to this point, Tugendhat's reformulation of the old ontology is clear. But it reveals a weakness when, before any intervention of logic, it patterns the manifold forms of living speech on the single mode of a predicative statement of the form 'Fa'. The Aristotelian introduction of ontology as a new science loses its

[35] Cf. Aristotle, *Metaphysics*, IV, 1004b15.

point, if all sentences are construed in the same way in terms of their form because the logician has already treated them *uniformly*, contrary to the variety of manifold modes of discourse which are precisely not such as to allow any recognition of a single relationship between them. The ontological theme which is latent in language as it is does not need to be further disclosed. The semanticist has already taken command and defines the theme of ontology from his interpretation of the structure of the sentence. In opposition to his starting-point in Heidegger and Aristotle, who first wanted to uncover the problem of Being in language, Tugendhat thus follows by turning in this direction a projection of the professional semanticists. This line of thought proceeds from a schematized preconception of language as a referential system of signs and, in the manner of Quine for instance, allows 'ontological commitment' to follow from this as a second step.

Tugendhat does not confine himself to the example of ontology alone in order to open up a discussion between the form of linguistic analysis which he favours and traditional positions in philosophy. Another example to which he has recently given copious attention[36] is the theory of *self-consciousness*. This has been the guiding motif in the development of modern thought, culminating in the speculative heights of German Idealism. That is well known: equally familiar are the constantly recurring doubts of common sense about the outbreak of philosophical madness which then occurred. Astonishingly, the German epidemic of speculation crossed the Channel in the nineteenth century, until the healthy powers of English empiricism successfully rallied to resist it. Thanks to Russell and Moore, an *empiricist* component has become part of the inheritance of analytical philosophy, the impetus to which was given not least by criticism of Bradley's and McTaggart's neo-Hegelianism. Similar considerations inspire Tugendhat's contribution.[37] Great acumen is shown in supplying arguments to support the misgivings of sound common sense about the philosophers' offences against normality. Now it is safe

---

[36] *Selbstbewusstsein und Selbstbestimmung, sprachanalytische Interpretationen*, Frankfurt, 1979.

[37] Although he chooses as his starting-point quite a different position, namely D. *Henrich*'s impressive exploration of the paradoxes of a conception of self-consciousness in terms of the subject–object schema. Henrich's study, *Fichtes ursprüngliche Einsicht* (Frankfurt, 1967), for all its criticism, is in sympathy with its subject.

to say that common sense would have been hostile even without such philosophical support, so that giving it such argumentative support does not make it into a philosophical position.

The inflexible stubbornness with which Tugendhat ignores the central conceptions of German Idealism, to which he nevertheless devotes a whole book, is remarkable. Particularly with Hegel, a final reckoning ought to be made – a kind of 'last dance'. I do not dispute by any means the value of Tugendhat's excellent interpretations of *Wittgenstein*'s private language problem, of *Heidegger*'s existential description of an elementary 'self-to-self-relation' of human Dasein and of similar insights to be found in *Mead*'s enlightened social behaviourism. Undoubtedly, these alternatives to the Idealist concept of the ego do suggest themselves for various reasons, but they are, as in Heidegger's case, drawn up on the lines of Kierkegaard's earlier critique of Idealism. This shows an underlying continuity in Tugendhat's argument which makes it less original and which, when occasionally made explicit, must leave anyone who is familiar with these questions with great doubts.

> You see that, from an analytic point of view, the
> scandal of the Hegelian conception does not by any
> means lie so much in the thesis of real contradictions and
> in the 'Dialectic' which results from it, but in the
> manner in which the concepts of identity, negation and
> so on are in the first instance descriptively applied . . .
> What bewilders the linguistic analyst is the carelessness,
> inspired by primitive models, with which in German
> Idealism the logical categories were and still are
> descriptively applied by those who philosophize in this
> specifically German tradition. In a way, this means a
> relapse to the stage before Plato and Aristotle, to the
> level of logical development achieved in the Eleatic
> school and the Sophists who followed it; at that time,
> when men first began to reflect on such concepts as
> Being, Alteration, Identity and Predication, the lack of
> linguistic reflection – the interpretation of determinations
> which are really linguistic in terms of objects, and the
> neglect of ambiguities – led to paradoxes. The same
> paradoxes, now indeed deepened and seemingly

reinforced by the direction of interest towards the problems of subjectivity, are repeated in German Idealism, except that they are now accepted, objectified and systematized. The enthusiasm for the idea of the philosophical system – a system which is essentially characterized by the notion of a single derivation of all logical and ontological categories from a single principle – was bound to consolidate still further the naivety of the descriptive approach . . . Hegel contrasted his 'speculative' ('rational') interpretation of the concepts with that of the 'understanding', of the 'natural consciousness', but he rightly saw that in his speculative interpretation the contradictoriness which is already implicitly ('in itself') present in the concepts of the natural consciousness, as he interpreted them, is merely made explicit ('posited').[38]

To begin with, it is quite mistaken to accuse *Hegel* of logical naivety in comparison with Plato and Aristotle. Hegel's 'Science of Logic' is, as is shown precisely in its well-articulated relationship to the ancient 'founders' of logic,[39] of extreme subtlety.[40] There is no question either of any lack of methodological awareness of the linguistic character of the logical concepts generally.[41] Above all, however, Hegel's much discussed doctrine of the 'speculative proposition',[42] whether one agrees with it or not, is quite unintelligible without reference to the indissoluble connexion of logical structure with linguistic form. One might even reduce the whole content of the despised speculative philosophy to the single formula, that philosophical thought becomes conscious of its links with the pre-given modes of our customary and universally understandable speech in predicative sentences and comes to terms with them. Speculation is not an automatism of pure thought, detached from language and rendered autonomous in a naive attitude. It arises first against the background of a

[38] *Selbstbewusstsein*, pp. 304ff.
[39] Cf. *Hegel's Lectures on the History of Philosophy* (translated by Haldane and Simson), London, 1896, Vol. II.
[40] On this point see Gadamer, 'Hegel and ancient dialectics', in *Hegel's Dialectic* (translated by C. Smith), New Haven, 1976.
[41] See the Preface to the 2nd edition of the *Science of Logic*.
[42] *Phenomenology of Spirit* (translated by A. V. Miller), London, 1977, Preface, and many other places in Hegel's writings.

well-reflected relationship to the modes of understanding and speech which are at our disposal and which we constantly exercise before we begin philosophy.

Tugendhat's repeated criticism that it is a matter of an attempt, never made fully explicit, carelessly to alter the normal use of words is thus neither correct nor particularly original. In fact, it is merely a recurrence of that *protest of the natural consciousness* against philosophy which has been raised since Hegel's own time and which he himself anticipated – indeed took up. The version derived from linguistic analysis has furnished the protest with modern weapons, but does not alter anything in the heart of the objection. The protest is always raised at times when philosophers appear to speak differently from people in everyday life. The philosopher, however, ought to be the last person to be surprised by this. He ought to know from the history of philosophy that he, as a philosopher, is in principle incapable of eliminating the difference.

Above all, he ought not to indulge in the illusion that the deliberations of linguistic analysis in the Wittgensteinian therapeutic style, with their obsessive concern with detail and their wrestlings with paradox, which are meant to make a precise diagnosis of deviations from the normal use of words and to cure them, are themselves an example of the ordinary use of language. Linguistic analysis, which deliberately refrains from all high-flown terminology, does not for that reason become everyday language. It does not speak the language of everyday because it speaks *about* it. The natural consciousness is very much aware of the difference of the special language of philosophy, even in forms of address which are less pointedly contrary to common sense than, for example, Hegel's Dialectic. It does not allow itself to be deceived by the familiar forms in which is expressed, with great artificiality, what genuinely natural language ought to look like. In spite of everything, for the natural consciousness on the level of everyday language, linguistic analysis still remains philosophy. Linguistic analysis never genuinely returns to the area of pre-philosophical normality of speech, however much it might like to. I do not even see how it is supposed to be such a great philosophical act to pursue the self-annihilation of philosophy, that is, to concern oneself that we should in future speak only in the way that everyone has always spoken and will continue to speak whether or not there is any philosophy. The problem of self-consciousness, at all events, will not be dissolved into thin air in this way.

A word on the theory of science

Theory of science in the true sense is a product of the nineteenth century. Even before that, of course, philosophy had had things to say about the sciences which found a justification for existence beyond its own. Aristotle, Bacon or Descartes, for instance, dealt with the conception and the procedures of science within an explicit framework of philosophical logic and methodology. It needed, however, the headlong advance of the special empirical sciences in the nineteenth century, and the simultaneous decline in the credibility of encyclopaedic systems based on the resources of pure reason, to reduce philosophy, which had formerly occupied such an exalted position, to a much more modest role. In view of the undoubted fact of science philosophy was totally converted into a logic of scientific knowledge and enquiry. This is no longer a part of philosophy: it is the whole concern of philosophy. To the extent that philosophy still seeks some chance of survival in a climate of decidedly scientistic rationality, it has to surrender all pretensions which go beyond this. The positivism of the Vienna Circle had for everything which went beyond the logic of scientific sentences only the verdict of 'metaphysics', seen as a kind of 'poetry of thought' which was not to be taken seriously.

But it has been known for a long time that the positivist creed has proved full of cracks. The philosophically interesting developments are taking place without doubt at the point where orthodoxy is disintegrating and the resumption is thus made possible of fruitful contact with the historical sciences of man and society, radically interrupted by the rigid 'physicalism' of the Vienna school. Since the fifties and sixties there has been a resolute movement away from the classical positions, making it permissible to imagine syntheses which would have horrified the positivists. German philosophy, with some exceptions, has played only an indirect part in this movement, apart from responding to the state of discussion in Britain and America. The founding generation of classical theory of science, such as Carnap, Reichenbach or Hempel, had either already left Europe earlier or were compelled to emigrate. It was in the emigration that there then arose, in collaboration with indigenous traditions such as pragmatism, the dominant school which until recently defined what theory of science was.

The political situation in Germany cut off native philosophy for almost a decade from international developments. Then after the war the phenomenological school and Heidegger's blatantly anti-scientific thought for a time formed a barrier to understanding. Since then, however, theory of science, in much the same way as analytical philosophy of language, has returned and has occasioned spirited efforts at assimilation and productive consolidation. It is not really unfair to say that, apart from the group assembled round P. Lorenzen, there have been scarcely any original contributions made to the fundamental canonical questions of theory of science by German philosophers in the post-war period. Instead, however, there has been a mass of stimulating and occasionally ingenious attempts at mediation. Anyone who is convinced that the future of theory of science, so far as it has one at all, lies in this direction will hardly complain of that as a defect. The classical paradigm of the 'philosophy of science' from Schlick to Quine must at all events represent a completed chapter in the history of philosophy. This diagnosis by no means rules out the possibility of further meaningful investigation in this style, but one may doubt if any significant new territory can be won by following these well-trodden paths.

As a sign of the response mentioned above and the associated endeavours to achieve a synthesis, three recognizable centres of interest have developed in German philosophy in recent decades. One centre is under the influence of *Carnap and orthodoxy (Stegmüller)*; the second under that of *Popper and his followers (critical rationalism)*. The third centre of interest has developed as a purely German movement from the earlier beginnings of *H. Dingler (Lorenzen and the Erlangen School)*. Between all these camps there are fluctuating lines of connexion and disagreement. Above all, the debate with the positions of *hermeneutics* and *dialectic* has mobilized a good deal of intellectual energy. Things are in a complete state of flux, so that the sketch which is offered here certainly represents an over-simplification.

The picture can be seen most clearly, in my opinion, if one follows up the challenge presented by Popper and his successors (such as Kuhn and Feyerabend). The philosophical responses to this challenge are the most deserving of our attention. In comparison with them, Stegmüller's magnum opus, the product of his solitary labours, in which he seeks to make an independent compilation and a perceptive analysis of 'problems and results of the theory of science and analytical philosophy' in many volumes,[43] becomes much less important than its own merits deserve.

However, Stegmüller's voice, which defends the orthodox point of view, is important for the outlying regions of the theory of science, while to echo the acknowledged doctrine in the strongholds of theory of science in the Anglo-Saxon world would necessarily sound somewhat second-hand. Hence the relative omission of this point of view may be permissible for our purposes.

In what follows, I have chosen to concentrate, in three representative main sections, on:

(1) Critical rationalism, inspired by Popper;
(2) Irritation by and adaptation of Kuhn's quasi-hermeneutics and Feyerabend's quasi-dialectics.
(3) The so-called Erlangen school of constructivism.

Since at least the first two sections could not be written without Popper, a brief account of his approach, which has inspired so many developments, would not be out of place.

Popper's position

Popper was the first to deliver a successful blow against positivism. He was close to the fashionable Vienna Circle in the twenties and thirties of this century, although he tended to play the flirt with his existence on the fringes of the Establishment. Popper's *Logik der Forschung* of 1935 may be seen in the first instance as an intelligent continuation, though one essentially loyal to the tradition of the Vienna Circle, of the discussion of the empirical basis of scientific theories.[44] The explosively liberating force which is contained in the book perhaps became clear to Popper himself only by degrees. Its more extensive influence was delayed by the

[43] *Probleme und Resultate der Wissenschaftstheorie und analytischer Philosophie*, Berlin/New York, 1970– .
[44] See e.g. the review by Max Black in *Mind*, 45, 1936; also M. Reichenbach and R. Carnap in *Erkenntnis*, 5, 1935.

emigration and came to be felt comparatively late. It began after the Second World War from Popper's place of work, the London School of Economics, and not least as a result of writings like *The Open Society and its Enemies* or *The Poverty of Historicism*, which drew *political* conclusions from the fundamental ideas of the *Logik der Forschung*. As a result of the impression created by them, there appeared for the first time in 1959 the English translation of his masterpiece of theory of science from the thirties under the title *The Logic of Scientific Discovery*.[45] Popper's influence in Germany emphatically dates from this time.[46] Even this originally German-speaking philosopher had to make a detour through the Anglo-Saxon world before finding in the sixties wide understanding in Germany even outside academic philosophy. Thus it is not without significance that, for instance, German Social Democracy, when it wanted openly to disavow its founder, Karl Marx, chose to substitute Karl Popper as its ideological patron saint.[47] Many find it possible to identify with his blend of Kantian Enlightenment and reformist social engineering.

Popper's new beginning in the *Logik der Forschung* sprang from an inherent difficulty in positivism. The Vienna theorists of science thought that the unity of all genuine sciences should be based on the physicalist model: they assembled in one comprehensive system all the propositions with empirical content which the sciences furnished and organized them with the philosophical help of logic. In the system of propositions, therefore, the scientists are responsible for the 'matter', the philosophers on the other hand for the 'form'. The system of propositions, constructed through and through in accordance with formal structural rules, stretches from the highest, most general, propositions – the universal propositions of natural law or their unification in a scientific theory – right down to the simplest, not further analysable, propositions which form the *basis* for the whole. Regarded from the analytical standpoint, they are called atomic propositions, but from an empirical point of view they are observation

---

[45] Cf. Popper's autobiography, *Unended Quest* (which first appeared in the Schilpp volume *The Philosophy of Karl Popper*), published separately, Glasgow, 1976, pp. 113ff., 148ff.

[46] The 2nd edition of the German original of *Logik der Forschung* appeared in 1966, and was soon followed by several further editions.

[47] *Kritischer Rationalismus und Sozialdemokratie*, with a Preface by Helmut Schmidt (eds. Lührs and Sarrazin), Berlin/Bonn, 1976².

sentences, protocols or basic propositions. The basis endows the whole system with its empirical content, and it is here, as it were, that crude experience originally takes on propositional form.

However, the way in which the adjustment of experience and propositional system is properly to be understood remained the subject of intense debate. For on the one hand the questionable propositions of the basis are just as much propositions as all the other parts of the system constructed from them; but on the other hand the basis ought to involve an immediate contact with reality, not further structured by logic. This is not the place to reconstruct the doctrine of the empirical basis with all the proposals, revisions and alterations.[48] In truth, the problem of the basis, however averse it may be to all forms of subject–object schema, and however completely directed towards the logical analysis of a system of propositions, is the heir to the traditional problem of epistemology: how do we come to know anything about reality?

It was thus a liberation when Popper turned philosophical attention away from the logic of propositions and towards the logic of *enquiry*. He reminded philosophers that no science proceeds in a way which precisely conforms to the positivist ideal. The much talked of fact of science had secretly been replaced yet again by a clumsy construction of the philosophical mind which was scarcely inferior in dogmatism to the older, reviled metaphysics but was certainly so in subtlety of thought. If one looked at the process of enquiry as the true mark of scientific rationality, however, then one did not see a well-ordered system of propositions, but rather an interplay of 'conjectures and refutations' in the intersubjective framework of the participants in the enquiry. Theories and hypotheses are proposed and subjected to critical testing, they are accepted or rejected in the light of experimental evidence and observation, which are also in their turn open to further critical testing. The final court of appeal is not any kind of 'logical construction of the world', strictly reflected by unified science, as Carnap wanted it to be, nor yet any special set of protocols or basic statements saturated with experience, such as Neurath or Schlick[49] had in mind. The final court of

---

[48] On this point, cf. the first volumes of the journal *Erkenntnis* (1931–).

[49] Cf. Schlick's critical remarks on Popper ('Über das Fundament der Erkenntnis', *Erkenntnis*, 4, 1934, § II, translated in A. J. Ayer (ed.), *Logical Positivism*, Glencoe, 1959).

appeal is the criterion of *criticism*, to which all enquirers submit themselves. This critical rationality, which first sets in motion the process of enquiry as an interaction between subjects bent on knowledge, cannot be derived from anything else. It does not even coincide with the rules of formal logic. It comes down, in the final analysis, to a free decision. Critical rationality originates in a decision.

If appearances are not entirely misleading, the faint outlines of a *Kantian* position can be seen in this, at all events in J.F. Fries' 'anthropological' version. Fries thought[50] that Kant's 'transcendental prejudices' ought to be swept away, while recognizing in the a priori activities of subjectivity facts of empirical psychology. The realistic reinterpretation of Kant is a protection especially against the later errors of Idealist exaggerations of the critical transcendental philosophy. Popper was familiar with Fries' approach through Leonard Nelson and Julius Kraft.[51]

According to Kant, 'critique' means the systematic limitation of our reason to the world of experience. We spontaneously project theoretical forms of organization of reality, which we allow to be determined, that is, limited by empirical data. Philosophical critique restricts reason to the given reality instead of leaving it free to its own projections. Nothing at all outside reason itself motivates us to this attitude of critical self-limitation of reason. Critical rationality, which seeks its own path between the exuberance of metaphysics and vulgar sensualism, owes its existence to a decision of reason. I do not wish to overestimate the Kantian elements in Popper, but I believe that this analogy has subterraneously assisted his reception in contemporary German philosophy. As earlier the call 'Back to Kant'[52] was to the struggle against Idealist exaggeration, so again today, critical sobriety, legitimated by scientific method, is an appropriate weapon to

---

[50] Fries, *Neue Kritik der Vernunft* (Heidelberg, 1807, e.g. Introduction xxxvff.); cf. Popper, *Logic of Scientific Discovery*, §§ 25, 29.

[51] *Unended Quest*, pp. 74f. Popper's previously unpublished early work *Die beiden Grundprobleme der Erkenntnistheorie* has since become available (Tübingen, 1979). It shows the development of Popper's conception, with its similarities to Fries', especially pp. 431f. and many other passages.

[52] O. Liebmann, *Kant und die Epigonen* (1865); F. E. Beneke, *Kant und die philosophische Aufgabe unserer Zeit* (published in 1831 as part of the Jubilee celebrations for the fiftieth anniversary of the publication of the *Critique of Pure Reason*).

repel the assaults of hermeneutic obscurantism and the dialectical myths of history and society. At all events, that is the view of 'critical rationalism'.

Critical rationalism

The leading representative of critical rationalism is *Hans Albert*. An economist by training, he became Popper's interpreter in Germany, because he sought a theory of science which had shed the narrowness of outlook of positivism, applied to both natural and social sciences alike and permitted a bridge to be built between scientific knowledge and political decision. All these merits critical rationalism hopes to combine in itself. Its applicability to the most varied domains has attracted support from many sides for the programme, which radiates the plausibility of enlightened common sense. The alleged strength, however, immediately comes to be accounted a weakness when it is a question of bringing philosophical clarification and precision to bear on the principles of criticism.

Albert begins with a brilliant attack on the traditional model of rationality in philosophy and science. Rationality has always been associated with *foundations*. This is however a deep-rooted error. Recalling the fabulous Baron von Münchhausen, who pulled himself out of the quagmire by his own hair, Albert forces the usual understanding of rationality into what he calls the 'Münchhausen Trilemma'. That is, either the quest for foundations falls into an infinite regress and does not fulfil its appointed task, because every foundation itself requires further foundation in turn; or else the foundation proceeds in a circle and presupposes what it is supposed to prove, in which case it is again doomed to failure; or finally the foundation ends at an arbitrary point, in that without any reason the decision is made to stop at certain kinds of evidence.

The conception of rationality as resting on a foundation of certainty which has been generally accepted since the time of Plato and Aristotle and right through the whole modern period is consequently to be abandoned. Not only is the certainty thus aspired to not to be attained, but to cling to this ideal leads to a paralysis of enquiry and has a conservative effect, favouring established theories for which confirmation is merely sought in a dogmatic spirit. It is worth understanding once and for all on the contrary that 'All certainties in knowledge are self-fabricated and so valueless when it comes to the comprehension of reality.'[53] Instead, the '*idea of critical testing*' ought to be given pride of place: it does not indulge in the illusion of finding an Archimedean point on which our knowledge can be based, but starts from the deceptiveness of all knowledge and so does not withdraw anything from the scope of criticism. Anyone who does not aspire to absolute certainty and also does not immunize himself dogmatically against objections, must, in the interests of solving the problems which constantly emerge, take part in the business of critically testing any hypothesis and any proposal whatsoever.

> Methodology is, so to speak, nothing but a fundamental technology for the conduct of problem-solving, which is directed towards particular evaluative viewpoints – to those, namely, which are connected with the human aspiration towards knowledge of reality and so towards truth. The *acceptance* of a particular method, even that of the *method of critical testing*, involves to that extent a *moral decision*, since it signifies the assumption of a methodical practice with important consequences for social life – a practice which is of great significance not only for theory-formation, for the formulation, elaboration and testing of theories, but also for their application and so for the role of knowledge in social life. The model of rationality proposed by criticism is the sketch of a mode of life, a social practice, and so has ethical and beyond that political significance. It is in no way an exaggeration, but simply the assertion of a simple and easily intelligible connexion, when one refers to the fact that the principle of critical testing, apart from anything else, creates an *association* between *logic and politics*.[54]

Now that is a large claim. Is there really a single procedure which can be applied to any problem whatever? Can this be what is meant by 'critique'? Does morality oblige us to adopt the critical position? Does the solution of the ancient enigma of the unity of theory and practice lie in the association of politics and

[53] *Traktat über kritische Vernunft* (1968), Tübingen, 1975³, p. 30.
[54] Ibid., pp. 40f.

logic? Let us examine the matter more closely. *Technologies* represent well-adapted and highly developed instruments for overcoming definite problems. Instruments have a function but always in relation to an end. Without exact information about the particular end, the task to be overcome or the special character of the problem which confronts us, technologies cannot be made precise or perfected. If I do not recognize the nature of the problem, all I can do is muddle through ad hoc in a way which is highly contingent and dependent on luck, and which can hardly be given the fine-sounding title of a technology.

The problems, however, do not remain vague. They are clearly characterized: it is a matter in the first place of the knowledge of reality or of truth. And for that there are certainly very specific methods of proceeding. The theory of knowledge and science has furnished more and more refined concepts for that purpose. Certainly, the knowledge of reality is a problem of quite a different kind from the problems to be solved in politics. The problems of truth are not directly the problems of human social life. Of course, political and social problems may not ultimately be soluble without an element of the truth or of appropriate knowledge of the relevant area of reality. Philosophy of practice, for as long as it has existed, has always defended this line. But the presupposition of knowledge *for* the purposes of politics and practical life is by no means the same as the special problems of this domain itself. One must be aware of the peculiarities of the problems which emerge in practical life and make it explicit that they are concerned with action directed to specific goals. In this respect, practical problems differ from problems about reality, and the two should not be mixed up in the interests of efficient practice itself. The awareness, presupposed by practice, of the peculiar character of the problem to be solved in action first opens up in a very real sense the true way for practice. In a word: if talk of technology is to have any meaning, the specificity of the problems to be solved must be recognized, and it must surely be conceded that the *difference between knowledge of reality and politics* is important here.[55]

The failure to make such distinctions in the conception of the problem directly corresponds, in the programme of critical

<hr>

[55] Albert once again categorically denies this in his *Traktat über rationale Praxis*, Tübingen, 1978.

rationalism, to the *emptiness of the concept of criticism*. 'Criticism', as a term, originates from Greek legal language and originally meant 'separation' or 'judgment'. Right was separated from wrong, and critical judgment was passed, always with special regard to something. Criticism thus required a standard against which what was given in any particular case could be held and critically assessed. Even in Kant, the idea of the 'tribunal' of criticism is still a living one,[56] where the pretensions of human knowledge are assessed by the standards of reason and either recognized as legitimate or rejected. With regard to theoretical knowledge, reason applies the standard of the understanding of empirical reality, with regard to practical questions, that of the moral law.[57]

A critique without a *criterion* would be an absurdity. The assessment of something can be carried out only with reference to something else: the former is the thing to be assessed, the latter the applicable standard. Of course, standards themselves can also be critically assessed, and this will be done in terms of their suitability or unsuitability to fulfil the function of a standard. But even here there is a criterion of assessment, namely, the function of a standard in general. The universalization of criticism among Popper's followers certainly tends to lead to a refusal to state the appropriate criterion for assessment. Problems seem to be seen as all on the same footing, so that for all cases, for those of science as for those of politics, one and the same solution is recommended: criticism, whatever that may mean.[58]

If one looks more closely for the true definition of criticism,

[56] *Critique of Pure Reason*, A, xi.f.
[57] This explains why, in the Kantian system, it is *pure* reason, that is, metaphysics, which is criticized in the first *Critique*, but in the second it is *merely* practical (and not pure practical) reason, that is, empirical prudence (cf. the Preface and Introduction to the *Critique of Practical Reason*).
[58] The later Popper, however, has been aware that the free extension of the idea of criticism does not absolve one from the need to indicate a standard. He has complied with this requirement in two ways: by his determined move towards the Platonism of 'World Three', where beyond the physical and psychic worlds the purely ideal contents of proposed problem-solutions are preserved; and by the construction of successive approximation to truth (verisimilitude), which brings together the historical process of enquiry and the ultimate aim of all real sciences – to understand reality without remainder (*Objective Knowledge*, London, 1972). Both ideas seem to me untenable (see my 'Dialektische Elemente einer Forschungslogik', in *Dialektik und Wissenschaft*, Frankfurt, 1973).

one finds in Albert that it coincides in the closest possible fashion with the basis of rationality. To be *critical* means to be *rational*, while rational procedure is always characterized as critical. How is this to be understood? Rational procedure is contrasted in a perfectly general way with dogmatic procedure, which rests on arbitrary postulates and protects itself from questions and objections. Dogmatism is thus the refusal of further information. What information could be required, however, to make a dogmatist into a rational arguer? What is it that one is questioned about in critical discussions? It is *justifications* for beliefs or for assertions which are asked for in discussions and with which the arguer supports his position. Anyone who argues rationally is prepared, instead of making dogmatic assertions, to provide justification of a kind which anyone can appreciate and which can be accepted, rejected or made the subject of further enquiry. The general plausibility of grounds for assertions corroborates these assertions in the face of critical questions. The argumentative task of adducing grounds can be carried to the point where the grounds are so valid and generally perspicuous that criticism comes to an end, so that the position which is being defended is seen to be rational.

To say that, however, is to return once again to the traditional model of justification, from which Albert had so emphatically taken his leave. Certainly, in the framework of rational argumentation what is required is not *ultimate justification* in the sense of principles which are absolutely unsurpassable, ultimate and necessarily compelling to all rational beings. To that extent, Albert is right when he erects the Münchhausen Trilemma to confront the postulate of ultimate justification. Adequate justification, however, is not to be understood exclusively in the sense of ultimate justification, and Albert persistently evades this point. Certainly, the concept of rationality remains connected, as it always has been, with a more broadly understood concept of justification in the sense of the *logic of argumentation*. Thus, the following possibilities are open to the defender of critical rationalism. Either he provides a criterion of relevant assessment, in the light of the given type of problem to be solved, which is independent of the concept of criticism purely as such, or he elucidates the idea of criticism in terms of rationality, where a 'rational procedure' means the readiness for argumentative justification in the context of critical discussion. At all events, the 'idea of critical testing', just in itself, has no clear sense.

The gravest risk threatens this idea – that of a covertly insinuated *dogmatization of criticism*. If the concept of criticism is not explicated by the fact that criteria are indicated which are distinguishable from the activity of criticism itself, which possess validity and prove their validity for criticism, in that even critical activity is still subject to them, then criticism and standards of criticism coincide indistinguishably. Then everything which is distinct from the standpoint of criticism is liable to criticism simply on the grounds that it is distinct from this standpoint: for everything can be involved in a critically testing comparison with this standpoint. The standpoint of criticism, which is at the same time established as a standard for all criteria of testing, becomes unassailable. That would amount to the most extreme hardening of dogmatism, which is not merely shielded externally against criticism, but cuts the ground from under the feet of all critical objections, because the idea of criticism in general is already identical with the standpoint.

Against such self-delusion there is only one remedy – *self-criticism*. The critical testing applied to another position must also be ready to exercise criticism of itself. Instead of that, however, Albert, in his enthusiasm for criticism, has consistently accused those positions with which he does not agree, or which have criticized critical rationalism, of dogmatism and immunization against criticism. That has happened to the dialectical sociologists,[59] the Marxist psychologists,[60] and all hermeneuticists,[61] whether they belong to the 'communication theory' school[62] or to traditional theology.[63] This shows that even criticism is liable to the insidious threat of dogmatism: self-righteousness impedes self-criticism.

[59] On this see below, on the so-called positivist dispute in sociology.
[60] Albert and Keuth (eds.), *Kritik der kritischen Psychologie*, Hamburg, 1973.
[61] 'Hermeneutik und Realwissenschaft', in Albert, *Kritische Vernunft und menschliche Praxis*, Stuttgart, 1977.
[62] Albert, *Transzendentale Träumereien, K.O. Apels Sprachspiele und sein hermeneutischer Gott*, Hamburg, 1975.
[63] Albert, *Theologische Holzwege, G. Ebeling und der rechte Gebrauch der Vernunft*, Tübingen, 1973.

Explanation of understanding

In opposition to hermeneutics, Albert demands an *explanation of* understanding which would lead out of the long-familiar but outmoded contrast between natural and human sciences. If understanding can be explained, then there is ready to hand a deductive-nomological method to be applied to the specific objects of understanding. In this way the autonomy which is claimed for understanding would be disproved and the ascendancy of 'naturalism' would be finally established. Albert refers first to Dilthey, who associated himself with the older hermeneutic techniques by conceiving of hermeneutics as an '*ars interpretandi*'. For Albert, this is to annul the mythologization of hermeneutics stemming from Heidegger and Gadamer and to move towards sober rational explanation. He is mistaken, however, when he attempts to make Dilthey into the chief witness in support of a naturalistic model of explanation which allows to understanding no special and irreducible powers. Dilthey's decidedly methodological mode of expression, which makes such an impression on Albert, is intended precisely to lay claim to an adequate autonomy of procedure for the understanding of meaning alongside explanation in the manner of the natural sciences. Dilthey is to that extent the founder of a dualism of method which critical rationalism seeks to reduce to a unity and so overcome.

Albert's second authority is Max Weber, and here the situation is more complicated. Weber believed, as is well known, that sociology is a 'science whose object is to interpret the meaning of social action and *thereby* give a causal explanation of the way in which the action proceeds and the effects which it produces'.[64] Since action is characterized as human behaviour 'when to the extent that the agent or agents see it as subjectively meaningful', the scientific demand for explanation is met only if understanding is presupposed because otherwise meaningful action is inaccessible.

Much has been written in the attempt to make a passable methodological bridge between understanding of the subjective meaning of action and explanation of the objective causality of the way in which the action proceeds. As we have seen, it has been

---

[64] *Wirtschaft und Gesellschaft*, § 1; the translation is from W. G. Runciman (ed.), *Weber, Selections in Translation*, Cambridge, 1978, p. 7 (my italics).

recognized at least since the work of Alfred Schütz that even the *subjective understanding of meaning* implies more than the extremely abstract maxims of empathetic 're-living' by the investigating subject of the experiences of his object of investigation, who for his part is also an acting subject. It is not enough simply to take as one's starting-point that the giving of meaning to actions is somehow already accessible to us because we are all, agent and investigator alike, human beings.

The variety of forms which subjective meaning may take are classified by Weber as 'rational in the sense of an attempt to realize some absolute value', 'affective', 'traditional' and 'rational in the sense of employing appropriate means to a given end'. From the outset this represents an abstraction, which is methodologically based on *means–end rationality* and is defined in terms of a gradual divergence from that point. Means–end rationality takes precedence because it motivates the kind of action which is most 'intelligible' from the scientific point of view. All other forms thus lie on the 'limits' of meaningful action. In this there is evidently a preference on the part of the objectifying scientist with regard to what he finds intelligible and what he does not. The construction of science as such thus limits, prior to all investigation, the domain of possible objectivity and structures it in accordance with the prevailing interests of enquiry.

Still more complicated is the form taken by the transition from *understanding to explanation*, or the translation of the meaning borne by the action into lawlike hypotheses to be used in a possible explanation.[65] Since sociology, unlike history, is not interested in the adequate comprehension of the individual case in its particularity, but seeks to discover the general regularities of social behaviour, it must, where it starts from the 'subjectively intended meaning', construct the generality of its theme itself in a certain fashion. Weber does this with the help of the so-called '*ideal type*', which is clearly characterized as a heuristic assumption of science, intended to reduce the variety of given reality to a unity which is the most scientifically intelligible because it is the most rational in the means–end sense. The ideal type of the objectively correct coordination of end and means, action and

---

[65] On this see Weber, 'Über einige Kategorien der verstehenden Soziologie' (1913), in *Soziologie, Weltgeschichtliche Analysen, Politik*, Stuttgart, 1956; see also W. G. Runciman (ed.), *Weber*, pp. 23–5.

intended outcome, permits sociology to formulate lawlike hypotheses, to which reality conforms, though always only to some degree of approximation. This construction, however, proves to be necessary if the step is to be taken from understanding to nomological explanation.

I do not want to pursue further Weber's programme and the replies which have subsequently been made to it, right up to the present day.[66] It must anyway be obvious that the interests of the construction of sociology as a real science have controlled the design of the categorial scheme in terms of which the relevant objects are from the beginning classified. This fact must be borne in mind if a correct evaluation is to be made of the reiteration of Weber's programme in the course of the criticism of more recent hermeneutics. Albert of course sees the difficulties in the construction of ideal types, but regards Weber's model of explanation as superior to hermeneutics. At all events, he objects that the interpretation of the situation from the side of the agent, on which Weber's concept of subjectively intended meaning is irreducibly based, must once again be made into an object for science and illuminated by sociological or psychological theories of perception, behaviour etc. That amounts ultimately to the elimination of even that residue of understanding which was conceded by Weber, in favour of a nomological procedure, the competence of which, in Albert's view, is subject to no further restriction. Where everything is explained, there remains nothing to be understood.

Our brief sketch of Weber's conception must already have shown the extent to which the problem of establishing a real science of social life has left its mark on the way in which its objects are perceived. Before the science begins to work at all, its field of vision is already so narrowed that it sees only certain objects and even those only in a very definite light. All the *prior decisions* which belong with the interests of science in general and define sociology as the equal partner of the recognized sciences of nature are already forgotten and lie in the back of the scientist's

---

[66] E.g. Hempel, 'Typological methods in the natural and social sciences' (1952), in *Aspects of Scientific Explanation*, New York, 1965; J. W. Watkins, 'Ideal types and historical explanation' (1952), in A. Ryan (ed.), *Philosophy of Social Explanation*, Oxford, 1973; W. G. Runciman, *A Critique of Max Weber's Philosophy of Social Science*, Cambridge, 1972 (esp. ch. 3).

mind. He may thus, in his role as a scientist, even not reflect upon them, unless he ceases to be an empirical scientist. Hermeneutics saw its philosophical vocation as being to draw attention to the limitations and one-sidedness which always accompany the establishment of a methodical science, while not lapsing into a wholesale verdict on this necessary condition for all scientific activity or even wanting to compete with scientific knowledge. Philosophical reflection quite naturally has a different status from that of the special sciences.

Hermeneutics poses those questions which science by definition neither can nor ought to pose. Whether the questions are legitimate cannot be decided in advance. This becomes clear from case to case when the questions touch on something worth questioning, that is, on something which is not, or could not be, treated of otherwise by science and the elucidation of which represents a gain in insight. Such questions must, for instance, be raised about Weber's theory of science, with its peculiar bias in relation to social reality, which is treated as an object of enquiry, because they cannot be raised within the framework of this science. The critical rationalists' attempt to reduce hermeneutics to a sort of technology of understanding, which is in turn subordinated to the all-embracing nomological model of explanation of real science, has the effect precisely of cutting off these questions and wantonly sacrifices the insight gained by hermeneutics to the self-confirmation of the dominant scientism, without adding any new insights of its own.

This is all the more astonishing in that *Karl Popper* himself has for a long time dissociated himself from the kind of scientism which is predominantly modelled on the natural sciences and has taken the findings of hermeneutics seriously. He had earlier spoken at length in general terms about 'situational logic',[67] meaning by this a kind of historical understanding of the particularity of a situation and its conditions (for example in the case of scientific 'discoveries'). He has furthermore, quite consistently, outlined a 'rational theory of tradition',[68] in which the determining role of the state of knowledge as it exists and is current at any given time is given its full value. Finally, it is possible to infer from a late essay of Popper's on 'The objective mind' that he

[67] *The Open Society and its Enemies*, Vol. II, ch. 14.
[68] In *Conjectures and Refutations*, London, 1963, esp. pp. 129ff.

would concede the primitiveness of a hermeneutic dimension, which embraces even natural science, instead of being contrasted with it in the usual fashion or even being subordinated to it in the way that Albert wishes. Popper says:

> I oppose the attempt to proclaim the method of understanding as the characteristic of the humanities, the mark by which we may distinguish them from the natural sciences. And when its supporters denounce a view like mine as 'positivistic' or 'scientistic', then I may perhaps answer that they themselves seem to accept, *implicitly and uncritically*, that positivism or scientism is the *only philosophy appropriate to the natural sciences*. This is understandable, considering that so many natural scientists have accepted this scientistic philosophy. Yet students of the humanities might have known better. Science, after all, is a branch of literature; and working on science is a human activity like building a cathedral.[69]

If one accepts the validity of Popper's plea for a productive role for hermeneutics, then all sciences, not just the humanities, come within a general framework of meaningful human activity. What is more, it becomes obvious that criticism itself is inconceivable *without a background* of unquestioningly accepted preconceptions and fundamental presuppositions. The background against which critical activity is first able to develop is determined at any given time by the tradition to which we belong. The tradition governs the direction of the criticism and influences even its standards to a certain degree. Without this element of the given, criticism would be suspended in mid-air. The mere good intention to be as critical as possible in every respect is not enough to set concrete activity in motion. A simple call to arms, no matter how moralistic in tone, ignites no fires, if it is not known at what point to begin amongst the infinitely many possible subjects for criticism, all exactly similar to each other. Without a background, criticism is formal and abstract.

This observation does not in any way involve a conservative dogma. The background of tradition which is necessary for criticism, that is to say, is by no means permanently excluded from

---

[69] *Objective Knowledge*, p. 185.

criticism. It may itself be criticized in a second step. To be sure, that requires yet another background against which what was formerly accepted as self-evident now seems questionable, because now something else is accepted as self-evident and removed from all possibility of questioning. This process can take place only step by step. It is extremely laborious, since no unified schema covering all cases is available for use in the business of questioning preconceptions, which has to be undertaken case by case. What is to be criticized and in regard to what and in which context becomes clear only ad hoc and must be decided in each particular instance.

Historical processes of enlightenment in the political consciousness ought to develop in a similar fashion to the widening of the horizons of scientific enquiry from age to age, from generation to generation and between different schools. The process develops step by step, sometimes along side-tracks or by circuitous routes, hardly ever in a dead straight line. One situation can never be reached in reality, although the critical rationalist treats it as the normal case: that is the situation in which criticism is exercised on the basis of background knowledge and at the same time the background which makes the criticism possible is also subjected to criticism. The situation of *unconditioned criticism* feeds on a fiction. The idea of criticism becomes in this case self-satisfied and functionless, because it no longer admits anything which is excluded from criticism and possesses validity.

In reality, however, there is no reason to be concerned about this fiction. Critical rationalism is the best illustration of the point that convictions about the correctness and absolute validity of the 'idea of critical testing' – convictions which are never themselves criticized – form an ultimate background. To surrender these would be to nullify the work of criticism. No reader of Popper or Albert will be able to dispute that there are massive convictions at work here which regulate the critical impulse but are themselves never exposed to the assaults of criticism. This state of affairs is perfectly natural and so affords no scope for objections. Nevertheless it limits the claims of criticism and confirms the propriety of hermeneutic considerations.

The problem of values

Let us consider in this connexion one more final point, namely, the problem of values as it has existed since the time of Max Weber. '*Value*' was originally a concept derived from classical economics. In the course of the nineteenth century it came to be more and more fashionable also in theoretical philosophy. In this connexion it is interesting to see that it became in some ways the heir to the discredited concept of the 'Idea'. H. Lotze, now forgotten but in his own day extremely influential, was one of the first to prefer the concretely intelligible concept of value, using it first in aesthetic enquiries and then also in logic.[70] 'Value' now denotes an ideal moment which we observe in a thing, going beyond our empirical awareness of facts.

Value-contents can be recognized above all in the life of the historical spirit. It is to them that the cultural or human sciences are devoted. Neo-Kantian methodology sets alongside the natural sciences, with their 'nomothetic' procedures, aimed at subsuming the individual under general laws, the cultural sciences with their 'idiographic' methods, concerned with description directed towards the value of historical individuality.[71] Hegel's much-abused Idealism was rehabilitated in the bosom of the neo-Kantian logic of science,[72] in that value-relevance was admitted as a specific method of knowledge for the structure of historical meaning.

Weber essentially took over the concept of value from the neo-Kantian Rickert[73] – the two men were colleagues in the University of Heidelberg during a period of fruitful common activity. Weber's doctrine, now celebrated, means that the social sciences proceed on the basis of a *theoretical value-relevance* in that they endow the objects of their enquiry in general with a cognitive interest, which is responsible for selection and approach in

[70] E.g. 'Über den Begriff der Schönheit' (1845), in H. Lotze, *Kleine Schriften*, Vol. I, Leipzig, 1885, pp. 300ff., 333ff.; 'Seele und Seelenleben' (1846), in ibid., Vol II, p. 175.
[71] W. Windelband, *Geschichte und Naturwissenschaft* (Rectoral Address, 1894), Strassburg, 1900.
[72] W. Windelband, '*Erneuerung des Hegelianismus*' (Festival Address at the Heidelberg Academy of Sciences, 1910).
[73] Rickert, *Grenzen der naturwissenschaftlichen Begriffsbildung* (1902), Preface to 4th edition, 1921.

dealing with the quantity of material. Value-relevance does no more than indicate certain theoretical objects in preference to others, but in no way implies any practical evaluation; 'for we are of the opinion that it can never be a task for an empirical science to determine binding norms and ideals, in order to derive from them prescriptions for practice'.[74] To be sure, science can introduce clarity about ends–means relations, and thus improve techniques, without thereby removing from the agent the decision for or against an end. Science can also shed critical light on decisions once made and make fundamental beliefs themselves into subjects for enquiry. But what it may not and cannot do is to advocate or justify such value-positions: 'politics does not belong in the lecture-hall'.[75]

The thesis of the *value-freedom of science* continues to arouse as much passion in men's minds as it ever did. The so-called 'debate about value-judgments' which has a history of a good three-quarters of a century has broken out again in recent times with fresh intensity. The lines of battle, however, have changed as compared with the opponents of Weber.[76] From several quarters the rigid distinction between knowledge and evaluation, between 'is' and 'ought', which Weber wanted to make obligatory for the scientist, is disputed. Either it is claimed that enquiry is inextricably involved with universally accepted social value-positions which go beyond the theoretically instrumental and methodically controlled value-relevance which was alone recognized by Weber. Or else the special position of those values which cannot be made a subject for science is denied on the grounds that all choice of methods ultimately also implies a value-position. In both cases, the criticism of Weber results in the abandonment of the bounds set to the value-problem, although the motives of the criticism are very different in nature. So we come to the threshold of a controversy between the adherents of Popper and those of dialectic, which has come to be known by the not entirely happy title of the 'Positivist Dispute'.[77]

---

[74] 'Objektivität sozialwissenschaftlicher Erkenntnis', in *Soziologie, Weltgeschichtliche Analysen, Politik*, p. 187.

[75] 'Wissenschaft als Beruf', ibid., p. 325.

[76] On this see the account in C. V. Ferber, 'Der Werturteilsstreit 1909/1959', *Kölner Zeitschrift für Soziologie*, 11, 1959.

[77] Adorno, Albert, Dahrendorf, Habermas, Pilot, Popper, *Der Positivismusstreit in der deutschen Soziologie*, Neuwied, 1969 (translated by

The attitudes adopted towards the demand for value-judgments offer a good point of entry into the debate. It is complicated at a number of points, since the opposing parties seem to be in agreement, but the arguments they adduce for this are irreconcilable with each other. Complaints about misunderstanding and the need for repeated attempts to make the respective positions more precise run right through the debate, but in the end there are no entirely clear lines of battle to be discerned. Popper and his camp, that is, are in several respects nowhere near ꜣ as far from dialectic or as subservient to positivist dogma as their critics suppose. Conversely, the critics from the Frankfurt School ꜰ are not in every respect dialectical enough to escape the suspicion of a new dogma consisting in belief in the totality of Reason.

For Popper, the postulate of value-freedom is perfectly simple to deal with: it is a matter of one value among others! It would be as artificial as it would be unnecessary to attempt to abstract from all preferences and practical points of view contributed by the scientist as a human being on the basis of his experience of life. On the contrary, one must be aware that methodological principles and scientific ideals represent norms in the same sense as the extra-scientific value-positions of practice. The scientist indeed pursues a special goal – he commits himself to the quest for knowledge and subjects himself to the norms of criticism.

> The phrase 'the passion for truth' is no mere metaphor . . . Objectivity and freedom from such attachments [viz. to values] are themselves *values*. And since value-freedom itself is a value, the unconditional demand for freedom from any attachment to values is paradoxical. I do not regard this argument of mine as very important; but it should be noted that the paradox disappears quite of its own accord if we replace the demand for freedom from attachment to all values by the demand that it should be one of the tasks of scientific criticism to point out confusions of value . . .[78]

G. Adey and D. Frisby, *The Positivist Dispute in German Sociology*, London, 1976); cf. on this P. Lorenzen, 'Szientismus vs. Dialektik', in Bubner, Cramer and Wiehl (eds.), *Hermeneutik und Dialektik, Festschrift für Gadamer*, Tübingen, 1970.

[78] Popper, 'Die Logik der Sozialwissenschaften' (14th Thesis), in Adorno, et al., *Positivismusstreit* (this translation, revised by the author, from Adey and Frisby, *Positivist Dispute*, pp. 97f).

Thus the postulate of value-freedom becomes unproblematic, since it proves to be a variant of the decision to adopt the critical standpoint which Popper otherwise advocates. This decision, which can have no justification but can only be the result of free choice, already mediates between theory and practice. Albert loyally follows his master in the belief in a simple solution to this stubborn problem.[79]

Dialecticians like Adorno[80] and Habermas[81] see the problem in a more complicated way. The long recognized separation between 'is' and 'ought', or between factual propositions and evaluations, cannot be reconciled without further ado by an appeal to an idea of criticism. Rather, the need is to expose the element of *ideology* which is concealed behind the postulate of value-freedom in the sciences. That means that the questionable distinction is false, but at the same time necessary. For under the cloak of alleged abstinence from evaluation and the illusion of objectivity which is thus produced there lies concealed a very definite cognitive interest aimed at the technological domination of nature. The purposes which are actually in control are not admitted or accepted as unquestionably self-evident, so that the scientific and technological disposition places itself, by means of the well-established separation of a sphere of values which is withdrawn from all possibility of discussion, in an independent position above the neutral middle ground. Such uncontrolled knowledge for its own sake represents a danger, for here rationality turns suddenly into irrationality and coercion.[82]

[79] *Traktat über kritische Vernunft*, Ch. 3; 'Theorie und Praxis, M. Weber und das Problem der Wertfreiheit und der Rationalität' (in the Festschrift for S. Moser, *Die Philosophie und die Wissenschaften*, Meisenheim, 1966).

[80] 'Zur Logik der Sozialwissenschaften', reply to Popper (*Positivismusstreit*, pp. 137ff.)

[81] 'Analytische Wissenschaftstheorie und Dialektik', a contribution to the controversy between Popper and Adorno (*Positivismusstreit*, pp. 170ff.).

[82] *Herbert Marcuse* has applied the scalpel of the critique of ideology to Weber in an even more radical fashion. He implies a secret complicity between the thesis of value-freedom and the national power-state of the imperialist period. Marcuse's polemic was delivered at the Heidelberg Congress of Sociology on the occasion of the centenary of Weber's birth in 1964 ('Industrialisierung und Kapitalismus im Werk M. Webers', now in H. Marcuse, *Kultur und Gesellschaft*, Vol. II, Frankfurt, 1965; translated in *Negations*, Boston, 1968). This interpretation has provoked various reactions: J. Habermas, *Technik und Wissenschaft als 'Ideologie'*, Frankfurt, 1968, pp. 48ff. (translated in *Towards a Rational*

Adorno does not hesitate to bring the methodological problem of value-freedom fully into the light of the Marxist demand for practical change through theoretical criticism.

> The false separation of value-freedom and value is revealed to be the same as that between theory and practice . . . The subjective reason of the ends–means relation suddenly turns, as soon as it is not in fact restrained by social or scientific authority, into that objective Reason which contains the axiological moment as one of knowledge itself. Value and value-freedom are dialectically mediated by each other.[83]
>
> The dichotomy of 'is' and 'ought' is as false as it is historically necessary; it is not simply something to be ignored. It first becomes clearly understood in its necessity through social criticism. Actually, value-free procedures are forbidden not psychologically, but objectively. Society, knowledge of which is the ultimate aim of sociology, if it wishes to be more than a mere technique, crystallizes itself in general only around a conception of rightly ordered society. This is, however, not to be contrasted with the status quo abstractly, simply as a supposed value, but arises from criticism, and thus from society's consciousness of its contradictions and their necessity.[84]

Cognitive interests

The debate about the correct relationship between knowledge and values, which was closely connected with the methodology based on Weber, has more recently developed into a doctrine of *cognitive interests*. Habermas has sought to re-establish the broken connexions between science and the life-world by elevating the influence of value-positions on cognitive processes into a topic for the theory of science in the form of a threefold conception. Instead of simply detaching the values which are influential in the back of the scientist's mind, they should be subjected to explicit reflec-

Society, London, 1970); H. Albert, 'Wissenschaft und Verantwortung', in *Plädoyer für kritischen Rationalismus*, Munich, 1971.

[83] *Positivismusstreit*, pp. 74f.
[84] Ibid., p. 139.

tion. If they are, the following typological distinctions become clear. The empirical sciences of nature obey a technical or instrumentalist cognitive interest. The sciences of historical understanding correspond to a practical or communicative cognitive interest. The critically oriented sciences, finally, originate in an emancipatory cognitive interest. How is this threefold classification of cognitive interests to be understood?

Behind the first two types can readily be discerned the traditional scheme of a dualism of explanatory and interpretative methods, which are determinant in the natural and the cultural or human sciences respectively. To that extent we are treading a familiar path. Habermas has referred the old classification, which used to be based on the *procedures* or *aims* of knowledge, back to specific sets of interests appertaining, *prior* to any kind of science, to the domain of practical life. The reflections, originating in phenomenology, on the reciprocal relations of life-world and science have here borne fruit.

What, on the other hand, of the third type of cognitive interest, which, as is well known, the author favours? It would be a hard task to associate any existing sciences at all with the emancipatory cognitive interest. Habermas calls the two examples the *critique of ideology* and *psychoanalysis*. Both kinds of endeavour connected with knowledge could not really be described without qualification as 'sciences', even if within the Frankfurt School a perfect blend of questions arising out of the critique of ideology and psychoanalytic motifs has been developed. The modes of thought associated with the names of Marx and Freud belong rather to philosophy than to any of the usual forms of scientific procedure. Habermas has not the least hesitation, in his dispute with positivism and value-theory, in making his starting-point a 'comprehensive concept of rationality' in the sense of the 'convergence of reason and decision which was immediately in the mind of the great philosophers'.[85]

It is in the name of a third, specially proposed, type of science that there emerges a cognitive interest which ought to be called the original *interest of reason itself*. This cognitive interest is disting-

[85] 'Dogmatismus, Vernunft und Entscheidung – Zu Theorie und Praxis in der verwissenschaftlichten Zivilisation', in *Theorie und Praxis*, Neuwied, 1963, pp. 244, 256 (translated by J. Viertel, *Theory and Practice*, London, 1974).

uished by contrast with the first two types, in that knowledge does not serve an interest different from itself, be it that of the domination of nature or that of intersubjective communication. There is no further difference to be discerned between knowledge and interest: the interest goes to knowledge as such, or knowledge is the only interest which counts. In other words, the questionable value-position and the rationality which the usual methodology differentiates from it blend completely with each other.

With a certain amount of good will, one can feel some sympathy with Habermas' efforts to stir up the methodological debate, which has become somewhat stagnant. One then sees that aspiration towards absolute rationality which is properly the idea of philosophy resurrected as a new type of critical and emancipatory 'science'. But whatever label one chooses to attach to it, it is still a matter of a form of *theory*. This theory may quite possibly be such that the value-positions of practical life, in the context of which science necessarily moves, are not alien or opposed to it. It will then come back to practical orientations and convictions in critical reflection. The task of theory can even be largely defined by the fact that it is to shed rational illumination on the dominant ideologies of social life. At all events, however, it will remain theory. It will never succeed in overcoming instantaneously the distance between it and the practice which is its object.

In Habermas, however, it sometimes looks as if the third type of science is to move into the place of practice, so that practice and rationality become the same thing. Habermas operates with a many-faceted concept of practice. On the one hand, it means the sphere of the life-world prior to methodically practised science, together with the elementary value-positions and interest-situations of the agent. There is also the appeal to that special practice represented precisely by the activity of the theoretician, in which rationality itself is elevated to the level of a value which is aspired to, and all interest serves knowledge alone. The practical interestedness in theory as such or the philosophical and scientific evaluation of reason is, however, simply one aspect of the wide variety of meaning which can be given to 'practice', 'interest' and 'value'. Reference to the practical characteristics of theory never includes the rest of the totality of practical life.

Basically, what Habermas has in mind is the following idea: the *ideal society* would be that in which everything proceeded with the same rationality which is found in unrestricted rational science. If the barrier between rational science and practical evaluation is ideological, then it must in critical reflection be set aside. If it is set aside, then the picture of the ideal communication community, as outlined by Apel and Habermas,[86] represents a scientific discussion projected on to the whole of social practice. I do not wish to argue about whether this counterfactual ideal is a pure utopia or a criterion for rational criticism of existing relationships or a real practical directive for the establishment of that rational state of affairs. My doubts are rather about whether the ideal of rational practice, without any regard for the possibility or impossibility of realizing it, is as rational as it appears. This doubt thus goes deeper: that is to say, it concerns the question of the appropriate concept of practice and a correspondingly appropriate ideal of practical reason. Precisely in the name of the critique of ideology, it is important to be on one's guard against a merely rhetorical mediation between theory and practice.

The danger of a subreption in Habermas' methodology is obvious. Talk of a special kind of practice which is called theory, which follows the norms of rationality and is subordinate to a critical cognitive interest of the third type turns all too quickly into talk of practice in general, which deserves to be called rational in a broader socio-historical sense. There is no common denominator, however, between theoretical and practical reason. The practice of enquiry is not the practice of life. A special cognitive interest does not turn into an interest of activity without transformation. The approach to theory of science with which we are presently concerned obviously glosses over these difficulties. We shall return to this question in the third chapter, on 'Dialectic and philosophy of practice'.

The historicity of the paradigm

The moment has come to pass on to another position which may be classified among the developments of Popper's pragmatic and critical logic of scientific enquiry. In the literature, *Thomas Kuhn* is counted as belonging to the tendency inaugurated by Popper. I

---

[86] See the beginning of this chapter.

do not wish to enter into any detailed discussion of Kuhn's originality.[87] Without doubt, his book *The Structure of Scientific Revolutions* (1962) led to a revolutionary paradigm-shift of the kind analysed in the book itself. It has become customary to speak of post-Kuhnian theory of science in contrast to the classical positions of Carnap, Hempel etc. What is new in Kuhn's conception is the emphasis on the *role of history*. Theory of science and history of science work hand in hand, and the logic of enquiry must be relativized in the perspective of historical change and social conditions. Mountains of literature have since accumulated, expounding or taking further Kuhn's ideas (Feyerabend),[88] opening up a debate with alternative positions (Popper, Lakatos),[89] putting Kuhn in his place from a classical point of view (Scheffler)[90] and so on.

Discussion of the theory of science, which in Germany has taken place predominantly under analytic influence, has reacted with remarkable sensitivity to the shock of Kuhn. That is hardly surprising when one recalls the strongly historical alignment

----

[87] In the preface to his book, Kuhn refers to the stimulus given by an almost forgotten study: L. Fleck's *Einführung in die Lehre vom Denkstil und Denkkollektiv* (Basel, 1935; new edition, Frankfurt, 1980; English translation, 1979). Fleck demonstrates by means of a medical example the collective and historical constitutive conditions of what we usually call a fact. 'We cannot escape from the past with all its errors. It lives on in the concepts which we have taken from it, in the formulation of problems, in what is taught in our schools, in everyday life, in language and in institutions. There is no "spontaneous generation" of concepts: they are as it were determined by their ancestors. The past is much more dangerous – or, to be precise, only dangerous at all – when the association with it remains unconscious and unrecognized' (p. 28). Fleck was certainly greatly influenced by the *sociology of knowledge* of the twenties (he cites 'Jerusalem, die soziale Bedingtheit des Denkens und der Denkformen', in M. Scheler, *Versuche zu einer Soziologie des Wissens*, 1924). The following remark on positivism is very illuminating: 'The epistemologists of the so-called Vienna Circle (Schlick, Carnap et al.), with their training in the natural sciences, committed the mistake of having far too much respect for logic, a kind of religious reverence for logical conclusions' (p. 58).

[88] *Against Method*, London, 1975.

[89] Lakatos and Musgrave (eds.), *Criticism and the Growth of Knowledge*, Cambridge, 1970.

[90] *Science and Subjectivity*, New York, 1967; see also the positive reply by C. Hempel: 'Die Wissenschaftstheorie des analytischen Empirismus im Lichte zeitgenössischer Kritik' (in Patzig et al. (eds.), *Logik, Erkenntnistheorie, Theorie der Geisteswissenschaften*, Acts of the XIth German Congress for Philosophy, Hamburg, 1977).

which has been a constant element in German philosophy since the nineteenth century. The thesis of paradigm-shifts which provide a constructive basis for scientific rationality came just at the right moment. Whereas in the analytic camp the thesis has had the irreversibly liberalizing effect of breaking down the positivist dogmas of the official theory of science, such a critical effect was not so necessary in the climate of continental philosophy, with its *hermeneutic* and *dialectical* character.

The content of Kuhn's thesis was taken up with all the greater vigour and pursued with an exclusiveness which probably goes beyond the author's rather cautious claims in philosophical matters. Kuhn's analysis of revolutions was supported by excellent evidence from the history of science, which carried conviction anyway in the name of the *historicity of thought*. It was hardly an accident therefore that, in reaction to the historicist euphoria, W. Stegmüller made a particularly sophisticated attempt to save the orthodox point of view once and for all, without simply accusing the Kuhnians of heresy. In what follows, I want briefly to sketch the reasons for Kuhn's reception and the forms in which he was assimilated,[91] in order to set Stegmüller's reaction in its context.

Hermeneutics has long maintained that scientific knowledge finds its place in a broadly conceived context of '*pre-understanding*'. The pre-understanding of activity in the life-world, prior to methodically regulated scientific operations, actually makes enquiry possible and is not opposed to it in the way suggested by a widespread conception of the difference between science and life. The conditions for the possibility of scientific activity lie in an original familiarity with reality, in skilled practical dealings with things and implements, in the ability to acquire techniques and to master special procedures and not least in the interest in problems which require solution. These are presuppositions without which science would not be possible, but they are in no sense part of the subject-matter of science. If science retreats to a second level to consider its own presuppositions and to make its theme, for instance, the psychology of enquiry, the social context of scientific education, the historical

---

[91] The following items from the literature may be mentioned: 'Tendenzen der Wissenschaftstheorie' (with contributions by L. Krüger, E. Ströker and others), *Neue Hefte für Philosophie*, 6/7, 1974 (Göttingen); W. Diederich (ed.), *Theorien der Wissenschaftsgeschichte*, Frankfurt, 1974; K. Hübner, *Kritik der wissenschaftlichen Vernunft*, Freiburg, 1978.

institutionalization of methodical knowledge and so forth, then it is only at the price of repeating in the form of a regress that pre-scientific presupposition without which the approach to science would be inconceivable.

Owing to the fact that relevant presuppositions exist for strictly regulated processes of knowledge, science is retrospectively reconciled with history. More has always been 'known' than is made into the object of investigation in particular sciences in the context of methodical enquiry, and more must be known if the process of highly stylized objectification which is institutionalized as science is to be carried out. On the other hand, the surrounding surplus of knowledge fades into the background as science concentrates on definite objects and the grip of method becomes more complete. The supporting pre-understanding necessarily moves into the background. Thus the direct consequence of the primary definition of objects, with which specialized enquiry generally begins, is that the presuppositions under which it stands are forgotten. The historicity of science is its dependence, unbeknown to itself, on given conditions in the social world and in the tradition as it exists at the time.

Kuhn's concept of the *paradigm*, which in spite of his critics[92] owes its theoretical fruitfulness precisely to its lack of precision, brings out with reasonable accuracy these historically given contextual conditions for scientific activity. The loose combination of a variety of elements of a theoretical, practical, technical, psychological and other kinds makes the paradigm open to penetration by the general life-world and by history. Nevertheless, Kuhn formulates the concept of a paradigm so narrowly that it refers only to that background-knowledge which is definable in relation to actually established sciences. Now this must be a fiction covertly influenced by the ideal of science; for it would scarcely be possible to differentiate the constitutive presuppositions for the 'normal science' of an epoch with the clarity with which the concept of the paradigm is defined amid all the variety of elements which it comprises. The limits to the remainder of a whole stream of tradition are difficult to draw.

Evidence for this can be found in all those 'renaissances' in which allegedly superseded and out of the way knowledge is

---

[92] Cf. M. Masterman, 'The nature of a paradigm', in Lakatos and Musgrave, *Criticism*.

revived. In the historical sciences such renaissances are a frequent phenomenon. But even in the natural sciences, with which Kuhn is concerned, there are unexpected reversions and revaluations of the past which leave behind the narrow framework of the dominant paradigm. The answer which Feyerabend has given, with his methodological anarchism of 'anything goes' across the ages, in fact seems to be an exaggeration. In a polemical form he nevertheless draws attention to the limitation imposed on Kuhn's latent historicism by his concept of a paradigm, solidified as it is by being projected on to an ideal of science.

The *hermeneutic* insight into the historical character of all knowledge is free from such limitations. If there are conditions without which science cannot work normally as a functioning enterprise, then such conditions precede science and transcend the clearly demarcated area of objects admitted by a particular theory. Connexions with the life-world which everybody shares are established; the social and ideological constitution of a society may not be left out of account, and the historical development of practical needs and the level of consciousness achieved in the general public have a role to play as external factors. Wide scope exists for historically orientated contextual investigations of the immediate and more remote vicinity of pure history of science, in the sense of a succession of exact theories and the discoveries of genius. The first attempts to cultivate this field already exist, though frequently they in turn lapse into formulating the questions in a highly specialized manner. Thus there is the sociological and economic investigation of science, which is principally interested in the controlling authorities or in the elaboration of planning directives. Furthermore, there is a small number of Marxist-inspired studies which go beyond the general thesis of the relation between base and superstructure and enter into historical detail.[93] They can seldom be satisfactory, however, since they either have prior knowledge of what the outcome is to be, namely the predominance of economic determinants, or are written entirely in the service of a preconceived critique of the so-called 'bourgeois' forms of social embedding of science. Recently there have been some improved attempts along these lines to attach to Kuhn's

---

[93] E.g. the papers by a former member of the Vienna Circle, E. Zilsel, which were published in German by W. Krohn under the title, *Die sozialen Ursprünge der neuzeitlichen Wissenschaft*, Frankfurt, 1976.

concept of the developed paradigm a necessary tendency towards the 'finalization' of science through the pursuit of external goals of a social and practical kind.[94]

Finalization of science amounts, more or less, to the instrumentalization of mature, that is, technically applicable, theoretical sciences. According to this model, the phase of finalization inevitably ensues when the articulation and consolidation of a paradigm is complete, whereas the initial phases of the first orientation and slow formation of a paradigm are still subject to a neutral, purely theoretical, interest. Certainly, the extent of technical application increases when the theoretical questions which provided the initial stimulus have been solved and the business of 'puzzle-solving' has come to preoccupy concrete work. At the same time, of course, the theoretically determining influence of external factors on the work of enquiry at the front line declines. The technical transplantation of the results of a confirmed paradigm always happens subsequently: it no longer affects the paradigm itself at its heart and is rather a matter of external developments. The thesis of finalization is thus not very fruitful for the theory of science, since it is related to consequential phenomena in the social context of science.

More important to clarify, but more difficult to grasp, are the practical interests of the historical situation, which initially, as more or less consciously followed guiding threads, point the direction to be pursued at the *origin* of a paradigm. How does genuinely theoretical curiosity[95] stimulate the scientific community in the periods of revolution and how important are transferred needs from extrascientific practice? The dispute over the internal or external explanation of scientific development is unsettled. Plainly, it is scarcely possible to say more about it at this stage than that there is a mixture of factors with no neat line to be drawn between them. The pressure of social needs and the chance of the existence of a wealth of scientific talent work together according

---

[94] Studies with a view to producing models of a connexion between theory and practice on the basis of the history of science have been undertaken above all in the Starnberg Institute, directed by Habermas and von Weizsäcker (cf. the contribution reprinted in Diederich, *Theorien*, by Böhme, van den Daele and Krohn, 'Die Finalisierung der Wissenschaft').

[95] Cf. H. Blumenberg, *Der Prozess der theoretischen Neugier*, Frankfurt, 1973.

to circumstances. If one is genuinely to develop further the structural consideration of scientific revolutions, however, one must go beyond such platitudes. So far there has been a concentration on studies of individual cases, which without question furnish important material that cannot be ignored, but from which it is difficult to draw more general conclusions.[96]

Dialectic in paradigm-change

We alluded from a hermeneutic viewpoint to the dilemma which arises in connexion with Kuhn's concept of a paradigm, to the extent that it represents a projection of established science on to its background conditions. From this there follows an undervaluation of the whole extent of the historical dimension in which knowledge moves. The undervaluation of history is expressed in a different form as an over-emphasis on the extent of the change between normal science and revolutionary periods. The objection has been made to Kuhn that he exaggerates the difference between normality and revolution, because he basically takes the side of normal science and correspondingly dramatizes in an artificial way critical and revolutionary change. Popper[97] on the other hand has forced the problem unduly into a psychological and moral direction, in that he elevates the revolutionary attitude into the rule and degrades normal science to a phenomenon resulting from a deplorable lack of criticism in the consciousness of scientists. It is however not merely a question of correct education and good will whether the radically critical attitude which Popper regards as a duty for the scientist spreads out from the rare moments of revolutionary upheaval into the everyday practice of normal science. Those of Kuhn's interpreters who accept that there is a close *interpenetration of the normal and the revolutionary*, which cannot be divided into clearly demarcated phases, come closest to the truth. What must be understood is how the two work together. It seems to me that dialectical ideas may be helpful in this regard.

---

[96] An example is: Böhme, van den Daele and Krohn, *Experimentelle Philosophie*, Frankfurt, 1977.

[97] 'In my view the "normal" scientist, as Kuhn describes him, is a person one ought to be sorry for' ('Normal science and its dangers', in Lakatos and Musgrave, *Criticism*, p. 52).

The interpenetration of the normal and the revolutionary should not be attributed to the completely accidental succession of narrow-minded and enlightened forms of consciousness, either in the mind of one and the same individual scientist or in the competition of schools and talents. The demand for a *structural interpretation of the historical development* arises quite naturally. The state of the long-continued debate about incommensurability or incompatibility between paradigms does not suffice to meet that demand. Basically, we are still at the point where Kuhn talked of the 'incompleteness of logical contact' and left the transitions in obscurity.[98] The structural interpretation of the inner connexion of normal and revolutionary elements must be in a position to make intelligible the reciprocal causal relations between the two. The stagnation which is represented by the dominance of normal science without alternatives must as such and without the intervention of external and contingent factors lead to revision through revolutionary crises. Correspondingly, the general confusion which exists at a time of revolutionary change must in itself require renewed stabilization and firm guidance by norms. The reciprocal relations of the two elements and their mutual causality result from one premise, namely, that of rationality. This premise is indeed immediately posited with the acceptance of science.

Under the *premise of rationality* the normal character of science appears as a successful narrowing of vision on the basis of a general renunciation of fundamental alternatives. Where only quite specific possibilities of realization are admitted by science, which are simply equated with rationality in virtue of an unquestioningly accepted norm, the danger of the limitation of rationality threatens. The limitation has indeed the factual force of the existing state of affairs on its side, but not a foundation explicitly earned in the interplay of alternatives. A limitation of rationality which remains unnoticed is however equivalent per se to a certain measure of irrationality. The premise of rationality, which is present as part of the supposition of science, itself gives sufficient ground to call for the revision of possible irrationality in the state of organized knowledge. The penetrating criticism which takes the form of the shaking of an accepted paradigm is thus not a

---

[98] *The Structure of Scientific Revolutions*, Chicago, 1970², ch. 9.

mysterious natural event, which recurrently afflicts the scientific community every few generations like an epidemic. The criticism arises from the *conflict between the dogma of rationality and the questioning of rationality* in the case of a given paradigm.

The conflict appears, in view of the formal premise, as a *logical* one. The field in which the contest takes place is nevertheless *history*. The structural interpretation, which contributes to the problem of paradigm-change by using dialectical categories, moves between logic and history. The resolution of that conflict in which the dogma of rationality disputes with criticism in the name of rationality is the change of paradigms as it occurs historically, while the reason for the change is of a logical nature and does not exhaust itself in the description of a change in any given situation.

Consequently, the resolution takes the form that the expectation of rationality which structurally connects the fulfilment of science with every paradigm which is assumed is in fact satisfied. The crisis of the old is in effect the postulation of a new paradigm. The transition between the two has rational grounds. The logical relation of the second to the first paradigm implies, simply on the basis of the intelligible succession, that at least the shocks and uncertainties which led to the downfall of the first paradigm are eliminated in the second. Otherwise this paradigm would not take over the function assigned to it in accordance with the structure of scientific activity. An unsatisfactory successor paradigm would not even be a successor.

The elimination of the particular limitation of the first paradigm in the second by no means guarantees that inadequacies of quite a different kind may not appear here. The new limitations may in several respects amount to a decline below the level attained already in the superseded paradigm. A priori and independently of information about the history of science, at all events, no decision can be reached about this. The ordered sequence of paradigms relative to each other conforms to no teleological pattern for the whole process. In his later work, Popper has reacted to Kuhn's historical relativism by advocating the exaggerated concept of 'verisimilitude'.[99] The intended teleology of a linear progression of knowledge to ever more perfect forms

[99] *Objective Knowledge.*

governed by the ultimate vanishing point of a definitively true theory of the whole of reality is, however, indefensible on the basis of the history of science, without the support of quasi-metaphysical hypotheses.

The rather free interpretation which I have given of the theory of paradigm-change starts from the fascinating, though not fully clarified, mixture of history and logic which has also attracted other interpreters of the theory. I certainly believe that the neglect of the historical dimension in a teleological interpretation based on the model of the inclusion of one paradigm in the next up to an ultimate paradigm, or the reduction of history to the 'quantité négligeable' of a group-psychology of individual scientists, undermines the decisive connexion of logic and history in Kuhn's conception. The author himself, indeed, even fails to do justice to it when he deviates into a quasi-Darwinistic view of scientific development.[100] What is lacking is a logic of the structural evolution of theories. It would have, without any absolute prejudgment about the ends of the process, from the limitation of rationality in the concrete form of a paradigm, to grasp the supersession of that paradigm and the search for a new one as a *transition* which is necessary in the name of rationality. Anyone who looks for help in this very complex problem finds notable hints in the dialectical method. Feyerabend has quite correctly seen this analogy, although he makes undesirable associations between dialectic and the political liberalism of Mill or anarchistic calls for radical freedom. The purest exposition of the dialectical method is to be found, as is well known, in Hegel's Logic.[101] For present purposes, I have extracted some motifs from it which may be of some use towards a 'logic of transitions'.[102] The logic of transitions would have to be concerned for rationality even in the conditions of the crisis of rationality, while the historical dimension takes on a constitutive role for situations of imperfect rationality. What happens in the transitions is analysed by logic.

[100] *Scientific Revolutions*, ch. 13.
[101] Stephen Toulmin's contribution to the debate follows Collingwood in relying less on Hegel's Logic than on his theory of history (*Human Understanding*, Vol. 1, Oxford, 1972); on this, compare Imre Lakatos' criticisms (*Philosophical Papers*, ed. J. Worrall and G. Currie, Vol. II, Cambridge, 1978) – Lakatos indeed in an obscure passage admits to his own dialectical beginnings (*Philosophical Papers*, p. 70).
[102] On the revival of Hegel see also below, Ch. 3.

That they happen at all and are endlessly repeated with every paradigm-change is a mark of the historicity of our knowledge.

This brief outline can prima facie claim at best a certain plausibility. It ought to provide a stimulus for a fresh consideration, by recourse to dialectical reflection, of the questions which are constantly debated in the wake of the structural analysis of scientific revolutions about the logical status of those transitions which lead from one rationality-fixing paradigm to another. That may sound startling to Hegel's professional detractors. Sometimes, however, contempt is merely the protective colouring of ignorance. In this case, there might be a need for a critical paradigm-change!

Stegmüller's defence of orthodoxy

Far removed from such dangerous speculations is *Wolfgang Stegmüller*, who encyclopaedically elaborates the theory of science and language of analytical empiricism and defends them with great subtlety. The phenomenon of historicist dissolution which appeared within the school with Kuhn and the movement which followed him requires intensified efforts on the part of the defensive forces. The best defence always consists in not entirely denying the rights of the heretics, since that would give rise objectively to a competition which would necessarily relativize even one's own point of view. It is better to concede a modification of relative rights in the wider context of one's own position, into which the supposed deviation fits in such a way that it can be explained adequately in this framework. The strategy of such an outflanking movement tends to be given the sonorous name of 'rational reconstruction'. This designation implies that

(1) a reconstruction is necessary, because without it the disputed proposition would be quite unintelligible and impossible to discuss;

(2) only the rational content is reconstructed and inessential or irrational accessories escape and

(3) the proper reconstruction conforms to the criteria of rationality in general.

Stegmüller's fundamental reconstruction[103] of the dynamics of

---

[103] *Probleme und Resultate*, Vol. II, Pts D and E; 'Theoriendynamik und logisches Verständnis', in W. Diederich (ed.) *Theorien*; 'Theory-change

theories seeks to replace the objectionable paradigm-change, together with the accompanying phenomenon of a shock to the firmly built structure of rationality by a concept of *theory-dislodgment* which exorcizes the danger of irrationality in the gaps between paradigms. Stegmüller depends essentially on J. Sneed's book, *The Logical Structure of Mathematical Physics* (1971). With Sneed, he starts from the mathematical core of a theory as distinct from its empirical interpretations. He further accepts with Sneed a criterion of theoreticity according to which the mathematical calculation of quantities or functions within a theory is possible only by reference back to the theory itself. In this way the mathematical core of the theory may be stabilized and the old dispute about the theory-dependence of empirical observation sentences, which had led amongst other things to the concept of paradigms, may be bypassed. At the same time the way is prepared for an elucidation of the dynamic development of theories. One should not hope, like Popper, for the falsification of a theory by an experience which must be thought of as a falsifying instance independently of the theory. But equally one need not, like Kuhn, resign oneself in the face of a logically unintelligible and suddenly occurring 'Gestalt-switch' between paradigms.

The stable core of the theory permits one to talk of 'holding' a theory, that is, of having the possibility of empirically applying the theory in a number of respects through the formulation of testable hypotheses. Holding a theory in this sense represents Kuhn's condition of normal science. The empirical interpretation of the core may lead, with different scientists, to inconsistencies between their respective hypotheses. Since an indefinite number of possible interpretations must be supposed, it would be precipitate to ascribe the inconsistency of a number of proposed applications to the core of the theory, which is in itself rational. There is no need to draw the radical consequence of abandoning the whole paradigm which is based on the core of the theory. That would be to make the mistake of throwing out the baby with the bathwater. What is certain is rather 'that the inability to find a solution with

---

and theory-dislodgment', *Erkenntnis*, 10, 1976, with a reply in the same issue by Kuhn, 'Theory-change as structure-change', in which Kuhn says, 'In fact the Sneed formalism supplies no basis for Stegmüller's counter-revolutionary formulations' (p. 190); finally, Stegmüller, *The Structuralist View of Theories*, New York, 1979.

one's theory never discredits the theory, but only the scientist'; so that radical consequences show only that the human being has failed in his vocation.[104]

Stegmüller's strategy is obviously aimed at defending the inherent rationality of a theory as such and relegating the troublesome phenomena to the status of contingent psychological factors. This is to reintroduce the abstract and unrealistic separation of theory in its own right on the one side and on the other the finite subjects who always recede behind it – that separation which it was precisely Kuhn's great merit to have overcome. Under the explicit motto '*In dubio pro theoria*',[105] Stegmüller then explains revolution as follows. First it is worth making use of all kinds of modifications of the empirical interpretations in order to keep the mathematical core of the theory unshaken. Then one should think of an expansion of the core, which nevertheless still has a conservative function. Finally, however, one theory may dislodge another, though Stegmüller does not explain in any detail when, why or in what conditions. The mystery of paradigm-change as such remains, though the name is changed to 'theory-dislodgment'.

Only one postulate is laid down to close the gaps in the transition: the dislodged theory must be reducible to the newly emerging substitute theory. In this way an advance would be guaranteed which would come about without any teleological total schema. Stegmüller wants in this way to mediate between Popper's 'verisimilitude' and blind Darwinism *à la* Kuhn. Stegmüller meets the expected objections that it would be difficult to reduce the whole history of the sciences in all its stages to the formula of the reduction of the old to the new by separating the domains of the historian and of the logician of science.[106] The one cannot ultimately judge what the other knows – so we should once again be in the situation which Kuhn's synthesis helped productively to overcome.

A half-hearted appeal to *Kant* also does not help to get out of the dilemma.[107] The stable core of the theory is to be compared to Kant's a priori principles of knowledge, while the empirical applications a posteriori permit a change which may be interpreted in historical terms. However, the a priori is not so a priori,

[104] In Diederich, *Theorien*, p. 190. [105] *Probleme und Resultate*, p. 230.
[106] Ibid., p. 249. [107] Ibid., pp. 250ff.

since even Stegmüller wants in principle to take account of theory-dynamics involving the firm core. If, however, the a priori status of the principles of all knowledge is surrendered, there remains only the relativization of a specific core in relation to a specific set of applications and this relationship will always be played out in the historical dimension. We must follow up this thought just one step further to find ourselves back at the dialectical interpretation of paradigm-change.

The relativization of absolute principles in relation to that which they succeed in explaining proves to be flexible even in regard to that which cannot be successfully explained on the basis of these principles. For from the insight which has now become possible into the limits which the claimed achievement runs up against there results a movement to attempt a new project which faces a similar fate. Through the relativization of the principles to what they achieve and what they do not, various forms of actualization of rationality become comparable with each other. They come into the kind of immanent connexion in which the one form can be related to the shortcomings of the other. The movement which thus emerges, which holds on to the idea of rationality without identifying it with one of its realizations, is called in the tradition 'dialectic'. After all, *Hegel* was the first to relativize Kant in the sense indicated. The dialectical method, which horrifies Stegmüller, has the advantage over the vacillation between the Kantianism of the firm a priori and the historical relativization which disavows the a priori that it thinks this connexion consistently through to the end.

Stegmüller's efforts at being a conservative about theories while at the same time recognizing the advances made by Kuhn are bound to miscarry: as the children's saying has it, you can't have your cake and eat it. The stabilization of rationality against revolutionary convulsions which at first sight makes dexterous use of the distinction between structural core and empirical applications achieves nothing if it must in the end still accept inexplicable processes of theory-dislodgment. So it comes at most to an elaborate reformulation, with an impressive use of formal techniques, of Kuhn's insights which systematically misses the real point of the conception.

Constructivism

One tendency in theory of science which is argued for in an original way and clearly allows of extension beyond the narrow field of the traditional objects of the theory of science is what is called *constructivism*. Constructivism has developed independently of the positivist principles which the Vienna Circle established and which were extended as a school by the official 'philosophy of science'. Constructivism, however, has equally little attachment to the opposite party, the 'humanities', which in all their transformations return to the venerable dispute between the methods of the natural and human sciences. The constructivist conception represents a development which is to a certain extent separate, and which goes back to some half-buried ideas of an idiosyncratic philosopher by the name of Hugo Dingler. The continuation of these beginnings, for which Paul Lorenzen has been primarily responsible, has come to be known as the Erlangen School. Such labels say little; they are principally ways of appeasing the interest in general views and classification. What does the constructivist tendency seek to achieve, philosophically speaking?

The fundamental idea of constructivism is the demand for a *construction, rigorously regulated by a method,* of all concepts and procedures which are important for a specific science. Scientific rigour requires not only that relevant definitions and special techniques are acknowledged and utilized. The correct scientist has to give account of everything with which the various specialisms customarily work without giving a complete account of all foreknowledge which is simply given with the establishment of the specialisms. Against that constructivism sets the ideal of total foundation. Dingler started from the problems of the foundations of geometry and physics which had been prominent since the first half of the century. The characteristic formality of the programme of construction, however, permits its extension to all theoretical sciences, and even beyond into the practical sphere, which, according to the prevailing conceptions of ethics, can neither be treated methodically nor regarded as cognitive in the strict sense. At all events it is in this extended version that constructivism is discussed today.[108]

---

[108] Cf. P. Lorenzen, *Methodisches Denken*, Frankfurt, 1968; *Normative Logic and Ethics* (the John Locke Lectures at Oxford), Mannheim, 1969;

The rigorous demand for a methodical construction of all
concepts and procedures implies the set of problems connected
with an *absolute beginning*. Only if one is certain that beyond the
constructive sequence of steps there lies nothing more that is
uncomprehended and still in need of methodical treatment does
constructivism acquire that force of conviction which makes its
programme so attractive for many. Dingler writes on this
point:

> There are two different possible ways of arriving at the
> beginning. We can either begin 'in the middle' or 'at the
> null-point'. The first attempt would mean that we
> commence our endeavours 'anywhere' in civil life. In
> this case, enquiry could take two directions from this
> starting-point – 'downwards', in that we seek to find
> 'foundations' for our initial assertions. Or on the other
> hand, we could seek to move 'upwards', in drawing
> consequences from these assertions. This procedure of
> starting from the middle is generally in use in the
> existing sciences and in philosophy. All positivism, all
> empiricism proceeds in this way. The other approach,
> starting from the null-point, has likewise been repeatedly
> attempted (first of all by Descartes), but without
> complete success. The latter approach is the one which
> we shall adopt here.[109]

The constructivists know, of course, that no one can remove
himself from the conditions of the ordinary pragmatic context, of
'civil life' as Dingler puts it in his rather old-fashioned way. No
one can simply set aside the prior knowledge developed in everyday life and the point of view implicit in ordinary language. The
constructivists deny, however, that these given factors are bound
to exert an irresistible or even decisive influence. They want
constructively to bring under control all relevant elements of the

Lorenzen and Schwemmer, *Konstruktive Logik, Ethik und
Wissenschaftstheorie*, Mannheim, 1973; J. Mittelstrass, *Die Möglichkeit von
Wissenschaft*, Frankfurt, 1974.

[109] *Die Ergreifung des Wirklichen* (1955), new edition with an introduction by
Lorenz and Mittelstrass, Frankfurt, 1969, pp. 97f.; see also the older
work with the suggestive title *Der Zusammenbruch der Wissenschaft und
der Primat der Philosophie* (The Collapse of Science and the Primacy of
Philosophy), Munich, 1926.

actual life-situation and if necessary even to correct them. This contention is at first sight diametrically opposed to the hermeneutic interpretations of the life-world and the intersubjectively used language as a presupposition beyond which it is impossible to go.[110] At second glance, however, it can be seen that precisely for the most elementary steps of the construction it is necessary to refer back to data which lie in a sphere which is prior to all culture, all science and all philosophy.

The demonstration of presuppositions, of a beginning at the absolute null-point, cannot however succeed without some *presuppositions*, which are not indeed of a substantive kind, but which do concern the methodical procedure itself. That is to say, the constructivist method makes use of intersubjectively controlled confirmation of all information, steps in argument, techniques etc. which come into question in the construction of a science from the first beginnings. This confirmation, in the sense of the construction of the theoretical structure and the reconstruction of its prescientific presuppositions, occurs in the context of a dialogue, in which, following certain rules as in a game, one partner issues a challenge and the other must perform certain specific actions. The dialogue game permits the introduction of all necessary constituents in the methodically ordered advance from one stage to the next. But the dialogue itself and the successive introduction of the necessary concepts, activities and more complex modes of procedure do not arise in a vacuum. First of all, the very simplest practical capacities are presupposed. As in Wittgenstein's analysis of simple language-games[111] one must proceed on the basis that certain actions can be performed. Primitive *practical* handling of everyday things must already be learned before the methodical procedure can be set in motion at all. It is on that basis that the first constructive steps build: they require the simplest activities like drawing lines, 'producing' figures and 'realizing' signs. From the simplest actions more complex ones are then constructed, higher rules are introduced and general concepts formed. The clearly ordered advance can be easily made manifest in the sequence of steps. The elementary skills of a practical kind, however, cannot themselves be introduced; for in order for it to

---

[110] See Lorenz' and Mittelstrass' article, 'Die Hintergehbarkeit der Sprache', *Kant-Studien*, 58, 1967.

[111] Wittgenstein, *Philosophical Investigations*, §§ 2ff.

be possible methodically to 'introduce' anything at all, recourse must be had to them.

Still further presuppositions, which have to be taken over from 'civil life' prior to all exercise of methodical discipline, are essential for constructivism. The capacity to act appears from the outset as an ability to imitate on the basis of a request. The framework of the process of introduction is a dialogue with a *teaching or learning character*. The steps to be taken are externally directed. Thus it is necessary not only to have a command of practical dealings with objects, but also to understand requests, to be able to imitate what has previously been done and in general to have the capacity to learn. The capacity to learn is, all in all, even what gives the most important impetus to the methodical construction. Without it, no step would be possible and the ordered sequence of steps would make no progress.

One would not have to dwell on these presuppositions any further if the methodical claim did not stand or fall with them. In itself, the question of the origin of all these capacities in social psychology, anthropology or even cultural history is unfruitful, since we already presuppose them whatever we do, even when we pose questions of origin. Linguistic analysis, following Wittgenstein, has rightly shown that it is impossible to ask meaningful questions at a deeper level than the mastery of a language-game of ordinary language as a complex form of life. It has thereby merely reminded us of a certainty which no one could seriously dispute, although it contains a valuable prophylactic against the programme of an ideal language.

The constructivists are not addicted to the old illusions of an ideal language. Nevertheless, they pledge to lay a methodical foundation for what is given in the practice of life and in everyday speech, which they too acknowledge – a foundation which, from a wider point of view, is to make possible a decision about the *rationality* or irrationality which is there implicit. But since for the purpose of the methodical introduction itself, indeed right at its very beginning, a learning capacity has to be supposed which dialogically controls the individual steps and is to be acquired, not in the methodical advance itself, but already prior to it, the outcome turns out to be rather modest in comparison with the constructivist solemnities about beginning at the 'null-point'.

It is scarcely possible to dismiss the fact that, along with the supposed framework of dialogue, the instructions, their execution, the prior exercises and imitation, the understanding of the different roles of the partners, there exist certain premises about the rationality which determines methodical procedure and cannot be further elucidated; for to make them into a theme for themselves would necessarily be to repeat the methodical schema. The measure of rationality which can on the other hand be grasped directly in the process of construction is in the highest degree abstract. 'Rational' here means simply methodical and 'methodical' means proceeding step by step without sudden leaps or circles. The general demand for methodical thought undoubtedly deserves a hearing and ought to become, to a greater extent than it usually is, a self-evident obligation in philosophy.

The requirement of method as such, however, provides only a modest amount of information about possible degrees of rationality or even about irrationality to be avoided if it cannot be explained in terms of content. *In terms of content*, the abstract call for method has absolutely nothing to say, since it is emphatically related to the formal ordering of abstract succession. Which step is to be taken after which, in what context which concept has its place, after what preparations which procedure is to be introduced and so forth – these are all questions of content, which cannot be answered by recourse to the idea of method. A capacity for judgment on the part of the introducing partner in the dialogue comes into play, which of course also reflects his preunderstanding. The appeal to the abstract succession of steps confers no authority in this matter.

That becomes plain on all possible alternatives. A different sequence of steps could look equally methodical and would have turned out equally rationally, although it represents an alternative to the first proposal. Whether the alternatives are compatible or not, whether one is better, that is, more fruitful, more stringent or whatever than the other – these are new questions which inescapably present themselves. It is impossible to see who should decide in such cases of conflict, since there are no criteria which transcend the idea of method. Constructivism has no answer to hand, since in general it does not take such cases into account. For it, methodical procedure takes only one form and the doubt-free validity of the constructivist path has its foundations in formal considerations.

Decisionism or transcendental foundation

The limits of a programme which abstracts from questions of content become very evident at decisive points. Thus the constructivist foundation, as far as its beginnings are concerned, can never completely free itself of an element of *decisionism*. In Dingler, the peculiar character of the beginning – its appearance as a decision – is even emphasized. The nature of decisions, which, in contrast to theoretical foundations, have no argumentative connexions and emerge spontaneously, seemed to offer a way out of the problem of the regress of justification. Of course, it is not arbitrary where the beginning is made, since the beginning is clearly posited. But the act of beginning does not require any further reasons. Constructivism bases itself quite consciously on the presuppositionlessness of practical activity as such.

Incidentally, this inevitably brings it very close to *Fichte*. The Cartesian beginning which Dingler refers to started, as is well known, with an activity of consciousness which no form of thought, not even the radical doubt of all presuppositions, can neglect: *ego cogito*. For the problems associated with presuppositionlessness with which more recent philosophical systems grapple, however, this solution is inadequate. For it immediately came to be recognized that the self-consciousness which accompanies all consciousness of something does not represent any sort of absolute beginning, since the subject referred to cannot be thought without an object. Thus something is presupposed here, be it only the world of objects from which the doubting consciousness must first separate itself in order to find itself. But what is sought is a beginning such that its positing presupposes nothing further. That can only be a beginning which posits itself.

Fichte was the first to understand this, basing his 'Theory of Science', which was supposed to unfold all sciences of the theoretical and practical domains from a first principle, on the primordial 'Deed' of the I. The I does not exist at all before it says 'I' to itself and thereby posits itself. The appearance of this original act of self-identification evidently requires no further presuppositions. Fichte's Absolute I has from the beginning been accused of exaggerated egocentrism by popular but entirely superficial critics. A fair judgment, however, ought to recognize that the I which initially posits itself was for Fichte's Theory of Science the decisive key to the problem of a presuppositionless beginning. This problem of construction, even if not its solution in the concept of the I, is clearly analogous to the more recent conception of the constructivist theory of science.

Certainly this comparison also throws light on the prejudices of constructivism. The decisionistic element at the beginning of the methodical construction, which corresponds to one of the three horns of the Münchhausen Trilemma mentioned earlier,[112] simply has to be accepted. The beginning chosen is never the true, unique and ultimate one, since this qualification already calls for foundations outside itself. The beginning is rather posited, and indeed at a perfectly specific point. With activities of methodical clarification it is usual to begin, that is, at the point where they seem *necessary*. The beginning is made, not at any arbitrary point, but controlled by the exigencies of proof, the requirements of the search for foundations, debates about principles and disputed questions in science. The beginning of the construction is deliberately made at the point from which the pressing requirements can best be covered. For instance, Dingler begins his search for a foundation of mathematical natural science with the concept of the 'something'. The reason for his starting here becomes clear from the consequences which he draws from it, but not from the argumentative debate with alternative starting-points like Fichte's I, Hegel's Being etc. The positing of the beginning in this way, free of all argumentation and dissociated from any justification, fits in perfectly correctly with the constructivist strategy. But at the same time it makes clear the necessary incompleteness of the work of methodical construction.

The fact that all construction or reconstruction of a scientifically significant sequence of concepts begins, not at some arbitrary distance, but naturally at '*neuralgic points*' should not be at all surprising. The decision to engage in thorough methodical clarification is usually motivated by an awareness of a problem which grows out of the actual state of enquiry and the current debate going on in the disciplines at the time. A total, would-be continuous, introduction of anything and everything which subscribes, uncontrolled by any interest of enquiry, to the illusionary ideal of systematic completeness is bound simply to lead to the

---

[112] See section above on 'critical rationalism'.

machine's running idle. [113] Who is interested in the exact statement
of the steps in the derivation of completely unproblematic or
self-evident concepts? What kind of clarification would be needed
where there is nothing essential that is unclear?

To engage in constructivist work in the problem areas of the
existing sciences which are to be defined in terms of their epistemological status helps to relax the rigidly universalistic claims
and makes a contribution towards the task of laying a concretely defined foundation. The Erlangen School has coined for
this the term 'proto-science'. The 'proto' part is the definitory
and normative preliminary to a particular science which rests on
this foundation. So there is to be a proto-mathematics, proto-
physics, [114] proto-sociology and so on. In the proto-scientific part
there is a normative definition and methodical legitimation of
concepts and procedures employed in the associated scientific
activity.

This distribution of tasks between science and proto-science
and also the rank-ordering between the foundational part and the
special science which it makes possible have provoked a comparison with Kant's *transcendental philosophy*. The constructivist
programme might be understood as a modern (meaning one
which accords with present-day science) reformulation of the
kinds of philosophical problems which concern Kant in the *Critique of Pure Reason*: how is mathematics or natural science possible?
Although it is always easy to find supporters for a reading of Kant
from the point of view of theory of science, since it brings
philosophy into a necessary cooperation with the recognized
sciences, it is still worth taking a closer look at it here.

Strictly speaking, *Kant's question* is: how are synthetic judgments a priori possible? It is a matter of the possibility of judgments which originate from reason alone prior to all experience
and are nevertheless informative, that is, not tautological. The
answer to this general question includes the answer to the two
more specific questions mentioned above, about the possibility of

---

[113] The rigid standardization of a pure and all-embracing 'Ortholanguage',
which has created the temptation to establish a whole 'ortholexicon' on
a constructivist foundation, tends towards an autonomy which is in
many ways functionless (Lorenzen and Schwemmer, *Konstruktive
Logik*).

[114] Cf. P. Janich, *Protophysik der Zeit*, Mannheim, 1969; G. Böhme (ed.),
Protophysik, Frankfurt, 1976.

strict sciences.[115] The division of functions is explained by the fact that the sciences are being treated as a paradigm, against which the prospects and limits of a quite different theory can be tested. And this theory is metaphysics as the pure doctrine of reason, which the critical testing is in fact aimed at. In this respect, the *Critique of Pure Reason* yields its much-discussed consequences for theory of science only incidentally. Its true purpose is revealed by the title of the parallel elucidatory work, which Kant called 'prolegomena to any future metaphysics which is to be regarded as a science'. The intention was to raise metaphysical knowledge derived from reason to the already attained level of a science. The epoch-making outcome in a sense ran counter to the intention, since the overthrow of dogmatic metaphysics was confirmed by Kant's influence in the same way as the rational legitimation of scientific knowledge.

As against the perfectly general question of the possibility of synthetic judgments a priori, which concerns reason in general without any limitation to individual sciences, Kant was very well aware of the necessity to offer a suitable foundation for the *special empirical disciplines*. In doing this, the need for substantive specification in regard to the contemporary empirical sciences certainly becomes apparent. Such a specification cannot be required of the general critique of reason. Kant chose a systematically thorough form in order to deal with the problem of an a priori and yet substantively specified *foundation for the individual sciences*. He did at least produce a model in his *Metaphysical Principles of Natural Science*. The introduction of relevant basic concepts such as force, motion etc., which covers the 'proto-scientific' part of contemporary physics, is by no means based on transcendental philosophical considerations of a formal kind. The 'principles of natural science' can rather be derived only from a substantive theory which develops the concepts independently of experience, since these concepts are to guide specialized empirical enquiry. Such a substantive and a priori theory must however again be called 'metaphysical'.

The return to metaphysics in that work of Kant's may be felt to be awkward, since the radical destruction of metaphysics in the *Critique of Pure Reason* precedes it and the declared Kantian aim of

---

[115] Cf. *Critique of Pure Reason*, 2nd edition, Introduction, § VI; *Prolegomena*, §§ 4f.

a 'dogmatics' which was to supplement the 'critique', and which would take the form of that future metaphysics which would satisfy all scientific criteria, has not been realized. Nevertheless, the *Metaphysical Principles of Natural Science* reveals a clear awareness of the methodical and systematic problems of an a priori pure foundation which is yet related to the problems of individual sciences. It is precisely that that the constructivists, comparatively naively, aspire to in fulfilling their programme. The thought may nevertheless strike one that what they call 'proto-physics' Kant still called *metaphysics*.

Practical rhetoric

A final aspect of the constructivist enterprise which deserves some attention transcends the dimension of theory of science in the direction of the *philosophy of practice* and thus belongs, strictly speaking, to our third chapter. Certainly, the adherents of the school consider it to be one of its particular merits that it extends theory of science in this way into practical philosophy. The philosophical object-domains of ethics, technics and the historical cultural sciences, which frequently lack any clear ordering or general view of their relative positions, are to be subjected to the salutary discipline of the methodical principle. How can that happen? The text-book says: 'An ethics which seeks to lay down principles of argumentation for or against particular ends and which does not permit every general proposition to be accepted as an argument, but which is ready to speak of (practical) argumentation only when it serves as a preparation for action, ought to be limited to the task of laying down principles for settling conflicts through discourse.'[116]

Ethics appears to be limited to a logical and methodological aid to *settling conflicts*. Its theme is not how to act, but how to speak if conflicts arise between the parties in the given flow of action. Argument is used where no further action is possible without argument. In this way ethics is limited to the special cases in which a dialogue between subjects helps to prepare for action and it is subordinated to the general logic of argumentation. The

[116] Lorenzen and Schwemmer, *Konstruktive Logik*, p. 109; see also
    P. Kambartel (ed.), *Praktische Philosophie und konstruktive
    Wissenschaftstheorie*, Frankfurt, 1974.

principles of dialogue with practical intention are just as teachable and learnable as in the case of the theory of knowledge and science. The constructivist is committed to the possibility of methodically conducted dialogue about practice.

The restriction of ethics to special cases[117] may be regarded as involving an increase in definitional precision over older ideas, although it seems to me that the only kind of practical philosophy which properly bears that name is one which is ready to speak of practice in the original and unrestricted sense. The most important doubts arise, however, when one recognizes that the commitment to methodically regulated discourse about practice in cases of conflict represents a '*metabasis eis allo genos*'. Ethics is surreptitiously being transformed into *rhetoric*. Rhetoric, that is, has always claimed to know how to teach and to train men to speak correctly when some matter is in dispute and the conflict which arises is to be settled by argument. The ethical problem of correct practice appears as the rhetorical problem of correct speech.

The replacement of the guidance of action by the logic of argumentation also expresses the oldest objection to rhetoric. Since Plato's criticism of the Sophists and Aristotle's consequent separation of practical ethics from logico-rhetorical topics, philosophy has sought, with more or less success, to avoid the *fallacy* that the principles of rhetoric are the rules of action. The methodical ideal of a constructivist elaboration of concepts, which guarantees the teachability of correct speech, unconsciously brings back into play the rhetorical fiction of a competence for practical matters. Thus it is only in form that practice is integrated into a programme which never really gets away from its origins in theory of science and the aims which it derives from those origins.

It is easy to feel the dilemma in the inevitable affirmation that ethics should recognize only those utterances which 'serve as a preparation for action'. The principles of argumentation which govern the structure of discourse may be completely observed, in such a way that the methodical instructions are correctly learned and sucessfully applied in discourse. If the speaker does not also contribute the sincere intention to realize the results of the dia-

---

[117] W. Wieland puts forward cogent criticisms in 'Praktische Philosophie und Wissenschaftstheorie', in M. Riedel (ed.), *Rehabilitierung der praktischen Philosophie*, Freiburg, 1972.

logue in his actions subsequent to the argument, the most correct argumentation remains without effect. That is certainly an adequate description of what really happens. But if the clause which makes this proviso is absorbed into the definition of ethics, one gets the rather uninformative assertion that discourse becomes practically relevant only when it is in fact practically relevant. One of the oldest, and so far never satisfactorily solved, puzzles of ethics consists precisely in guaranteeing the transfer of correct insight into action.

Kant's *Categorical Imperative*, which the constructivists suppose they can rationally reconstruct by their methods,[118] was designed entirely in order to solve this problem. The imperative, that is, is not just a formulation of a 'principle of transsubjectivity', as the methodically established version has it, but also an inseparable combination of the '*principium dijudicationis*' with the '*principium executionis*'. In other words, the rule which says how one ought to act and the unconditional duty to observe it are one and the same. Kant went as far as it is possible to go towards connecting the self-understanding of a rational subject and the unconditional *realization* of those maxims of action which are understood to be rational. The true autonomy of reason is to be found only in reverence for the moral law: anyone who is interested in the former must submit to the latter. However the dispute about the validity of the Categorical Imperative or its adequate reformulation may turn out, it would mean a substantial loss if the built-in function of preparation for action had to be added to the established norm as a rhetorical appeal. An ethics whose assertions were systematically disconnected from practice and which for that reason had to hope for the contingent circumstance that the arguer allowed his action to follow what he said, would in the end be simply preaching to the converted.

---

[118] Lorenzen and Schwemmer, *Konstruktive Logik*, p. 117; see also Schwemmer, *Philosophie der Praxis*, Frankfurt, 1971.

3

Dialectic and philosophy of practice

Dialectic as a method

Everyone knows that dialectic is a thing with many aspects. To some, dialectic appears suspect for that very reason. Others see precisely in the flexibility of its use the theoretical potency, even the proof of the universal validity of dialectic. In view of the familiar controversies it is necessary to remember the origins of dialectic. It arises from the formally regulated discourse of the *Platonic dialogue*, where several partners seek, with regard to a subject of common interest, to advance knowledge through the to and fro of the different arguments. Even in Plato, dialectic appears as a formalized method, intended to establish in the discourse the structural ordering between the *one* theme and the *many* contributions. Hegel, who was the source of all the more recent forms of application of the dialectical method, referred quite explicitly to the Platonic example.[1]

Considered as a method, dialectic determines the relation of the one and the many. Between the two there exists an immanent logic, in so far as the many only appears as the many in relation to the one, and conversely the one first becomes intelligible as what is not the many. This formal structure constantly stands the test in relation to all possible substantial themes, and always in the same way: individual given aspects, which reciprocally balance each other in their relativity, are combined and transcended towards what is common to them, or unity is established in the passage

[1] E.g. in the final chapter of the *Science of Logic* on the method of dialectic (ed. Lasson, Hamburg, 1951, Vol. II, 484ff., 411ff.; translated by A.V. Miller, London, 1969).

through the manifold of the correlated aspects. The schematic text-book version of dialectic as a sequence of thesis, antithesis and synthesis gives only a very pale reflection of this methodical process, even leading to error through its false fixing of three positions. Originally, therefore, dialectic referred to a reproducible path to knowledge and not a separate complex of objects, for instance those of the historical Spirit or of society in contrast to those of nature.

The forcing of dialectic into a special field of objects is rather a *product of decadence*. When the global presentation of all contents of knowledge in an encyclopaedic system of the Hegelian sort ceased to seem convincing, dialectic began to be defined in terms of content. Any field of objects which is either so indeterminate or so mysterious that it cannot be grasped in any better or more solid fashion is abandoned *faute de mieux* to the bewildering play of the dialectic. Where the methods monopolized by the sciences no longer suffice, dialectic begins to lead a marginal existence. Accordingly, to positivism from the nineteenth century right up to our time dialectic is simply suspect on the grounds of irrationality and obscurantism. On the other hand, the dogma of dialectical materialism has become established, above all in the Marxist camp, which is united by an assured political conviction. Not only is it already fundamentally undialectical just on the grounds that it is a dogma, but its massive prior substantive decision in favour of materialism, in the sense of emphasis on the economic motive forces of society, also contradicts the formal principle of knowledge of the dialectic. If one wishes to form an unprejudiced judgment of the philosophical significance of the dialectic, one must be clear that the forms in which it has predominantly appeared for such a long time in themselves represent the loss of original understanding.[2]

Any noteworthy results produced in our century by a philosophy which argues dialectically have always emerged from a

[2] The most recent example of the reduced angle of vision from which the dispute about dialectic between positivists and Marxists is still conducted even now is furnished by the debate which, under the title of the 'positivist dispute in German sociology' (Adorno, Albert, Dahrendorf, Habermas, Pilot, Popper), has passed into the ideological annals of the sixties (Adorno et al., *Der Positivismusstreit in der deutschen Soziologie*, Neuwied, 1969, translated by G. Adey and D. Frisby, *The Positivist Dispute in German Sociology*, London, 1976). On this see above, Ch. 2.

reaction against the decadence of classical dialectic. Against the petrifaction and constriction of dialectical thought the wide validity and vitality of the old universal method of knowledge and art of argumentation was once again to be restored to favour. This has happened essentially in two ways, which here and there intersect and which have grown above all in recent decades into broad highways of philosophical activity. The one way developed out of the neo-Kantian dispute about method, in which the side which proclaimed the distinctiveness of the human or cultural sciences tended more and more towards a revival of Hegelianism. From this there has recently emerged a whole tendency which seeks to present Hegel's philosophy in its systematic range and inner structure, with the intention of correcting the one-sidedness of its early followers. The *reconstruction of Hegel*, to be sure, is carried out, not in the interests of the history of philosophy, but as a paradigm for the tasks and possibilities of a dialectical mode of philosophy in general.

The other tendency, less confined to academic circles and thus with more public influence, includes the Hegelianizing form of neo-Marxism. From Lukács, via the critical theory of Horkheimer and Adorno and the existentialist variants of Sartre and Merleau-Ponty, to the New Left, whose political prophet has come to be Herbert Marcuse and whose point of contact with the theory of science has been Jürgen Habermas, one theme has remained influential throughout. Marxist orthodoxy, which controls the one true doctrine in a manner which is obviously highly unsatisfactory, has been burst open or enriched by elements of Hegel's original dialectic. Marx's theory promised to stand Hegel's Idealism on its feet instead of on its head. Since becoming established as a rigid school and rooted in political organizations, it has time and again been shown not to stand firmly enough on its feet as a theory to be able to do without the assistance of the head. The constant references back to Hegelian categories in fact keep the Marxist doctrine alive. Although the role of dialectical philosophy in the structure of neo-Marxism is altogether wider in its influence than the renewed preoccupation with Hegel himself, I shall begin by describing the latter.

The Hegel renaissance

In the tradition of the historical sciences of man, Hegel was hardly more than a source of important insights into the nature of society and history. For those domains of reality which did not, like external nature, submit without resistance to objectification his philosophy of Spirit as the subjectivity which is actualized in historical structures plainly offered fruitful suggestions. The *Phenomenology of Spirit*, the *Philosophy of Right* and his *Lectures on World History* seem to be the parts of his general *oeuvre* which have something substantial to say even to a time which is sceptical in regard to Idealism. The revolution created by the philosophies of existence since the twenties intensified the urgent search for concrete content behind the web of abstract concepts with which the dialectic, as an encyclopaedic system, had earlier inspired fear.

Hegel's philosophy[3] is, however, in the same position as other great philosophies: it is impossible with impunity to extract parts which seem necessary for certain interests and in so doing to neglect the whole. The dialectical mediation of all parts by each other is precisely what, in the case of the Hegelian system, lends to individual assertions their power of conviction. Croce's famous division of Hegel into the useful and useless has secretly taken its vengeance, since even what seems useful becomes useless without its context. If the total dialectic, with all its methodical sophistication, is not reproduced, isolated theses of Hegel, for instance about world history or the state, are bound to seem extremely rash and dogmatic. The presentation of Hegel's philosophy as a quarry of ideas which may be specially interesting for the problems of social history is thus beginning slowly to yield to the awareness that it is only a representation of the whole which really makes it possible to judge the value or lack of it of the dialectical mode of philosophy.

The guiding thread is to be found in the *systematic reconstruction of the Hegelian philosophy*. The concern with pressing on to the real structural principles of the system does not by any means result only in philological or exegetical corrections to previous pictures of Hegel. The methodological function of the dialectic is more

---

[3] The best and fullest account in English is certainly Charles Taylor, *Hegel*, Cambridge, 1975; see also the collection of essays edited by A. MacIntyre under the title *Hegel*, New York, 1972.

clearly revealed as a kind and manner of comprehensive philosophical reflection in relation to, and involving the overcoming of, the given forms of consciousness, the possibilities of understanding inherent in science and simply the actual spirit of the age. I should like to try to make the significance of this general question plausible and I shall begin from the certainty that it is seldom possible clearly to separate in thought so-called 'historical' problems in philosophy from so-called 'substantive' problems. Just a glance at contemporary discussions makes that plain.

Even those who follow in the footsteps of authors whom we still do not yet feel to belong to the distant past are part of the tradition. The classics of the present day have as their only advantage over the older classics the semblance of proximity, which simply conceals the actual distance which one always feels to exist between oneself and such authorities. Carnap or Wittgenstein and Hegel or Kant are in this respect on the same level. But it never harms philosophy to go and learn from the classics, as long as this is not a matter of satisfying purely antiquarian needs. The wholesale depreciation of past authors, in the name of the scientific progress which culminates in whatever happens to be the present time and of which each new present is readily convinced even with regard to its immediate predecessor, easily takes on the appearance of a kind of intellectual provincialism.

The philosophical task which can be pursued with particular advantage in Hegel is the clarification of the *interactions of thought and history*, with the help of an analysis which makes it possible to see both without favouring one side over the other. The problem finds systematic expression in Hegel in the relationship of the *Phenomenology of Spirit*[4] and the *Science of Logic.*[5] It has long seemed particularly difficult to define this relationship in such a way that its clarification would represent a genuine advance. The leading schools of interpretation up to now have paid insufficient attention to the connexion. They have usually placed the *Phenom-*

[4] *Phenomenology of Spirit* (translated by A.V. Miller), London, 1977; W. Marx offers an introduction to the conception of the *Phenomenology* (*Hegel's Phenomenology of Mind*, New York, 1975). The text of the Preface to the *Phenomenology* is in W. Kaufmann (ed.), *Hegel, Texts and Commentaries*, New York, 1966. On the introduction to the *Phenomenology* cf. M. Heidegger, *Hegel's Concept of Experience* (translated by K. Dove), New York, 1970.

[5] *Hegel's Science of Logic* (translated by A.V. Miller), London 1969.

enology in the foreground on account of its material richness, its closeness to historical life and its vividness. The *Logic* has thereby gained a reputation as an example of speculative madness. Another school has advocated the view that the iron laws of the *Logic* possess an a priori validity, exhibited in the fact that these laws must be remorselessly applied in all possible contexts. It was difficult, however, to make sense of Hegel's genuine concern to relate the *Phenomenology* and the *Logic* to each other in such a way that the relationship between the two remained rationally perspicuous and that history does not triumph over thought nor, equally one-sidedly, does the Idea's conformity to law triumph over all historical reality.

It is notorious that the *Phenomenology of Spirit* does not merely structurally reflect the real course of history. As a 'doctrine of the phenomena' (or appearances) of Spirit it is throughout related to Spirit in its reality beyond the sphere of appearances in such a way that the realm of historical concretion is organized under a guiding perspective. Nevertheless, independently of the phenomenological treatment, there is available no direct insight into the truth of Spirit, or the 'pure ether' of the Absolute, as Hegel puts it. The autonomous truth of Spirit must be arrived at by passing through the historical forms in which it appears. In that consists the primary task required of philosophy. Without any a priori command of absolute principles, but with a view to pure theory and in the interests of the autonomy of thought, there must take place a dialogue with the incomplete forms in which Spirit appears in history.

The importance of the task lies in the fact that the incomplete and dependent mental formations, the world-views and contingently conditioned general interpretations of reality, by no means appear of their own accord as what the *phenomenological* treatment of philosophy recognizes in them. They appear on the contrary with truth-claims which are identical on all levels and thus mutually exclusive. It is precisely the direct pretension to truth which unites the manifold forms and simultaneously relativizes them in relation to what is common to them all. The historical appearance and the deficient consciousness of historicity belong very closely together. Every *individual form of truth* wishes to be the *whole truth*. Without consideration of the competing alternatives, the dogmatic truth-claims in this way always turn into illusion, which covertly takes the place of what it pretends to be.

Consequently, phenomenology has a completely *critical* obligation to analyse the unredeemed and reciprocally competing pretensions. Critical insight does not end, however, in the destruction of the determinate form and in the rejection of its candidacy for truth. Rather they are all, as it were, taken at their word and, after the false total claims have been stripped away, are recognized in their relative rights as forms in which truth appears. The reinterpretation of the forms as appearances is the act of establishing an unrestricted truth as the universal reference-point of all one-sided and dogmatized deputies.

The translation of the given forms of knowledge into mere appearances is carried through in detail again and again in the course of the *Phenomenology*. Taken as a whole, therefore, phenomenology is the critical preparation for that philosophy which does not any longer appear in a limited form and is alone able to compensate for its limitation through false claims. The philosophy for which phenomenology prepares the way proves its superiority by the fact that it recognizes, rather than disavows, its *historically conditioned character*, and works its way through it rather than blindly leaping over it. The task is what is meant by Hegel's famous dictum, 'Philosophy is its own time apprehended in thought', which, as a general obligation of thought faced with its own epoch, met with approval far and wide.[6]

Dialectical logic

In fact the whole sphere of the forms of existing knowledge is revealed to be the field of history. The facticity which is not removed from the knowledge constitutes that contingency which

---

[6] E.g. Karl Marx in his leading article in the *Rheinische Zeitung*, 14 July 1842 (in K. Marx, *Early Texts* (ed. D. McLellan,) Oxford, 1971). One surprising literary response is to be found on the other side of the Channel in J. S. Mill, who in 1831, the year of Hegel's death, published philosophical reflections on his times in a series of journalistic articles under the title 'The Spirit of the Age', at the beginning of which he said, '"The spirit of the age" is in some measure a novel expression. I do not believe that it is to be met with in any work exceeding fifty years in antiquity' (ed. F. von Hayek, Chicago, 1942, p. 1; on the German sources see the Editor's preface, pp. xi, xviii).

adheres to the forms of knowledge as partiality and conditioned character and cannot be controlled by the knowledge itself. Thus it is not the real history which is in question, but the whole series of historical vestiges in thought which must be illuminated. In this regard, thought takes history seriously as the realm of the conditions for the limited and incomplete nature of thought. Thought recognizes itself as historical.

The confrontation with the *historicity* of thought as a problem which centrally concerns philosophy is certainly not a response to any mere interest in history.[7] Historical considerations for their own sake always run the risk of historicism, which is totally concerned with the presentation of change and variety. Philosophy seeks, on the contrary, through reflective confrontation with the influence of history on thought, to make possible a form of activity which is no longer subject to such unnoticed influence. *Logic* is regarded by Hegel as the sphere of pure and autonomous activity of thought which is disclosed at the end of the phenomenological work. But what is the 'science of logic'?

First of all, it is clear that this 'science' is *not* meant to be a *formal* logic as understood in the tradition. Since Aristotle's *Organon*, this has been taken to mean a technique of thinking which is put at the service of something else. It was supposed to give instrumental assistance to cognition and argumentation. The Hegelian 'science of logic' does not serve anything else. Rather, it embodies theory iself which has *become autonomous*. Hegel understood his science of concepts as 'first philosophy', but saw it as making a clean sweep of the dogmatism of the traditional metaphysics. In it is to be found a remarkable sequence of concepts which recall more or less explicitly the fundamental categories of Western philosophy, such as Being, Nothing, Essence, Ground, Actuality, Idea etc. These concepts are not perhaps taken up in the way in which they have been expressed in the history of philosophy. The concepts are rather developed as they naturally emerge from each other, so that, taken together, they form a methodically ordered system.

---

[7] This mistake is made perhaps by Lukács, who in his influential book *Der junge Hegel, über die Beziehung von Dialektik und Ökonomie*, Zurich, 1948 (translated by R. Livingstone, *The Young Hegel*, London, 1975) reduces phenomenology to the expression of a progressive conception of history and of political sympathy with the time, while the systematic significance moves into the background (Ch. IV, 2).

The possibility of such a comprehensive representation in a methodical order constituted a proof for Hegel that everything essential which thought had produced was included here and to that extent a consummation of European philosophy had been achieved. So considered, Hegel's Logic is the final answer of philosophy to the relation of thought to history which has so oppressed it. The concepts of the Logic do not float freely up to a Platonic heaven of Ideas, since their basis is the history of thought. Nevertheless, theory thus become autonomous is liberated from historical limitations, once it has confronted them in the *Phenomenology of Spirit*.

This may be noted first of all as Hegel's declared intention. It cannot be said that the programme is in itself and from the outset unintelligible or meaningless. To make good the intention of a dialectic which has been liberated into a condition of methodical autonomy, however, is a more difficult matter which has time and again challenged the sagacity of interpreters.[8] It is here that the obscurities begin. The determinate sequence of the concepts, the necessary transitions from one to another and the consistent process in which all of them develop from each other are here and there intelligible and then again become enigmatic. At all events, those interpretations must be less promising which suppose in the *Science of Logic* something like a confused system of formal syntax which is in need of being made more precise. Even those attempts at formalization which have occasionally been undertaken[9] do not offer any further help with the problem of understanding the dialectical process. In order to formalize, it is necessary in fact already to have understood.

A better suggestion is a *semantic model*, which aims to analyse the meaning-content of our general concepts. All concepts of the Hegelian Logic are to be interpreted with regard to their meaning and only this interpretation permits the development of all concepts in an entirely determinate sequence. The semantic model would have to explain consistently the plurality of the concepts

---

[8] I refer only to D. Henrich, *Hegel im Kontext*, Frankfurt, 1971; M. Theunissen, *Sein und Schein, die kritische Funktion der hegelschen Logik*, Frankfurt, 1978; also the contributions in R. Horstmann (ed.), *Dialektik in der Philosophie Hegels*, Frankfurt, 1978; H.-G. Gadamer, *Hegel's Dialectic* (translated by C. Smith), New Haven, 1977; R. Bubner, *Zur Sache der Dialektik*, Stuttgart, 1980.

[9] E.g. M. Kosok in the MacIntyre collection *Hegel*.

which arise from each other in such a way that no single concept can be understood without the others and all take their determinate place in the system of the whole.[10] The form of the methodical control of that plurality of concepts is nothing other than the dialectic itself.

The fact that the most general concepts, under which we categorially classify the totality of reality, appear in a plurality must have something to do with the connexion of our thought with language. By having recourse to the ancient concept of *'logos'*[11] Hegel particularly emphasized the role of language.[12] It is not hard for present-day philosophy to accept an autonomous theory on which it is incumbent to give a semantic analysis of all those concepts with which we make reality accessible to ourselves in categorial generality.

Frege had already spoken of an autonomous 'third realm' of thoughts alongside the physical and psychic spheres.[13] Popper followed Frege and directly recalled the Hegelian conception of Mind or Spirit.[14] Popper speaks of 'verisimilitude' as the teleological adjustment of knowledge to the definitively true theory of the whole of reality, in order to designate an inner developmental tendency in the Third World of Mind. Further support for the semantic model in the interpretation of Hegel's Logic can be found in the recent debate about 'meaning variance'. The study of meaning variances is addressed to the purely semantic investigation of the processes in which one concept issues from the 'Gestalt-switch' of another or takes over the function of a predecessor. Obviously, there are similarities with the processes of transition between determinate concepts which Hegel's Logic analyses.

One thing, however, is still not explained in this way and that is the heart of Hegel's *Science of Logic*. This theory is not just a matter of a plurality of concepts which stand in some kind of relation to

---

[10] Some suggestive hints are to be found in F. Fulda's paper, 'Unzulängliche Bemerkungen zur Dialektik', in Horstmann (ed.), *Dialektik*. Nevertheless, there is a whole new field for research here which is still waiting to be opened up in a thoroughgoing way.

[11] The interpretations of Hegel's Logic, equally beloved of both his critics and his followers, in terms of traditional metaphysics or even of theology have no adequate basis in the text.

[12] Preface to the 2nd edition, 1831.

[13] 'Der Gedanke' (1918), (translated in Geach (ed.), *Logical Investigations*, Oxford, 1977).

[14] *Objective Knowledge*, London, 1972.

one another or issue from each other, but of the *dialectical* pattern in the ordering of these relations. In the model of a semantic reconstruction of Hegel which has just been referred to, this essential characteristic of the Hegelian Logic can however be accommodated only with difficulty. Let us see whether we can make at least a little progress along this untrodden path. The debate mentioned above about Kuhn's structural analysis of scientific revolutions will afford some initial assistance.[15]

The dialectical pattern of relations under a plurality of concepts results to the extent that tensions or incompatibilities between the concepts arise. Such tensions arise to the extent that each concept makes a claim to totality for itself and thus makes every other concept which differs in content into a competitor. If the claim to totality is made, concepts become, despite their differences in content, incompatible with each other, since, although they designate something else, they allow no free space alongside themselves for the remaining concepts. In fact there is connected with the concepts of which Hegel's Logic treats a total view or a world-picture which endeavours to bring reality completely under one concept. The science of logic demonstrates the inadequacy of such world-pictures, by showing how one necessarily passes over into another, in such a way that no position is the ultimate and all-embracing one. In this regard the science of logic can be taken as a *critique of traditional metaphysics*. As far as the critical function of logic is concerned, there is an evident similarity to the procedure of the *Phenomenology of Spirit*. In both cases it is a matter of proving the lack of any basis for the claims of one-sided positions to totality. The autonomy of logic had been based on the fact that the dialectic was not subject to any further contingent limitations. How do the two things fit together?

The critique is still *on the way to* autonomy, while autonomous theory ought to mean something different from critique of points of view which do not satisfy the criterion of the autonomous theory. Yet autonomy simply cannot be achieved independently of the critique of one-sidedness and limitation. Autonomy is on the contrary associated with the process of stringently developing the concepts out of each other. Consequently, it is considered to be accepted that our knowledge of reality altogether disintegrates

---

[15] See above Ch. 2.

into a plurality of concepts which cannot be brought artificially or by force into a single ultimate unity. The relation of logic to language prevents the illusion of a transcendent point of view to which the totality would be present without remainder. The fact that our world-pictures are created entirely in language distinguishes them from the pure sublimation of Platonic Ideas. The linguistic character of our world-pictures confers on them a residue of finitude which forms a counterweight to the absolute intelligibility of the rational. There is no such thing as a pure intelligibility free of language. There are only attempts to realize in concepts of a linguistic kind the claim of theories to totality. One may call them 'conceptual frameworks'.

Since that *limitation* of rationality which is given with their linguistic origins is in general a feature of concepts, they all enter into competition with each other. All claim totality in the knowledge of reality, but the fact of their plurality disproves the claim anew in each case. Thus one concept stands to the other in the peculiar relation of denying its claim to totality in order to assert the same claim on its own behalf, while the succeeding concept takes over the same function with regard to the concept in question. Thus one concept drives the next forward, because all concepts intend the same, but none completely fulfils this intention. In view of the connexion with language which is common to all concepts, dialectical logic takes into account the finitude and limitation of our thought. But to the extent that the plurality of those concepts can be ordered in the form of an all-embracing system, it can also be brought back under *methodical* control. Dialectic is a method in so far as it is able to give rules for this highly complex situation of logical competition under one and the same claim to rationality. In this Hegel sees the greatest work of self-clarification of which thought is capable. All concepts with which thought operates gain clarification in the system about the possibilities and limits of their theoretical work. The *Science of Logic* may consequently be called the theory to which there is no further metatheory, because it furnishes its own metatheory.

Nevertheless it cannot be disputed that this is merely the indication of a suggested way in which dialectical logic might be given sense for present-day understanding. The usefulness of these suggestions could only be tested by going into detail and applying them to well-defined problems in logic and the analysis of language. A good deal of further effort would be required for that. We are at the very beginning.

The impact of Lukács

After this excursion into the lofty abstractions of the systematic reconstruction of Hegel, in which the status of dialectical philosophy in general has been discussed, let us forsake the thin air of speculation. At the outset, neo-Marxism was named as the second strand of present-day dialectical philosophy. The Marxists always hoped to replace speculation by the realism of concrete historical analysis. That is what is meant by the so-called 'materialist' approach. In the twentieth century, however, we find ourselves in the strange situation that the forward-pointing contributions of Marxist theory have always come about through going back to Hegel's dialectic! Thus 'Idealism' cannot be entirely out of date.

The first name which must be mentioned in this connexion is that of *Georg Lukács*. The intellectual ripples which spread from the work of his early and middle period can still be felt today. In particular, the ingenious use of Hegel's dialectic for the renewal and actualization of Marxist doctrine in *History and Class-Consciousness* (1923) has proved fruitful. The influence of this book on the wider development of Marxism, above all on so-called critical theory, cannot be overestimated.[16] It is therefore evidence of correct judgment if Party orthodoxy constantly accused Lukács of revisionism, although the incriminated author was not backward, especially during the period of Stalin's rule, in protestations of loyalty, public self-criticism and conformist production of inoffensive works.

In his later years Lukács mainly retreated into aesthetic studies. In any real sense, the only works which remain philosophically significant are those which resulted from his confrontation with Hegel's dialectic.[17] This includes the manuscript of a *Philosophy of*

---

[16] E. Bloch enthusiastically extolled Lukács' book in the expressionist style of the time (the review of 1923 is reprinted in Bloch, *Philosophische Aufsätze*, Frankfurt, 1969).

[17] Cf. the works of I. Meszaros, which are full of information though clearly marked by a pupil's loyalty to his teacher: I. Meszaros, *Lukács' Concept of Dialectic*, London, 1972; Meszaros (ed.), *Aspects of History and Class-Consciousness*, London, 1971 (with Hobsbawm, Bottomore, Milliband, Goldmann, Hauser and others).

Art written during his student years in Heidelberg (1912–17),[18] his study *Theory of the Novel*,[19] published in 1916 and to become famous, and the works produced in the twenties after his conversion to Marxism, of which, besides *History and Class-Consciousness*[20] and *Lenin, A Study of the Connexions of his Ideas* (1924),[21] *Moses Hess und die Probleme der idealistischen Dialektik* (1926) is also worthy of mention. We must content ourselves with a reference to *History and Class-Consciousness*, fascinating though it would also be to present, as a kind of mirror of the times, the spiritual development of the cultivated *haut-bourgeois* György von Lukács, through the revolutionary and the conformist, though occasionally rebellious, intellectual, until he becomes the Marxist classic.

The problem which Lukács seeks to obviate with a revaluation of the *reflection* on consciousness from Hegel's dialectical philosophy, which had been despised as Idealistic, is the solidification of the doctrine of Marx, once the inspirer of revolutionary hopes. The necessary self-dissolution of capitalism and the revolution in society because of the extreme contradictions historically to be found in it had been the practical future perspective which followed directly and of itself from Marx's *Critique of Political Economy*. Historical experience on the other hand had shown that the expected revolution had failed to materialize in the predicted form. That theory should in this way be contradicted by the practice which it had constantly invoked was for Marxists an intolerable thought. Something must have been wrong with the classical view. In general, it was bound to be questionable what 'contradiction' could mean in the complicated relationship of theory and practice. Instead of renouncing the theory, the preferred solution was to regenerate it by means of elements taken ad hoc from a supposedly outmoded tradition.

Lukács consciously commits the sacrilege of coming to the aid of a failed materialism with typically Idealist concepts.[22] He

18 Now available as Vols. 16/17 of the edition of his works published by the Luchterhand-Verlag (Neuwied/Berlin, 1974); see also the related essay, 'Die Subjekt–Objekt–Beziehung in der Ästhetik', *Logos*, 7, 1917.
19 English translation, London, 1971.
20 English translation, London, 1971.
21 English translation, London, 1970.
22 In Lukács' Foreword to the new edition of 1968 (*Werke*, Vol. II, Neuwied) it is even said that 'both the presentation of the contradictions of capitalism and the revolutionization of the proletariat

prudently appeals to the various laudatory mentions of the Hegelian dialectic in the classics[23] in order that he can then go on to give the evasive answer to the provocative question, 'What is orthodox Marxism?', that the correct use of the dialectical method must be the touchstone. Lukács' decisive thesis is that whether history is to take the revolutionary course which is in store for it depends on an act of *developing consciousness* and is not simply among the necessary consequences of material and economic conditions. The formation of the consciousness of the proletariat as the revolutionary class is the step on which everything depends. It is this class, according to Marx, which is the point at which the contradictions of the whole society are concentrated. The social system as such is supported by the labour of the proletariat, while this stratum which supports everything is at the same time forced, as far as its possibilities for subsistence and its human dignity are concerned, to the outermost edge of society. Only when the class recognizes this role which it has, and that means when it becomes conscious of itself, does the ideological camouflage of this state of affairs shatter and reality change at a single stroke. The act of reflective self-knowledge on the part of a class is thus necessary if the whole is to be changed.

> Such a relation of consciousness to reality alone makes a unity of theory and practice possible. Only if the growth of consciousness marks the *decisive step* which must be taken by the historical process towards its inherent goals – goals which are the result of human wills, but do not depend on arbitrary human choice and are not inventions of the human mind; if the historical function of theory consists in making this step practically possible; if a historical situation is given in which the correct knowledge of history becomes for a class a direct condition of its self-assertion in the struggle; if for this

> unintentionally contain overtones of a prevailing subjectivism. This has a constricting and distorting effect even on the concept of practice which is central to this book' (p. 20).

23   The references are as follows: Marx, Preface to the 2nd edition of *Capital* (1873); letters to Engels of 14.1.1858, 11.1.1868 and 7.11.1868, to Kugelmann of 6.3.1868 and 27.6.1870; the corresponding remarks from Lenin's posthumously published works (*Philosophische Hefte*, in *Werke*, Vol. xxxviii, Berlin, 1968, e.g. pp. 170, 315) cannot have been known to Lukács at that time. They were first published in 1929–30.

class its self-knowledge implies at the same time a
correct knowledge of the whole society; if consequently
for such knowledge this class is at once subject and
object of knowledge and in this way has an *immediate and
adequate* grasp of the theory in the revolutionary process
of history – only if all these conditions are fulfilled does
the unity of theory and practice, which is presupposed
by the revolutionary function of theory, become
possible. Such a situation has arisen with the appearance
of the proletariat in history.[24]

The trick which Lukács is using here consists in harnessing
together *conscious reflection* and the structural *totality* of the whole.
In Hegelian terms, there has been a shift from the *Phenomenology
of Spirit* to the *Logic*. The alteration produced by a reflection of
consciousness in reality, because reality is constituted by the
phenomenological consciousness in a way which it cannot understand, appears projected on to the total system of logical relations.
Consciousness, which is not aware of itself in its constitutive role,
automatically alters, if it comes to itself, the relations which it has
itself previously constituted. If one adds the category of totality
from the *Logic*, then every alteration of a part implies the transformation of the whole. After Lukács has, in terms of Hegel's
dialectic and not of Marx's economics, insinuated a whole which
builds itself up to a unity and which maintains itself as a unity
through the reciprocal relativity of the determinate, he manages
to prove that the proletariat's becoming conscious implies 'immediately and adequately' an advance in collective history.

Neo-Marxists

A further influence from the internal Marxist debate of the twenties, which, like that of Lukács, came back into favour in the
neo-Marxism of the sixties, stems from *Karl Korsch*. In his essay
'Marxismus und Philosophie' (1923),[25] Korsch seeks, as he says,
to apply Marxism to itself, in order to explain the degeneration
into 'vulgar Marxism'. The critical approach to ideologies, which

---

[24] *Geschichte und Klassenbewusstsein*, Berlin, 1923, pp. 14f.
[25] Republished, along with other texts, by E. Gerlach (Frankfurt, 1966);
there is also an English translation, by F. Halliday, London, 1970. A
Gesamtausgabe of the works of Korsch is appearing (Frankfurt, 1980–).

relates intellectual phenomena such as theories or political doctrines to a real historical basis, not only can but must in all consistency be applied in relation to the Marxist doctrine itself and its fate in the late nineteenth and early twentieth century. The widespread present-day arguments about the distortion, then just becoming known, of Marxism into a scientific legitimation of totalitarianism could appeal to Korsch among others.

The philosophical *self-criticism* of Marxist ideology must abandon the brazen claim of a materialist science to universal competence and falls back on to the pure dialectical method. In this way Hegel rebels against his alleged supersession by Marx. Of Marx's *Critique of Political Economy* there remains only the critical appeal, while the massive metaphysics of materialism, Engels' dogma of a dialectic of nature and all prophecy based on laws of history modelled on those of the natural sciences[26] are abandoned. Dialectic is useful only for the criticism of what exists, including official Marxism.

In its mission of criticism the brand of Marxist philosophy which reduced materialism to the critique of ideology was in contact with other tendencies, making common cause on the basis of philosophy against the prevailing self-understanding of the times. The early *Herbert Marcuse*, who mainly derived his philosophical education from Heidegger,[27] saw no difficulties at all in combining the anti-technological emotions of the Heideggerian analysis of existence with Lukács' call to form a revolutionary consciousness which can understand the general reification of the life-world.[28] Then, just at the right time, came the publication of the *Paris Manuscripts* of the young Marx which gave expression to a strong interest in philosophical anthropology rather than the economic science of his mature period. The philosophical notebooks of 1844, which were in the sequel to bring about a lasting change in the image of Marx, found in Marcuse one of their first

---

[26] Such as, for example, are emphatically postulated in Marx's preface to *Capital* and equally forcibly rejected by Popper in *The Poverty of Historicism*.

[27] Cf. the interpretation, inspired by *Being and Time*, of Hegel's ontology and the theory of historicity in *Hegels Ontologie und die Theorie der Geschichtlichkeit*, Frankfurt, 1932, Introduction (2nd edition, 1968).

[28] E.g. 'Über konkrete Philosophie' (1929); 'Über die philosophischen Grundlagen des wirtschaftswissenschaftlichen Arbeitsbegriffs' (1933) (now in *Schriften*, Vol. I, Frankfurt, 1978).

interpreters, directing his attention principally to the problem of alienation.[29]

The inner connexion of *labour and domination* or slavery refers directly back to Hegel's *Phenomenology of Spirit*, of which Marx says in his notebooks that it was the 'true birthplace and the secret of the Hegelian philosophy'. Hegel had here overtaken himself, secretly retracting his exaggerated Idealism and already preparing the way for the criticism of philosophical self-certainty in the style of the practical arguments of his successors. Marx writes:

> The *Phenomenology* is concealed criticism, still unclear to itself and mystificatory; but to the extent that it portrays the alienation of humanity – even if the human being appears only in the form of Spirit – there lie concealed in it all the elements of criticism and they are often prepared and elaborated in a manner which far surpasses the Hegelian standpoint.[30]

According to Marx it is thus worth emphasizing the radically *critical* work done by phenomenology, which makes it possible, despite the author's intentions, to escape from the false positivity of the Hegelian system; for here the dialectical thought-process becomes clear without any metaphysical prejudices. This view has been taken to heart by all neo-Marxists up to the present. We shall see what success they have had.

Before we come to this, one further contemporary parallel should be mentioned which continues to have an effect, only half recognized, in current debates. *Karl Mannheim's sociology of knowledge* found a ready reception in the twenties, since it translated the impulse given by Marxism to the critique of ideology, without dogmatic implications, into neutral language. The sociology of knowledge[31] investigates the 'existential determination' of knowledge relative to social formations. Mannheim was able to demonstrate this in a very obvious way using the example of conservatism. But where do the sociologists of knowledge themselves

[29] 'Neue Quellen zur Grundlegung des historischen Materialismus' (1932), *Schriften*, Vol. I.

[30] *Frühe Schriften*, Vol. I (ed. Lieber Furth), 1962, p. 644; see also pp. 640ff.

[31] Reference should also be made to *Max Scheler's* book, much praised at that time, *Die Wissensformen und die Gesellschaft* (1926). Scheler combines the ideas of the philosophy of existence with the American pragmatist tradition (William James).

stand? By which existential situation are they imprisoned when they assert the dependence of all knowledge? With all the sobriety of the sociologist, Mannheim posed this question, which gives rise to great heart-searchings among Marxist critics and ideologists, since they swear by a proletariat from which they have for the most part not come and to which they mostly do not belong. The reply of the sociology of knowledge admittedly has an escapist ring to it: it is a matter of a group of 'unattached intellectuals' with no place in society.[32]

This answer, which recalls ideas about social élites, may not satisfy anyone who had expected from a sociologist a more sociological account. Nevertheless, it is a poor testimonial for the application of Marxist theory to itself, if the critics of ideology were unwilling to recognize themselves in it. The theoreticians of the *Frankfurt School*, Max Horkheimer[33] and Theodor Wiesengrund-Adorno,[34] above all, put up a fierce resistance against the embrace of the sociology of knowledge. To be sure, they in the main came to battle armed with the conviction of their own unassailability, affirming that dialectical thought should not sell itself to sociological empiricism. Some of the polemic can be attributed to jealousy between colleagues: after all, Mannheim taught at the same university, Frankfurt!

Where criticism achieves a monopoly and dialectic affirms its immunity, a rigid position is surreptitiously taken up in the name of a theory which is averse to all kinds of dogmatism. The spectacle of the solidification of living thought is repeated yet again, so that once more dialectical criticism must go to work. The critical theory of neo-Marxism has in its turn become the object of fierce criticism. Here we have alighted right in the middle of the current debate.[35] The fruitful beginnings and open controversies of the neo-Marxism of the inter-war period suffered, because of the unfortunate circumstances of the emigration, an extraordinary interruption to the normal course of their

[32] *Ideologie und Utopie* (1929); translated by L. Wirth and E. Shils, *Ideology and Utopia*, London, 1936.

[33] 'Ein neuer Ideologiebegriff?' in *Grünbergs Archiv*, Vol. xv (1930).

[34] 'Das Bewusstsein der Wissenssoziologie', in *Prismen, Kulturkritik und Gesellschaft* (1955); translated in Arato and Gebhardt (eds.) (see next note).

[35] See the translations of important papers by Horkheimer, Adorno, Benjamin, Marcuse and others in *The Essential Frankfurt School Reader* (ed. Arato and Gebhardt), Oxford, 1979.

development. They were taken up and debated, first in more restricted circles in the fifties and then in the public domain in the sixties.[36]

Critical theory

The concept of *critical theory* was coined by Max Horkheimer. In the concept, the socio-economic theory of Marxism is finally reduced to nothing more than the critique of ideology. At the same time, the aspect of dialectic which is concerned with the philosophical method is rehabilitated in the face of slogans, political doctrines and mass propaganda. Marx's verdict that pure theory is definitively superseded and outmoded in the light of historical progress is expressly recanted.[37] Allowance is made for the existence of an esoteric 'correct consciousness' limited to the few who reflect and know: indeed this is even emphasized in view of the alienation and delusion which has now become total. The fundamental thesis of the critical theory speaks of a 'universal system of illusion' or of an ideology which has become total.

The historical experience of fascism, but no less the deep disillusion which the Stalinist perversion induced in all progressively minded Marxists, and finally the isolated situation of the émigrés brought them to the conviction that the illusion which leads society astray is in complete control, that reification has taken hold of all spheres of life without exception and that the tide of historical disaster is inescapably coming to a head. The Hegelian category of totality, which Lukács had already projected on to society in order to bring its contradictions into conscious illumination in one class and so to bring about revolutionary advance, remains valid. However, the confidence in the proletariat's capacity for reflection has dwindled. 'The situation of the proletariat does not, in this society, provide any guarantee of

---

[36] It is to an American historian that we are indebted for the most detailed and knowledgable account of the Frankfurt School in its external development from its foundation up to the high point of its influence (M. Jay, *The Dialectical Imagination, A History of the Frankfurt School and the Institute of Social Research, 1923–1950*, London, 1974).

[37] Cf. Adorno, 'Wozu noch Philosophie?' (in *Eingriffe*, Frankfurt, 1963, pp. 23f.): 'Anyone who engages in philosophy can do so only if the Marxist thesis that reflection is superseded is denied.'

correct knowledge.'[38] The *revolutionary class* exists no longer and so there is no longer a dialectical lever to move the whole.

What possibilities remain, then, for knowledge? Horkheimer considers it necessary to distinguish two types of theory; as the title of the programmatic essay of 1937 puts it, 'Traditional and critical theory'. Traditional theory presents a logically connected system of assertions, for which at the beginning of the modern era Descartes' *Discours de la Méthode* furnished the model which remained accepted, unchanged in principle, up to the sophisticated positivist theory of science. This must however be replaced by a '*critical attitude*', which is controlled by the 'interest in rational states of affairs' and which comes to expression only in certain subjects. The 'critical and oppositional theory' manifests itself in the activity of permanent and fundamental protest and opposition to the existing conditions of life.

> The disunited character of the social whole in its actual form is developed in the subjects of the critical attitude to the point of conscious contradiction. In recognizing the present economic forms and the total culture based on them as the product of human labour, as the organization which humanity has given itself in this epoch and for which it is suited, they identify themselves with this whole and grasp it as will and reason; it is their own world. At the same time they realize that society may be compared with extra-human natural processes, mere mechanisms, because cultural forms based on struggle and oppression are not evidence of a homogeneous self-conscious will; this world is not theirs, but belongs to capital. History up to now cannot be properly understood; what can be understood in it are only the individuals and particular groups, and even these cannot be understood without remainder, since, in virtue of their inner dependence on an inhuman society, they are still to a large extent, even in their conscious activity, mechanical functions. That identification is thus full of contradiction – a contradiction which characterizes all concepts of the critical mode of thought.[39]

[38] Horkheimer, 'Traditionelle und kritische Theorie' (1937), in *Kritische Theorie*, Frankfurt, 1968, Vol. II, p. 162 (translated as *Critical Theory: Selected Essays*, New York, 1972).   [39] Ibid., pp. 156f.

The contradiction which gives authentic information about the whole of historical society and the reality formed by it manifests itself only to *individuals* who are capable of thinking it through. Theories of the traditional type prove themselves unsuited to grasp the actual structures of the world. That is true above all of Hegel's Idealism, the dialectical method of which, correct in itself, has fallen victim to its author's 'extravagant concept of truth', which fails to recognize its proper role.

> Because Hegel does not recognize and affirm the existing historical tendencies which come to expression in his own work, but believes himself in his philosophical activity to be the Absolute Spirit, the significance of the temporally conditioned interest which is at work in the individual dialectical statements, through the direction which the thought takes, the selection of substantive material and the use of words and names, is concealed from him;

thus attention is diverted from the fact that 'his conscious and unconscious partisanship in regard to the questions of life necessarily has an effect as a constitutive element of his philosophy'.[40]

The illusion of the absolute objectivity and disinterestedness of theory, as well as the ideological function of thought which is based on such a traditional conception, is avoided by the critical attitude of the oppositional subject. Horkheimer creates the impression of a philosophical innovation. It looks as if, for the first time in the history of thought, reason seeks a refuge in critical individuals. In fact, however, this is just a repetition of a pattern which had already characterized the *Young Hegelian* movement. They had already tried to translate an esoteric theory into an open attitude of critical reflection in the face of changing historical circumstances. In this way, they believed, they could give actuality to the Hegelian system which was accepted at that time and make it politically applicable.[41] Feuerbach, Stirner, Bruno Bauer – the 'critical critics', as Marx mockingly called them in the *German Ideology* – regarded 'criticism as Absolute Spirit and

---

[40] 'Zum Problem der Wahrheit' (1935), in *Kritische Theorie*, Vol. I, p. 240 (also translated in Arato and Gebhardt, *Frankfurt School Reader*).

[41] For a useful introduction see D. McLellan, *The Young Hegelians and Karl Marx*, London, 1969; K. Löwith, *From Hegel to Nietzsche*, New York, 1964.

themselves as the embodiment of criticism'.[42] This certainty brought the critics together into a 'Holy Family', with which Marx polemically settled accounts.

The objection about individuals overestimating their own historical role which Horkheimer made to Hegel may obviously be returned. Marx had deeply mistrusted the unassailable exclusivity of those critics who spoke in the name of humanity and of Absolute Spirit. He was able to do so, however, only after he had turned his back on the Young Hegelian criticism with which he had at first been associated, in order to replace critical reflection with a 'traditional theory', as Horkheimer would have to say. The *Critique of Political Economy*, as Marx's programme of work was now described, is not merely a critique of ideology which sees through the objective illusion in classical economics, it is above all a systematic political economy.

This ambivalence between critical questioning and systematic economism has prevented any resolution of the debate about the theoretical status of Marxist doctrine from being achieved even now. The dispute about the methodology of his enterprise, which Marx himself neglected, retains a certain element of scholasticism even in those places in which it productively includes the findings of modern theory of science.[43] Much ingenuity is expended on the defence of fixed positions – that is the essence of all scholasticism. Conversely, the retreat to the inviolable rights of the freely reflecting subject condemns critical theory of the Frankfurt type to silence in the methodological debate. Everything methodical is suspected of belonging to the type of 'traditional theory' which has been in operation right up to modern positivism.[44] Faced with this, the Holy Family prefers to keep itself to itself.

[42] Marx, *The Holy Family* (1845) (German text in *Frühe Schriften*, Vol. I, p. 768).

[43] J. Zeleny, *Die Wissenschaftslogik bei Marx und das 'Kapital'*, Frankfurt, 1968 (translated as *The Logic of Marx*, Oxford, 1979); Lange, Fulda and Diederich, 'Marx' Methodologie', *Neue Hefte für Philosophie*, 13, 1978; L. Althusser, *Lire le Capital*, Paris, 1965 (translated by B. Brewster, London, 1970). A reply to Althusser's subjectless structuralism from the point of view of the Frankfurt School is given by A. Schmidt ('Der strukturalistische Angriff auf die Geschichte', in *Beiträge zur marxistischen Erkenntnistheorie*, Frankfurt, 1969).

[44] Horkheimer devoted his critical attention to the Vienna Circle in a shrewd study called 'Der neueste Angriff auf die Metaphysik' (1937), in *Kritische Theorie*, Vol. II. See also the parallel case in the sixties: Adorno et al., *Positivismusstreit*.

Paradoxes of the critique of ideology

Historical affiliations and cross-connexions are however of re-latively minor importance. The substantive content of the changed understanding of theory requires an unprejudiced inves-tigation. It is clear that Horkheimer wishes to replace the concept of theory as a complex of interconnected general assertions by a particular kind of *subjective reflections*. Of course, these acts of reflection should contain no element of the private and arbitrary. In them, rather, there comes to expression something universal which otherwise would not find expression anywhere, namely, the profoundly contradictory character of the social totality. No theoretical comprehension of this contradictory character seems possible other than that achieved in critical reflection, since every theoretical proposition of neutral universality which transcends the level of individual experience threatens from the outset to become ideological. That means that it would not have the capac-ity to state precisely what has to be stated: the falsehood of the whole.

The paradox lies in the fact that the retreat to the extreme point of subjective reflection in protest against the existing order ac-quires the function of enlightenment with regard to the whole only in a derivative fashion, because the category of totality, which asserts that the systematic illusion is all-embracing and complete, has previously been introduced. This assertion is neither legitimated by, nor achieved in, subjective reflection. It stands out as an unquestioned dogma, which is exalted above all doubt for the very reason that theoretical reasoning for and against the assumption represents a relapse of a suspiciously ideological kind into the traditional forms of theory. The danger of ideology can be avoided only if it is simply accepted and acknowledged every-where. Doubt and questioning increase the danger, only *a priori capitulation* gives immunity.

Looked at more closely, however, the thesis of the impossibil-ity of theory in the traditional sense involves an element of traditional theory of history and society. A suppressed assump-tion of a general nature about the condition of the whole is necessary in order to seek the unique route to knowledge of the truth of the whole by renouncing the universal propositions of traditional theory and having recourse to the ·subjective experience of the critically reflective thinker. If, however, the general assumption were to be articulated, it would refute what it is supposed to justify. Either, then, the very totality of the illusion, despite all appearances, is incomplete at least at one point, in so far as that knowledge lays claim to untarnished truth, or the illusion is indeed impenetrable, in which case even that proposition is untenable.

Thus, reflection vacillates to and fro between hope and despair. The totality of which it knows is the domination of the false. The doors to the open air are barred, but in this knowledge consists the most complete emancipation. *Walter Benjamin* perceived in this dilemma a kind of inverted eschatology and reformulated it above all in aesthetic terms.[45] Adorno was provoked by it to verify the diagnosis of the age primarily in products of *modern art* such as the works of Kafka or Beckett, where the insight into the absence of all possibility of escape from the situation appears to be the last remaining element of free humanity.

Adorno's mainly *sociological investigations* are combined with a note of complaint about the absence of the 'good life', which seems to be something in between the ancient concept of *eudaimonia* and a utopia of happiness in the future. Hopeless as the situation appears, the only hope lies still in unrelenting efforts to critically call by their proper names, case by case and in the concrete detail of the present and of everyday life, the expressions of the imperceptible dominance of fetishized illusion.[46] The superficiality of civilized progress, the pseudo-objectivity of sciences elevated into idols, the seemingly democratic diffusion of a 'culture-industry', the sophistication of advertising and not least the rhetorical defence of the freedom of the individual – all these are forms of alienation and heteronomy, which are not easy to diagnose because they proceed in such a different way from the classical forms to which the socio-economic analysis of the nineteenth century applies.

A brilliant attempt to achieve a unified conception of the theoretical dilemma along with the material critique of ideology

[45] *Illuminations* (introduction by H. Arendt), New York, 1970; see also *Aesthetics and Politics* (Essays by Benjamin, Bloch, Brecht, Adorno and others), London, 1979.
[46] A useful introduction is G. Rose, *The Melancholy Science, An Introduction to the Thought of T. W. Adorno*, London, 1978.

and the interpretation of aesthetic analogies was undertaken by Horkheimer and Adorno in their studies on the 'Dialectic of Enlightenment'.[47] The dialectic in question refers to a fate which overtakes rationalism from behind. Unlike Marx's usage, dialectical movement and progressive intention no longer necessarily refer to the same thing. The dialectic of Enlightenment is the self-destruction of Enlightenment, the withdrawal of the intended emancipation. 'Enlightenment is as totalitarian as any system. Its untruth is not what its romantic enemies have from the beginning cast in its teeth: analytical methods, reduction to elements, disintegration through reflection; but that for it the process is decided from the outset.'[48]

Without noticing or admitting it, the authors take up a theme from the young Hegel, who already in his early theological and political phase recognized the naked Enlightenment of the understanding as an element of fixation and division, which was to be overcome and abolished by the dialectical procedure of Reason. The Hegelian dialectic of Enlightenment also maintains a critical attitude towards the dangerous totalitarianism of the rational, in order to correct its lifeless one-sidedness, in which no alternatives exist, by means of the rational synthesis of the dialectical mediation. The radical critiques of Horkheimer and Adorno shrink from this consequence, however, for the Hegelian system of absolute mediation too seems to them to involve a forced reconciliation. From this follows the problem of stating on what grounds the dialectic of Enlightenment is denounced or else what standards are available for a radical critique of the domination of abstract understanding. The attempt to conjure up a comprehensive concept of Reason remains in a strange state of suspense between affirmation and denunciation.[49]

Adorno's shift to aesthetics

The question naturally remains unanswered, since Hegel is cited only as a critic and as a systematic thinker is regarded with

---

[47] Written in America in 1944, published in Holland in 1947, first republished in 1969 in the aftermath of the student rebellion (translated by John Cumming, London, 1973).

[48] Dialektik der Aufklärung, Amsterdam, 1947, p. 37.

[49] Cf. Horkheimer's The Eclipse of Reason, Oxford, 1947.

abhorrence. This remarkable process of decapitating Hegel is to be seen with particular clarity in one of Adorno's last works, which, despite all its horror of systems, is meant as the summation of a line of thought. His *Negative Dialectics*,[50] even in its title, takes the protest to the door of Hegel, who has robbed the dialectic of its critical salt by misusing it to give a positive legitimacy to an evil reality.

The enterprise of a strictly *negative dialectic* seems to me fundamentally a failure, not just because the enlightened essayist Adorno[51] uses his talents on almost the whole catalogue of the venerable themes of metaphysics. The sharp pen of the literary man is visibly blunted in the process. The attempt to apply dialectical methods and then to suspend them at one point, or to bring into play a logical process of reflection and then to call a sudden halt in a decisionistic fashion, falls short of being philosophically persuasive, however emphatic the protestations that may be made that precisely in this lies the higher wisdom. Philosophical thought must be such that it can be completely reconstructed, even when, as in the case of dialectic, the path of reflection methodically runs counter to the expectations of common sense. Precisely in the name of dialectic, it cannot be permitted to break off at one place, which is characterized only by private opinions and convictions which allow of no justification. The point at which, as it were, the tablets of the Law announce 'Thus far and no further' is not, as Adorno suggests, where dialectic begins but where it abruptly comes to an end.

A comparison with Hegel's argument of the *dialectic of the limit* may be helpful in elucidating this point.[52] Hegel cogently disproved Kant's thesis of the thing-in-itself in so far as he was able to show that to erect a formal limit already implies that one can stand on the other side of it. Limits which divide two domains can not be unilaterally established. The prohibition of knowledge of a thing-in-itself is *ipso facto* its conscious positing and thus already

---

[50] *Negative Dialektik*, Frankfurt, 1966 (English translation, New York, 1973).

[51] The programmatic acknowledgment of the essay as the only form of philosophy which is legitimate today can already be found in Adorno's academic Inaugural Lecture of 1931, 'The Actuality of Philosophy', in *Gesammelte Schriften*, Vol. I, Frankfurt, 1973, pp. 343f.; also in 'Der Essay als Form', in *Noten zur Literatur*, Vol. I, Frankfurt, 1958, pp. 21f.

[52] Cf. *Negative Dialectics* (German edition, pp. 396ff. and passim).

implies transgression of the limit which was supposed to be marked by the transcendence of that Something. Hegel inferred from his argument that the given limit of knowledge can ultimately be recognized by knowledge and thus relativized, or vice versa that nothing can limit knowledge as knowledge. It is precisely the recognition of the problem of the limit, instead of its denial, which constitutes the strength of dialectical thought. It is on this methodical foundation that Hegel's philosophy is constructed and not on the arbitrary absolutization of the Idea or the illusion of identity, as the objection which has been constantly repeated from the Young Hegelians up to contemporary critics would have it.

Kant's *thing-in-itself* is resurrected in Adorno in the form of the 'totally Other', the 'non-identical', which shuns conceptual identification in the clutches of the understanding and through such refusal affirms its rights. Plainly, the idea is based on the dialectic of the limit, which however is not carried through straightforwardly owing to a stubborn refusal. The Other, on the original autonomy of which the subject's drive to dominate theoretically runs aground, is in its limiting reality present in no other way than in the mode of negating identifying thought. The non-identical is by no means determined in and for itself; even its very name shows that it comes to determination exclusively by recourse to that form of thought which it opposes. Precisely this, at bottom dialectical, state of affairs, in which one aspect is dependent on the other which it uses in order to be able on the other hand to realize its own autonomy, is taken by Adorno as proof that the dialectic remains negative and does not admit of the continuation of reflection on the constitutive situation as a whole. That no further grounds can be adduced for this is for this philosophy grounds enough.

Nevertheless, Adorno's philosophy does not finally give up the struggle at a contingent point. The restriction imposed by theory on itself, which under the name of a negative dialectic contests the guilt in this act, puts reflection out of play merely in order to make the transition to *aesthetics*. Where theory ends, there art begins. The *Dialectic of Enlightenment* had already, with an apt appeal to Schelling,[53] conjured up the work of art in order to help out

---

[53] *System des transzendentalen Idealismus* (1800); *Philosophie der Kunst* (1802/4).

theory in its incapacity, since it could not break the ideological spell with its categories. The aesthetic illusion is the only illusion which does not lie, since from the outset it does not pretend to be anything else. In the world of the beautiful illusion, Adorno thus believes, is ultimately preserved the hope for infallible truth, in the face of which philosophy must resign. An ideology-free truth remains a utopia which appears in the meantime to be anticipated only by art. 'In illusion there is a promise of freedom from illusion.'[54]

Adorno's great posthumous work, his *Ästhetische Theorie*, first published in German in 1970, derived from this position of extreme retreat from theory brilliant insights into specifically aesthetic problems. *Ästhetische Theorie* is not, like many traditional works of aesthetics, the application of a systematic position already established to problems of art and of the aesthetic judgment. Adorno by no means wishes simply to extend to art a philosophy which is fundamentally certain of what it is about. He seeks rather to rediscover in art the totally uncertain subject-matter of philosophy. The fluctuating definition of the task of philosophy, which moves to and fro indecisively between the criticism of ideological illusion and the autonomy of theory, is surprisingly reflected in the phenomena of art, which also do not allow themselves to be tied down. They give the impression of autonomy and yet they are merely illusion. They wish to say something to us which is worth understanding and yet they do not stand up to any theoretical analysis. In sounding out these effects Adorno the connoisseur displays all the mastery of sensitive reflection of which he was capable. I believe that in *Ästhetische Theorie*, which frequently crosses the boundaries between literary criticism, musicology and history of art, his true legacy is to be found.

Habermas' conception

The most promising development of the idea of a critical theory can be traced back to *Jürgen Habermas*.[55] In a rapid series of

---

[54] *Negative Dialectics* (German edition, p. 397).

[55] A sketch of his main ideas and their development has been given by Thomas McCarthy in his *The Critical Theory of Jürgen Habermas*, London, 1978; see also the collection of essays edited by D. Held and J. B. Thompson, *Habermas: Critical Debates*, London, forthcoming.

writings, he has, following chiefly in the footsteps of his predecessors Adorno and Horkheimer (and unmistakably also those of Marcuse), carried on the critique of ideology in the present day with extremely subtle means. Unlike a loyal pupil, however, he has burst out of the pre-established framework and taken note of the alterations in the debate in philosophy, sociology and political science in order to react to them for the benefit of the further development of critical theory. In a masterly fashion he has seen how to integrate general theory of science, hermeneutics and contemporary philosophy of language. Thus he has more than a merely critical and defensive attitude towards all that was distrusted in the esoteric canon of the Frankfurt School as 'traditional theory'.

He even tends increasingly towards a rehabilitation of a type of *systematic philosophy*, which is capable of achieving a genuine reconciliation once more in the current state of knowledge between the sophistication of science and the practical questions of social life. The basic lines of such an integration, which bears the provisional label of a 'universal pragmatics', are clearly to be recognized, although Habermas intentionally chooses the literary form of 'prolegomena' and the outline sketch of ideas. The necessarily deliberate disavowal of traditional Marxism[56] and even of the 'Holy Family' of pure criticism has provoked all kinds of public polemics, but does credit to the philosophical independence of Habermas as a thinker. Future doctoral theses will find ample material in the detailed consideration of these controversies and in classifying the phases in their development.

It would be best to begin with the concentrated theses of the Inaugural Lecture at Frankfurt, 'Erkenntnis und Interesse'[57] (1965). At the outset, Habermas there appeals to Horkheimer's distinction between 'traditional and critical theory', and also to Husserl's discovery of the life-world as the foundation of the sciences, in order to pose afresh the question of the suppressed connexion between knowledge and interest. All cognitive processes are based on guiding interests which normally remain

---

[56] Cf. the earlier presentation 'Zur philosophischen Diskussion um Marx und Marxismus', *Philosophische Rundschau*, 5, 1957; also more recently *Zur Rekonstruktion des historischen Materialismus*, Frankfurt, 1976.

[57] English translation in the Appendix to *Knowledge and Human Interests*, 2nd edition, London, 1978.

unrecognized. The empirical-analytical sciences follow a technical cognitive interest which, on the basis of knowledge of laws, permits predictions to be made which assist in the control of the causal processes of nature. The historical-hermeneutic sciences on the other hand follow a practical cognitive interest, in so far as the understanding of the meaning of tradition and socially organized intersubjectivity serves to transform what is strange and thereby to assist a practical orientation in life. In this distinction the old dualism of natural and human sciences reappears, though it is no longer defined, in the way customary since the neo-Kantians, in terms of the difference of object-domains or methods. Rather, attention is focussed on a specific interest which guides the respective kinds of knowledge but remains unnoticed in the interests of the aspiration to scientific objectivity.

There is in addition a third form of knowledge, which is marked, in comparison with the two preceding, by conscious reflection on the interest which guides it. The critical sciences obey an emancipatory cognitive interest which insists on self-reflection and in so doing seeks liberation from the constraints of ignorance. This *ideal of enlightenment* is a properly philosophical one, since the interest here directly coincides with knowledge and no longer functions unrecognized in the background of knowledge. Cognition is not for the sake of something else – knowledge operates for its own sake. Although Habermas underlines how near this is to philosophy, he yet adheres to a threefold schema in the theory of science. He must consequently associate with self-reflection the 'sciences' of the critique of ideology and psychoanalysis. Habermas' successful book with the same title, *Erkenntnis und Interesse*[58] substantiates the triadic schema just outlined with sometimes brilliant analyses of Hegel and Marx, Peirce, Dilthey and Freud.

Of course, doubts are bound to be felt about whether the critique of ideology, if it is to be anything more than the 'critical attitude' of the Frankfurt School, should not always be thought of as a meta-institution in relation to science or world-view. Above all, however, there is dispute about the scientific status of *psychoanalysis*, which nevertheless was regarded as one of the

---

[58] Frankfurt, 1968; 2nd edition with Appendix, 1973 (translated as *Knowledge and Human Interests*, Boston/London, 1972, 2nd edition with Appendix, London, 1978).

standard courts of appeal of critical theory.[59] The psychoanalytic process of liberating the subject to assume his own identity by making him conscious of repressions can certainly not be interpreted without taking account of contextual conditions which define what is meant by 'healthy' and 'ill', or who is doctor and who is patient. Psychoanalysis represents a special case in science which can only be generalized on pain of being systematically misleading. If one sets aside the conditions of the social context and applies the psychoanalytic model to the whole of society, it instantly loses its meaning. It then becomes unclear who is healing whom, what the illness consists in and what condition is to be aspired to as constituting a cure. Account then has to be taken once again of the total delusion in which 'illness' means 'normality' and emancipation retreats into a utopian Beyond. In this way the old paradoxes of critical theory reappear.

Habermas naturally sees the difficulties and takes flight before them by appealing to contemporary philosophy of language.

> It is no accident that the criteria of self-reflection are removed from that peculiar suspension in which the standards of all other cognitive processes need critical examination. They are theoretically certain. The interest in emancipation is not merely before the mind, it can be understood a priori. What elevates us out of nature, that is to say, is the one fact that we can be acquainted with in its nature: language. With its structure emancipation is posited for us. With the first sentence, the intention of a universal and unconstrained consensus is unambiguously articulated. Emancipation is the one idea of which we are master in the sense of the philosophical tradition. Perhaps for that reason, the usage of German Idealism, according to which 'Reason' contains both moments – will and consciousness – is still not entirely obsolete.[60]

Language is a priori aimed at communication, but communication presupposes equal partners and freedom from external factors such as domination, scarcity, passion etc. As speakers we are always already participants in that Idea of a rational intersubjec-

[59] Cf. Herbert Marcuse's interesting book, *Eros and Civilization*, Boston, 1955.
[60] 'Erkenntnis und Interesse' (1965).

tivity which combines theory and practice, knowledge and interest. Habermas is quick to add that the *ideal dialogue* would of course take place only in a genuinely emancipated society, while under existing historical conditions it represents a counterfactual hypothesis.

> To be sure, it would only be in an emancipated society which had realized the liberation of its citizens that communication would develop to the stage of domination-free dialogue of all with all . . . The ontological illusion of pure theory, behind which the interests which guide knowledge disappear, confirms the fiction according to which the Socratic dialogue is universally and at all times possible. Philosophy has from its origins insinuated that the emancipation which is posited with the structure of language is not merely anticipated, but actual . . . Only when philosophy discloses in the dialectical course of history the traces of the force which has distorted the constantly renewed efforts at dialogue and has time and again driven them out of the paths of unconstrained communication does it advance the process whose retardation it otherwise legitimates: the progress of the human species towards emancipation.[61]

Objections

There is something crucial which does not fit in with these arguments.[62] Let us calmly disregard the fact that the historical reference fails, because the Socratic dialogue, as we know of it from Plato, is *not* in fact an *ideal situation* of pure reason, but is in its whole literary form realistically burdened with the unclarities and diversionary manoeuvres, the intersubjective asymmetry and material perplexities of all the dialogues which we conduct every day. The Socratic dialogue is no crystal-clear conversation of pure intellects, because it is meant to be a model for the cognitive path which

---

[61] Ibid., p. 164.

[62] See also the collection of papers on the theme of 'Hermeneutics and critique of ideology' (*Hermeneutik und Ideologiekritik*), with contributions by Apel, von Bormann, Bubner, Gadamer, Giegel and Habermas (Frankfurt, 1971).

leads out of ignorance and sophistry. What is false in Habermas' account is rather the systematic separation of ideal and actuality, which is then supposed nevertheless to bring about the mediation.

Habermas makes the dialogue into a fictitious situation, whereas he has to understand it as the guide of progress. The ideal dialogue becomes attached to an ideal world of the 'good life' in a genuinely liberated society. As long as that does not exist, it is merely the reflection of an antithesis to the status quo. Since, however, the ideal condition of society, like the Kantian 'Kingdom of Ends', is not of this world, indeed, since it is defined through negation of reality in general, even the dialogue as a model of social communication under conditions of pure reason remains a *utopian* postulate, which continues in permanent opposition to the actual forms in which human beings deal with each other.

If that is so, however, the model is of no value for the purpose for which it was introduced, namely, for the historical reconstruction of past societies on the basis of the degree of rationality realized in them or for the practical guidance of present-day society. In both regards, only the one identical answer is possible: that the ideal dialogue *did not* and *does not* exist. Since the dialogue was defined from the outset as being counterfactual, it was possible to know the outcome already, prior to entering into concrete investigation; and hence the dialogue model is devoid of any historically and socially informative content. All appearances of greater concreteness to the contrary, what is noticeable here is the Young Hegelian heritage in the criticism of the Frankfurt School, the abstractness of which had already been pertinently criticized by Marx.

Habermas sees quite correctly that the concept of critical reflection requires interpretation, and believes that he can depend for it on post-Wittgensteinian philosophy of language. It is certainly one of the genuine advances made by recent philosophy of language to have replaced the basically nominalist idea of symbols found in positivism by the pragmatics of the communicative function in language in the context of interaction. To that extent, Habermas can easily make connexions with certain linguistic theories of communication such as Searle's.[63] He has also sought support in

[63] 'Was heisst Universalpragmatik?', in Apel (ed.), *Sprachpragmatik und Philosophie*, Frankfurt, 1976; translated in Habermas, *Communication and the Evolution of Society*, London, 1979, ch. 1.

Chomsky's theory of linguistic competence,[64] in which an element of Idealist philosophy of language in the manner of W. von Humboldt[65] seems to reappear. Nevertheless, I consider it rash to project a *concept of reason* professedly borrowed from Idealism, with a few appropriate modifications, directly on to *language*.

Two reasons in particular speak against this. First, successful communication, which is to be conceived, in Wittgenstein's words, as 'part of a form of life',[66] affirms nothing about *reciprocal recognition* of the partners as equal subjects. If the process of coming to an understanding through discourse does not come to a standstill or generate misunderstandings, this indicates merely that all participants are correctly following rules in their use of language, whatever the practical situation may be – dialogue, command, lecture, game and many others. The presupposition of unrestricted rationality, which is supposed to be posited with the ideal dialogue, cannot be obtained from successful communication as such. For the abundant variety of established practical situations and social roles which are acknowledged, but not explicitly treated, as forms of life by the philosophers of language never contracts into a *single* principle of intercourse between free subjects under the direction of reason. Dialogue does not cover the entire range of practice. A theory of action would thus have to be set alongside the theory of communication.[67] Habermas, who initially wanted to combine the two things, has bowed to necessity and has since taken steps towards an analysis of *action* which is based on the philosophy of language but is independent of it. He thereby gets rid of exaggerated transcendental claims as well. We

---

[64] 'Vorbereitende Bemerkungen zu einer Theorie kommunikativer Kompetenz', in Habermas and Luhmann, *Theorie der Gesellschaft oder Sozialtechnologie, was leistet die Systemforschung?* Frankfurt, 1971 (translated in H. P. Dreitzel (ed.), *Recent Sociology 2*, London, 1970).

[65] *Über die Verschiedenheit des menschlichen Sprachbaus* (1827) (translated by Buck and Raven, *Linguistic Variability and Intellectual Development*, Philadelphia, 1972).

[66] *Philosophical Investigations* (translated by G. E. M. Anscombe) Oxford, 1953, section 23.

[67] To that extent, Searle's statement, 'a theory of language is part of a theory of action' (*Speech Acts*, Cambridge, 1970, p. 17) must be regarded, now as much as ever, as referring to a *desideratum*, which has not been adequately realized either among analytical speech-act theorists or among hermeneutic theorists of communication (cf. my book, *Handlung, Sprache und Vernunft, Grundbegriffe praktischer Philosophie*, Frankfurt, 1976).

saw earlier[68] that Apel argues along similar lines, making ideal conditions of rationality into indispensable presuppositions of any linguistic dealings between subjects – a claim that seems scarcely feasible.

The other objection which is to be raised against the original doctrine of the ideal dialogue concerns the *equation of language and reason*. The stumbling-block here is not the premise of freely interacting subjects: it is the thesis of an 'a priori intelligibility' of the emancipatory interest in the medium of language which gives rise to doubt. It is pertinent once again to recall the example of Platonism, which makes an essential contribution to clarifying the intricate relation between reason and language. Language is for the Platonic dialogues the indispensable *medium* of reason, which as a medium at the same time implies the possibility of opacity. The medium may bring together various points of view by concentrating them on the common theme, but it may equally distract from the common theme by the prominence which it gives itself. Here lies the clarifying task of reason, in differentiating between the medium and the understanding. In other words, *logos*, if rationally used, brings about true understanding among human beings who are subject to opinion. The medium may not, however, be confused with the truth itself, nor the *logos* with reason.[69] This confusion represents the essential problem of sophistry with which philosophy must be ready to deal, constituting as it does the menace of perversion which follows philosophy like its own shadow.

The *problem of sophistry* is an important and long-standing crux for the critique of ideology. Sophistry is not the 'false consciousness' of a separation of knowledge and interest which the critique of ideology seeks to investigate. It is precisely the appearance of 'correct consciousness', for in it all the external conditions of rationality are fulfilled and yet it is permeated by an unrecognized deception. The deception rests on the belief that, with the perfection of rational methods, with enlightened discourse regulated by mutual consent, one has possession of the rationality of the matter in question. Everyone is familiar, not only from political discussions, but even, and precisely, from academic debates, with the disturbing sense that, under the smooth surface of rationality,

---

[68] See above, Ch. 2.
[69] E.g. Plato, *Phaedrus, Seventh Letter* and passim.

extremely irrational processes are at work. The adherence to rational principles which everyone acclaims and self-consciously displays often contains an element of hypocrisy and from the outset wards off all the demands of criticism. Horkheimer's and Adorno's *Dialectic of Enlightenment* gave evidence of their perfectly proper misgivings about this problem of sophistry in the postulate of rationality.

The helplessness of the doctrine of the ideal dialogue in the face of the problem of sophistry shows how unsuited it is to be an instrument of criticism. The counterfactual postulate of ideal conditions is nothing more than an abstract antithesis to the actual situation. Because of its abstractness, it lacks precisely those substantive criteria on which a critique would have to be based. We want not merely to be made aware that everything about the way things are is false, or that what ought to be is simply the opposite of what is. We want, just in the interests of the critique, to be made aware of where and how improvements are to be instituted, in what direction and to what extent corrections are possible which would advance rationality.

The abstractness of the dialogue model can be seen also in another way. The ideal form of the dialogue turns out in reality to be *playful*. Under ideal conditions there emerge absolutely no questions which demand serious intersubjective treatment. The ideal dialogue turns out to be superfluous. If we nevertheless speak to each other in that anticipated society which would be different in all respects from the present, it will not be out of necessity but for pleasure.[70] Usually and originally, dialogues come about as a strategy for overcoming problems under the pressure of difficulties which are explained by the absence of ideal conditions in the social interaction. The topic of discourse results from the circumstances of theoretical unclarity and practical discord. If these circumstances, which are precisely what go to constitute the dialogue, are bracketed and the conditions for entering into dialogue are already defined in terms of its goal, namely, perfect rationality and achieved consensus, then the dialogical process loses its function.

---

[70] Incidentally, Marcuse clearly saw the playful and aesthetic character of the liberated society and depicted it with the aid of hints from Schiller (*Briefe über die ästhetishe Erziehung des Menschen* (1795); translated by R. Snell, London, 1965), see *Eros and Civilization*, esp. ch. 9.

Theory and practice

Habermas however believed that the long-hoped-for reconciliation of *theory and practice* could be achieved by the ideal dialogue, which later reappears under a somewhat more neutral name and linguistically modified as 'universal pragmatics'.[71] Let us once again get clear about the initial position. The critical theory of the Frankfurt School had elevated it into an intellectual duty to assist pure Reason to find expression in the face of the omnipresence of ideology and the dominance of Unreason; critique was conceived of, so to speak, as a Categorical Imperative. The restriction of effective reflection to a few subjects and the rather literary incantations on the fortunes of humanity no longer satisfied the demands of systematic philosophy. What was needed was a fundamental conceptual framework on which the role of critical reflection could be based. The conception of a communicative interaction which achieves its consummation in the ideal of dialogue makes actual that Reason which for mere critique is a vague and unlocated idea or a utopian anticipation in philosophical terms which admit of a sociological and linguistic interpretation. It is here that is to be found the potential of Habermas' project, which has led to the extension of its influence right across the disciplines.

If we are not to relapse into the old abstractions of the radical critics, however, it must also be explained how that reification which critique first challenges comes about in socio-historical reality. Moralistic condemnations or critical visions of cultural decadence are insufficient for this purpose. Habermas seizes on the concept of *labour* as the self-reproduction of humanity over against objective nature, developed by the early Hegel and reinterpreted by Marx in his *Economic and Philosophical Manuscripts*, and contaminates it with Weber's theory of purposive rational action. Labour, as a fundamental category of social anthropology, is thus contrasted with the communicative *interaction* which is portrayed in the dialogue model. The contrast of labour and interaction recalls the Aristotelian distinction[72] of *poiēsis* and *praxis*, made against the background of the ancient conception of the *polis* in the sense of that 'good life' (*eudaimonia*) so often invoked in

---

[71] 'Was heisst Universalpragmatik?', in K.-O. Apel (ed.), *Sprachpragmatik*
[72] *Nicomachean Ethics*, I, 1, VI, 4f.

Habermas. By distinguishing between labour, which is bound up with objects, and interaction between subjects, Habermas acquires a standard by which he can judge the misunderstandings of Hegel,[73] Marx,[74] and the more recent social sciences.[75] To confuse these two essentially separate domains, or to reduce the one to the other, turns out to be the root of all ideological evil.

Plausible though the distinction may be between labour, as instrumental, object-directed activity, on the one hand, and practice in the genuinely social sense on the other, the attempt to give this dualism a systematic grounding reveals several traditional weaknesses. Labour and interaction do not in the end define the specific cognitive interests of the empirical and hermeneutic sciences, which, as already shown, correspond to the old dichotomy of natural and human sciences. Strictly speaking, labour and interaction represent the anthropological fixations of a contrast in *theory of science*. Hence the real contents of labour and interaction occur in a peculiarly ethereal and diluted form. Labour shrinks to a deficient mode of communication and becomes something very like 'monological strategies',[76] while practice is to be thought of entirely as dialogical communication and thus comes to nothing more than talking to each other. It is easy to see that the structure of labour and interaction is replaced by the cognitively relevant features of a corresponding type of rationality. That may be a belated consequence of Weber's methodology of ideal types. In reality, of course, labour is something more than and different from a strategy and practice is something more than and different from a conversation. How are the essentially Idealist abbreviations of the forms of activity arrived at?

It is tempting to suspect that the Hegelian in Habermas has triumphed over the Marxist. Plainly, Habermas wants to rewrite the famous chapter on Master and Slave from Hegel's *Phenomenology*. A long succession of left-wing interpretations of

---

[73] 'Arbeit und Interaktion', in *Technik und Wissenschaft als 'Ideologie'*, Frankfurt, 1968 (translated in *Theory and Practice*, London, 1974, ch. 4).
[74] *Erkenntnis und Interesse*, ch. 1, §§ 2, 3.
[75] E.g. the controversy with Luhmann (*Theorie der Gesellschaft oder Sozialtechnologie*, Frankfurt, 1971); *Legitimationsprobleme im Spätkapitalismus*, Frankfurt, 1973, esp. Pt III (translated as *Legitimation Crisis*, Boston, 1975).
[76] E.g. Habermas and Luhmann, 'Vorbereitende Bemerkungen', pp. 251f., 277ff. and elsewhere.

Hegel[77] had sought to discover the secret of the dialectic in social philosophy, in the elucidation of domination and labour, which in Hegel was distorted by the Idealistic transfiguration into something spiritual. A rightly understood 'materialist' correction – one which did not lapse into a fresh heresy by substituting matter for Spirit, would have to consist in retaining the contingent and so not fully perspicuous moments of that dialectic which runs its historical course in the field of domination and labour; for it is here, in the dealings of humanity with nature and with each other, that we decide on the manner in which the social mode of life is organized. In one of his earliest works Habermas took up this theme and characterized as the real problem for modern Marxism the 'empirically testable philosophy of history'.[78] He has come back to that idea time and again. Let us see what it is all about.

Hegel's phenomenological analysis[79] has as its theme the contingent origin of regulated intersubjectivity without the premise of actualized Reason. Two self-consciousnesses which are in contention for the status of autonomous self-consciousness come to terms in that the one subjects himself to the other. The relation of Master and Slave manifests an accepted division of roles. The superior subject holds off from the pressing objectivity of the real world by interposing the inferior subject as a means. The Slave is compelled to labour, in which his subjectivity is bound to the world of things, in order to procure freedom for the subjectivity of the Master. The sovereignty of the Master, thus maintained by the intervention of the Slave, is however his weakness, since the Master is also dependent on the Slave. Herein lie the seeds of change.

As soon as the Slave becomes aware through labour, as the spontaneous transformation of the given reality, of the powers of his own subjectivity, he has made himself the equal of the Master. His being as a subject is 'the result of his labour' and is reflected

---

[77] E.g. A. Kojève's lectures contained in his *Introduction à la lecture de Hegel*, Paris, 1947, which were very influential in France and then extended their influence to even wider circles beyond those of French existentialism.

[78] 'Zur philosophischen Diskussion um Marx und den Marxismus' (*Philosophische Rundschau*, 1957), in *Theorie und Praxis*, esp. pp. 301, 314ff. (*Theory and Practice*, ch. 6).

[79] *Phenomenology of Spirit*, ch. IVA; cf. *Grundlinien der Philosophie des Rechts* (1821), § 57 (translated by T.M. Knox, *Hegel's Philosophy of Right*, Oxford, 1942).

by the solid product of his activities. In this way the intersubjective relationship is put on a different basis from the uncertain acceptance of the temporary roles by the temporary partners. Once the Slave has emancipated himself through labour, the inequality of their positions slips away. The dialectic is raised to the level of the equality of the subjects and the isolation of self-consciousness which had led to the struggle ends in the supra-individual unity of the ethical order. The form of intersubjectivity is Spirit: 'I that is We and We that is I'.

It is plain that the sphere in which several subjects participate in the principle of self-consciousness is that of *historical* struggle, which amounts to the division between the roles of domination and labour. Individual isolation can never transcend this sphere and thus moves within the forms of socialization which we are acquainted with from the whole course of history so far. Those forms of rational life which go beyond the given historical level originate in a different principle, namely, that of Spirit, in which subjectivity in general is preserved but individual self-consciousness is left behind. The Hegelian philosophy of law conceives of this transformed state of affairs as the ideal state of actualized freedom which marks the *end of history so far*.[80] Habermas avoids the momentous entry of the subject into the overall legal structure for reasons which are closely connected with the Marxist criticism of Hegel's state as a coercive institution under an ideological cover.[81]

[80] *Hegel's Philosophy of Right*, §§ 340ff., 360.
[81] For instance, one can read in Marx's *Critique of Hegel's Philosophy of Right* (which belongs to his Young-Hegelian and Critical phase of 1843): 'Hegel starts from the state and makes human beings into the subjectivized state; democracy starts from human beings and makes the state into objectivized human beings' (*Werke*, Vol. I, p. 293). It is however instructive to see, and something to which even Marxists too seldom pay heed, that the mature Marx, in the not exactly numerous passages in which he guardedly expresses his views about the prospects for a development towards a free society, counts on a sudden leap to a new level of a very similar kind to the one which he mentions in his discussion of Hegel, in the transference of the individual self-consciousness to the realm of Spirit. 'The realm of freedom begins in fact at the point where labour which is determined by necessity and external purposes comes to an end; in the nature of the case, therefore, it lies on the other side of the sphere of properly material production. As the savage has to struggle with nature . . . , so must the civilized man, and he must do so in all forms of society and under all possible modes of production . . . However this always remains a realm of

The reconstruction of the relationship of intersubjectivity from Hegel's *Phenomenology* in terms of Habermas' categories of labour and interaction avoids the *decisive difference of level*, in that alongside the form of life and action which is marked by domination and labour it sets another which is characterized by reciprocal recognition and dialogue. It looks very much as if the self-same subjects who initially came under the law of external determination and object-relations have the possibility of going over to a social condition defined in terms of self-determination and subject-relations. It is no part of my concern to establish or to call in question whether this possibility for subjects historically exists. I am concerned with the question whether in the transition the subjects remain *the same subjects* to whom, quite simply, two alternative forms of self-activity and development of powers are open. Does not Hegel's formula of the Spirit into the unity of which the competing self-consciousnesses are raised mean an alteration in the status of the subjects, who no longer oppose one another as self-conscious individuals? This indicates a structural shift which should not be ignored in any sociological reconstruction. The immediate interaction between subjects must be described differently from the sphere of law and ethical institutions, and differently again from the sphere of production in the world of objects. Habermas to a large extent suppresses these differences because he is seeking a *single* all-embracing social model.

Elements of the Social Contract

Once detached from the Hegelian model the problem may also be posed in a different way. The step beyond the form of life in which intersubjective relations are essentially determined through an unequal division of roles and the necessity for active reproduction does not lead to an alternative. It does not disclose another form of life in which *language* is suddenly the specifically *new* medium of exchange, such that the unequal division of roles would be eliminated and the pressure created by labour to come to terms with objectivity would disappear. Language, of course,

nature. Beyond this begins the development of human powers, which is an end in itself, the true realm of freedom, which can however blossom only on the basis of that realm of necessity' (*Das Kapital*, Vol. III, Berlin, 1953, pp. 873f.).

regulates the intersubjective exchange in that first realm too. Naturally, there is the language of domination, in which orders are given and norms of behaviour established, and there is the corresponding slave language of flattery.[82] There is, further, the language of technique, in the sense of instruction and guidance in the object-related production processes of labour. From this it becomes clear that the alternative realm of intersubjective action cannot be characterized by the linguistic medium alone.

The preconditions must be sought rather in an *altered relation* between the subjects concerned, who confront each other on equal terms in the name of Reason. For Hegel, consistent labour gradually, as an unintended by-product of that activity, produces the equality between the subjects which is anyway required by the idea of Reason and realized by the systematic advance to the higher, supra-individual, institutions of the objective Spirit. If that process is to be avoided because of its 'Idealistic' character, then the subjects, who as partners in dialogue insist on their roles as individual subjects, must leave it to a specific, collectively taken, *decision* that they pass over from the natural form of society based on labour and domination to a form of life determined purely by Reason. The subjects, who do not wish in a merely egoistic way to be subjects for themselves and so willingly to treat the other as an object, must collectively and indeed for themselves wish that the alter ego be a subject with equal rights and an equal share in universal Reason.

If the dialogue model is looked at in this way, then the outlines of an inter-subjective *contract theory of society* derived from the rich tradition of ideas about Natural Rights begin to become visible. To be sure, Habermas does not go so far as to revive the theory of the Social Contract.[83] Rather, in the context of the history of ideas, he takes up the liberal concept of a guarantee for subjective freedoms provided by the open criticism of public discussion and deliberation.[84] Whatever the historical interpretations, the concealed natural-rights element of a quasi-contractual agreement

[82] There are some very illuminating studies on this in the later chapters of Hegel's *Phenomenology*; the forms of literary publicity under French absolutism provide the historical background, but they can easily be replaced by modern observations.

[83] As, for instance, John Rawls attempts to do in his *Theory of Justice*, Harvard, 1971.

[84] *Strukturwandel der Öffentlichkeit*, Neuwied, 1962.

of free subjects to recognize each other's freedom, which is thought of as a rationally motivated decision, seems to me clearly discernible, precisely in the talk about 'counterfactual assumptions'.

Since, however, the rational decision in favour of reciprocal recognition is not transferred to a hypothetical initial founding of society, but represents a permanent possibility for the future or even an irrevocable condition here and now, certain questions arise regarding the reconciliation of this distinctive sphere with the complex of surrounding forms of life. How do we move from the given forms of life to rational interaction? Habermas makes use of the concept of an *interest* in order to bridge the gap. Does this work?

Everyone has a number of different interests which he follows directly in his everyday practical life. These interests have not passed through the filter of intersubjective understanding, they are simply given. The dialogue of free subjects, which guarantees equal rights and possibilities of expression, now constitutes a forum for critical reflection on, and explicit consideration and consensual treatment of, such interests. But are the interests in both cases the same? What exactly is the change brought about by entering into a dialogue on the interests which exist already?

Anyone who shows that he is prepared to allow discussion of his interests has already distanced himself from the direct identification with them which is demanded by action. He sees his interests refracted in the light of the theoretical regard for other subjects, who are possibly pursuing divergent interests. It may be that a new interest emerges, the interest in consensus. Reflection has thus already taken place and is given verbal expression in the dialogue. Nevertheless, intersubjective discourse about private interests does not without qualification amount already to the determination of *universal interests*, and thus the dialogue does not give rise to any normative authority belonging to a universally valid Reason. What the parties to the dialogue approve in the light of present interests does not from then on create any obligations for all agents.

The individual interests which are accepted in the dialogue by the critical subjects are, on the basis of this consensus, merely the possible, not the actual and certainly not the necessary, interests of everyone. To that extent, the dialogue with its constitutive rules cannot even guarantee the translation which always has to be made when one descends once more from the context of discourse to the area of practice. The dialogue, or 'communicative action', has no obligatory force in relation to the action which continues unabated and unchanged on the far side of the linguistic exchange. In short, the concept of interest is not enough on its own to bring about the urgent reconciliation of theory and practice. However, Habermas knows how to meet this objection.

We thus come to the *political implications* of the dialogue. If Habermas' model is considered from the political point of view, there is a conflict between a liberal and a rigorously ethical motif. Liberalism, for instance in the version of J. S. Mill,[85] refrains from interference in the private sphere of those individual interests which in fact motivate action. Only the preconditions for the rational coexistence of many individuals who are free in respect of their interests are to be created, while the reasoning public or enlightened deliberation forfeits its influence in preference to individual practice. Which interests the individual pursues and what he considers as his well-being concerns him alone, as long as he does not interfere with anyone else. The majority cannot issue decrees with any content.

Habermas diagnosed this restraint, following Mill's example among others, as a decline: 'Two dialectically interrelated tendencies indicate a decay of public opinion: it permeates wider and wider spheres of society and at the same time forfeits its political function, namely, the subjection of those states of affairs which have entered the public domain to the control of a critical public.'[86] To counteract this 'decay' means to concede to public opinion the right to total influence on the interests and concerns of the subject in his individual practice. A kind of Rousseauist rational will or '*volonté générale*' takes care that what proves, in the enlightened interaction of the dialogue, to be capable of giving rise to consensus is not merely permitted private interests but universal interests which impose obligations on everyone. Habermas makes no secret of the fact that in the perspective of the future he has in mind a 'universalist morality', which will annul

85 *On Liberty*, Introduction (1859).
86 *Strukturwandel der Öffentlichkeit*, pp. 156f.

the divorce which has come to exist in modern times between private morality and formal law.

> A resolution of the conflict (between the cosmopolitanism of 'humanity' and the loyalties of the citizen) . . . is *conceivable* only if the dichotomy between inner and outer morality disappears, the opposition between morally and legally regulated domains is relativized and the validity of *all* norms is associated with the discursive formation of the will of those potentially concerned.

> Only the *communicative ethic* secures the universality of the admissible norms and the autonomy of the acting subjects, simply through the discursive redeemability of the claims to validity with which norms are presented, that is, through the fact that only those norms may claim validity on which all concerned, as participants in a discourse, (unconstrainedly) agree (or would agree) if they engage (or were to engage) in a discursive formation of the will . . . Only the communicative ethic is universal (and not, like formalistic ethics, committed to a domain of private morality separate from legal norms); only it secures autonomy (in that it continues the process of fitting the motivational potential into a communicative structure of action, the process of socialization 'with will and consciousness').[87]

A circle

What Habermas is talking about in this somewhat laborious fashion is the requirement, projected in the dialogue model, but in essence belonging to the idea of Natural Law, that *reason* must assume the *character of a norm*. The dialogue is thus no longer merely a method of critical testing for interests or principles of action which originate in a pre-communicative sphere of real practice. The dialogue is the place in which the setting of norms and the discovery of interests themselves take place. The problem of the transference of the dialogical consensus to active practice

[87] *Legitimationsprobleme*, pp. 122, 125.

slips away. The old gap between theory and practice appears to be closed. For the miracle to be able to succeed, several conditions must be fulfilled.

First, the partners to the conversation are as such already actors, who preserve their concrete capacity for action and do not merely intermittently insert collective acts of reflection into the flow of action which is proceeding anyway. The situation is thus not that we originally act and then pause for reflection, in order to understand each other in the dialogue about points of contention so that we can unhesitatingly return to action. *Acting and speaking* must rather be taken as identical.

Furthermore, the speakers remain the *individual subjects* that they are, and do not turn into legal institutions and social organizations. At all levels of social and practical life they retain their full autonomy. Nevertheless, as partners to a conversation, they do not possess any longer the protective zone of individual freedom which liberalism required. They are, as individual subjects in all their concreteness, at the same time and without change rational beings who are subject to the universal laws of rational communication. Hence, what is discussed in the dialogue is also immediately relevant to action, or the interests which are its subject-matter are directly valid as binding norms.

These conditions, however, can be fulfilled only if the 'counterfactual assumptions' are reinterpreted as the factual preconditions of entry into the dialogue. The whole problem hinges on the question whether that is possible or indeed permissible. It would be a fallacy to think that what ideally *ought* to be, simply on the grounds that it is constantly taken for granted as a starting-point is what in some way or other *exists*. The radicalization of the norms of rational dialogue to something actually given in real dialogue, or the idealization of the parties to conversation into subjects whose whole practice consists in rational discourse, or even the expectation that anyone who is ready for conversation has already set aside all particular interests – these things contain the serious risk of an unnoticed blurring of boundaries in the name of a realistically concrete version of Idealist ethics or of Natural Law.

Rousseau and *Kant*, who were among the sources of inspiration for the model, had, after all, taken precautionary measures against such confusions. The '*volonté générale*' is not the '*volonté de tous*' –

that in which all in fact may concur is not for that reason that which is rationally to be willed. So says Rousseau: Kant expresses it as follows. For an empirical subject the purely intelligible requirements of the moral law remain an eternal imperative and only for the 'holy will' of a God would what ought to be also be directly what was willed. Finally, the universality of the Categorical Imperative must also be further developed into the 'Metaphysic of Morals', where established legal norms support that which ideally ought to be; for the actual potential for conflict among a plurality of individuals who are not harmoniously united in the metaphysical 'Kingdom of Ends' must be kept under control by means of external coercion. Habermas hopes to be able to pass beyond these well-established traditional distinctions between empirical and purely rational subjects.

In my opinion this belief goes together with a *misunderstanding of the Hegelian dialectic*. The dialectic can be understood as a procedure for methodically overstepping boundaries, in so far as the abstract distinctions of the understanding are reconciled in the higher unity of Reason. The aim is, as explained at greater length above in connexion with the relation between the *Phenomenology* and the *Logic*, to achieve a theory which is systematically comprehensive and which has become autonomous through having assimilated historical limitations. The aim of Habermas is to arrive by theoretical means at a point beyond theory where there is an ultimate unity of theory and practice. It is here that the contradiction is to be found. In reality the Young-Hegelian motif which runs through the whole of critical theory reappears. In this respect Habermas, for all his fruitful development of the fundamental ideas of the Frankfurt School, is still under the spell of his predecessors.

The Young Hegelians had already attempted to claim for themselves the superiority which Hegel's theory owed to the dialectical method, by applying the dialectical mediation to Hegel in his turn. Theory, that is to say, was seen by them as involved in an unmediated opposition (i.e. one which stood in need of mediation) to practice, such that the next step in unification was necessarily imminent. The paradox lies in the fact that this celebrated 'opposition' of theory and practice is nothing but a piece of theory, in so far as the two terms are put in the relation of negation to each other: the one is not the other and vice versa.

Theory, however, is also itself one of the terms related. Consequently, it remains completely obscure how the unification which abolishes the opposition is to be understood.

Theoretically, the unification cannot follow: this relapse into the initial position, where theory is unilaterally dominant, would be ideology. Practically, the unification cannot follow for the same reasons: it must be a matter of a practice which is blended with theory and is not purely 'pragmatic', without any element of ideas. The Young Hegelians usually made the excuse of 'history', which would in the future take care of the unity of action and reason. With all due respect to the progressive hopes for the work of history, so far it has not been able to persuade us that it alone can be relied upon where it is a matter of reason and correct practice.

The expectation of a situation of unity between theory and practice suffers, in the case of Habermas' dialogue model as in all his predecessors, from the fact that a theoretical method has been vaguely extended beyond the limits of theory. Dialectic, which originates in a meaningful methodological role, is bound when thus released from it to become a myth, which makes no contribution to the improvement of knowledge or even to a better life. It is obscure and dangerous. The urgent debate about the relation of theory and practice finds itself on firmer ground when closer attention is once more given to an insight which was one of the earliest achievements of philosophy, when it first began explicitly to concern itself with practical matters. Since Aristotle's 'invention' of '*philosophia practica*' it has been forbidden to mix this discipline with theoretical knowledge, since the respective themes are to be grasped in terms of their distinctive structures, and this implies a change in philosophical approach.

This ancient distinction does not arise from any unthinking caprice which has simply been passed on in the depths of the scholastic canon and ultimately stands in need of critical enlightenment. The special insitution of practical philosophy resulted rather from a critical reflection on the undifferentiated mixture of *logos* and *ethos* in Plato. To bring this background up to date will certainly make it easier adequately to understand the more recent contributions to practical philosophy which we shall now consider.

Philosophy of practice

The title which has become naturalized in German for the branch of philosophy with which we are concerned can scarcely be rendered in English without creating misunderstanding. '*Praktische Philosophie*' (practical philosophy) is a translation of the Latin title '*philosophia practica*', which has its origins in the Aristotelian tradition. Since Kant[88] the expression has been part of the general philosophical vocabulary. What is meant is the philosophy of practical matters in the widest sense and not an attempt to make philosophy as such practical. It is thus a matter of philosophical theory, though a theory of a special kind. It is not a question of 'applying' philosophical wisdom in some way or other to life, in the way constantly demanded by the pragmatic everyday understanding when it complains about the uselessness of pure speculation, or else in the way longed for by naive reformers who take their philanthropic attitudes for real action.

The question immediately arises why a philosophy which has to do with the practical in the wide sense sets such great store by the affirmation that it itself is merely a theory. An answer to this question can already be found at the origin of the *philosophia practica*. Aristotle separated off this special part within the whole range of philosophical themes on the basis of an argument which seems to me to be still no less valid.[89] The philosophy which applies itself to practical questions must take account of the peculiar structure of its object. Anything which has to do with practice never meets up to the same standards of perfection and exactness with which purely theoretical sciences operate. Everything practical implies, that is to say, a problem of *concreteness* which ultimately defies theoretical analysis. Theories can offer only generalities. Action, however, takes place here and now. Anyone who does not see this fails to do justice to his object and substitutes for practice a theoretical construct or an ideal projection.

Thus, if practice is to become an object for theory, then theory must be on its guard lest it unthinkingly encroach on the domain of practice. It is a fundamental *methodological* maxim for philosophy

---

[88] Kant had in mind eighteenth-century school philosophy, with its Aristotelian tendencies, and refers particularly to A. G. Baumgarten, *Initia Philosophiae Practicae Primae*, Halle, 1760.

[89] *Nicomachean Ethics*, I. 1.

to respect the peculiar structure of all practical objects. That means, however, maintaining the boundary between theory and practice. A theory of the practical does justice to its task only if it remains conscious that it is a theory, on the far side of which a practice begins which is to be protected against manipulation or replacement by a theory.

Aristotle developed this methodological maxim in the course of his disagreement with Plato, who tendentiously allowed correct knowledge and correct action to coincide. For Plato, practice was so much a matter of pure theory that the supreme science, namely philosophy, seems alone to be of any value for true statesmanship. The ancient polemics about the philosopher-king represent in this respect merely the outward manifestation of a set of problems the detailed consideration of which extends, however, much further. The methodological maxim which prescribes an appropriate philosophy of practice possesses an unquestionable actuality if one bears in mind the ever increasing attempt in modern times to cover all questions of life and politics with more and more complete and differentiated theories. The mental existence of the individual, the forms of intersubjective intercourse, all domains of social organization, the development of the economy, the forward movement of history – for every aspect of practice there is a science and nothing escapes the total embrace of theory.

There even prevails a widespread and deep-seated belief that all practical problems ultimately await scientific treatment and are suddenly solved or anyway become finally soluble at the moment when a special science applies itself to them. In this *scientific penetration* of the whole of human and social life the dominion of theory over practice which has been growing for so long reaches its maturity. At times it almost seems as if practice were merely an expression of embarrassment at the deplorable, but soon overcome, condition of incomplete theory. To be consigned to practice means to have to make do as much as needs be without a perfect theory. This impression that there are universal theoretical competences which leave no further room of its own for practice does not arise solely as a result of the wholesale ideologies of our time. It is also well established in the smaller dimensions of everyday life, where prediction, theoretical certainty and technical substitutes for action are more and more the rule. A heightened awareness of the special structure of what we call practice is thus by no means an obsolete philosophical theme.

Another consideration might come to mind in the light of our initial definition. If the philosophy of the practical has to do with action, why is it not simply called 'ethics'? The suspicion suggests itself that the objects mentioned properly belong to the ethical domain, so that the involved reference back to the outmoded term *'philosophia practica'* merely gives rise to unnecessary confusion. This objection can be met by referring to the astonishing process of dilution and contraction in the philosophical concern with practical matters in the course of recent centuries. Ethics is no longer a theory of social practice in the sense of ancient moral philosophy, but is reduced to the single question: what am I to do? Ethics has become *individual morality*.

The social framework of individual action, the historically developed forms of life and institutions, have faded into the background. The transition from private ethics to objective law becomes difficult once philosophy and jurisprudence have become distinguished from each other as independent disciplines. The situation is similar with the connexion between individual action and the economic conditions of society, not only in the comprehensible framework of the individual's life but also in the world-wide economic system of the present day. Here too the growing independence of the disciplines has made sure that actually existing relations have been broken off. The evil of specialization is most clear in the case of politics, which used, since the time of Plato and Aristotle, to be the crowning glory of the philosophical theory of practice, whereas at present there is virtually no acceptable philosophical theory of politics. The subject is by now in a state of theoretical crisis.[90] The flood of literature in political science cannot conceal the lack of essential concepts. Their place has been taken by a surrogate, an obscure brew of history of ideas, sociology, demography, group psychology, constitutional law, comparative study of institutions etc.

The philosophy of the practical originally embraced all those

---

[90] This is the explanation of the revival of a buried tradition, for instance in W. Hennis' interesting work, *Politik und praktische Philosophie, eine Studie zur Rekonstruktion der politischen Wissenschaft*, Neuwied, 1963. See also D. Sternberger, *Die drei Wurzeln der Politik*, Frankfurt, 1979.

domains which are relevant for the evaluation and direction of action.[91] Customs and social *forms of life*, the *economy*, the institutions of the *law* and *politics* all belonged together. As a result of the modern processes of individualization and isolation of the subject, the only remnant of all this is ethics, which prescribes rules for the actions of individuals or develops principles for their evaluation. The drastic reduction in the object-domain is evident. The questions which have little by little been separated off from philosophy, until only individual ethics remained, have been taken under the wing of specialized disciplines. That has certainly served to make them more scientific *'en détail'*. It has, however, allowed theoretical gaps to open up, which has accelerated the ad hoc development of the so-called 'linking disciplines', without really making superfluous the now-vanished unity created by philosophical understanding. The isolated scientific treatment of separated partial aspects lacks any direction and leads to misleading shifts in emphasis, as perspectives change and what was secondary becomes the main concern or what was central moves to the periphery.

Old and new tasks

The description of the general theoretical situation in the field of practice ought scarcely to be a matter of dispute in any decisive respect. The complaint about the lack of unity between the different subjects is even one of the few common themes which occasionally unite the disparate voices into some kind of harmony. For a long time, however, it remained impossible to see who was to take over the theoretical direction and how the main lines of a unified conception should look. Fairly recently, philosophy has begun to recall its long-neglected duty. Under the old title of the philosophy of practice it is beginning to pose the problems which are inescapable in the total view, but for which there exists no specialized competence. It would, to be sure, be to arouse false hopes if the renewal of a unified view with a long tradition behind it were to be passed off as in itself the solution of our contemporary problems! Fortunately, philosophy has become much too sceptical about its own claims to pursue such

---

[91] Cf. H. Arendt, *Vita activa*, New York, 1959; Stuttgart, 1960.

dreams. The renewal of the old thematic unity[92] merely provides a framework for theoretical *cooperation* on the basis of the knowledge which has now become available in the specialized disciplines.

The appeal to the tradition of philosophy of practice has a previous history which we may briefly recount here by way of illustration. It begins with *Hegel*, who, from the time of the political and theological studies of his youth, worked on the problem of reconciling the ethical demands of pure Reason with the historical reality of social life. Kant's Categorical Imperative had pushed the individualization of ethics to extremes. In Heaven and on earth only one thing was to be regarded as good in the practical sense and that was the 'good will'.[93] The good will is the purely subjective disposition to action prior to the entanglement with the world involved in the actual performance of action and in abstraction from all peripheral empirical conditions. Kant's ethical formalism and rigorism, which result from his approach, go back to reasons which are to be sought in the systematic constructions of his critical philosophy, especially the transition from the theoretical to the practical part, which need not however concern us here. Hegel and all later critics of Kant anyway remained dissatisfied that practical reason could not be enmeshed in the reality of intersubjectivity and historical life. The Categorical Imperative consequently had to be enriched in the dimension of social reality and historical practice. Hegel thus inferred the need to reconcile Kant's ethics of rational subjectivity with the thoughts of Plato and Aristotle about the *polis*. The reconciliation is achieved in the context of historical considerations which make intelligible the loss of the natural unity of the political in the systematic withdrawal to bare subjectivity.

Hegel's *philosophy of law*[94] corresponds to this programme, in that it allows the modern principle of subjectivity to realize itself in institutions of a social, legal and political kind, in such a way

[92] Representative expressions of this are two collections under the title *Rehabilitierung der praktischen Philosophie* (ed. M. Riedel, Freiburg, 1972 and 1974) which, as well as containing a number of historical contributions, give a say to hermeneutics, linguistic analysis, communication theory, political science, sociology, cybernetics, etc.

[93] *Fundamental Principles of the Metaphysics of Morals*, A1.

[94] On this cf. S. Avineri's excellent book, *Hegel's Theory of the Modern State*, Cambridge, 1972; and more recently C. Taylor, *Hegel and Modern Society*, Cambridge, 1979.

that conversely the concrete forms of social practice no longer stand opposed to the subject, who recognizes himself in them. The state which is born from Reason is more than a utopia, it converges with the real historical tendencies. Practical reason is Reason in history and history aims at the rational form of state organization – this is Hegel's teaching.

His philosophy of law was immediately interpreted as the most significant synthesis of the political and ethical thought of antiquity and the modern world. Precisely because the end result carried conviction, the Idealist premises remained in dispute. The passionate opposition to which the philosophy of law was subjected from the outset was not so much provoked by the way in which the problem was posed as such, but rather was directed against the solution which was proposed. From the Young Hegelians, via Marx, right up to the debates of our own century[95] the dispute has centred on the question whether philosophical thought alone is sufficient to grasp and to shape social reality in its full extent and substance, or whether there lurks in this attempt the perilous *hubris* of speculation or else an ideological glorification of the existing state of affairs. What is not in dispute, on the other hand, is that it is the task of philosophy to provide a comprehensive and adequate theory of social reality. On that Hegel's critics on the political left have been in accord with those Hegelians of conservative tendency who are loyal to the state since the dispute broke out in the first half of the nineteenth century.

The dramatic fate which Hegel's social philosophy and philosophy of history have suffered in the ideological struggles of our century between fascism and Marxism led the *bien-pensants* after the Second World War to revert to the traditional theory of *Natural Law*. From behind the back of the controversial Hegel there has once more emerged the reliable father-figure, Aristotle. At times – and this should not be overlooked – this increased preoccupation with Aristotle[96] has a subterranean connexion with

---

[95] Cf. K. Popper (*The Open Society and its Enemies*, 1945, Vol. II, 'The high tide of prophecy'), who charges Hegel with totalitarianism, and H. Marcuse (*Reason and Revolution, Hegel and the Rise of Social Theory*, 1941), who seeks to acquit him on the same charge.

[96] An important influence was the translation of Leo Strauss' book, a product of the emigration, *Natural Right and History* (Chicago, 1953). Later, a school formed round J. Ritter's studies on Aristotle and Hegel (*Metaphysik und Politik*, Frankfurt, 1969).

post-war tendencies towards a conservative Restoration. Since then, of course, the spirit of the times has noticeably changed and the conception of a universal philosophy of practice now serves as the point of intersection of a variety of attempts to establish contacts, from different points of view and in terms of connexions with different specialties, between philosophy and the highly specialized social sciences.

Anthropology and sociology

The social sciences, to the extent that they have not blocked off all contact with philosophy and replaced concept-formation by data-collection, have naturally exerted great influence on the philosophy of practice. The enormous presence of Max Weber, which extends right up into the contemporary debates about theory of science, has already been discussed. There will be more to be said about his leading role in the development of action theory. Another author, however, who has played a less central part in the development of his subject than Weber, deserves more than passing attention. *Arnold Gehlen* took over some suggestions from the philosophy of German Idealism and combined them with anthropological and ethnological investigations, finally reinforcing them with the categories of the functionalist systems-theory which Talcott Parsons established on Weberian foundations. Gehlen's work[97] is difficult to classify. He is too much of a philosopher to be an ethnological field-researcher, and too much of an anthropologist to be content with sociological descriptions. Theories which do not fit in to the usual division of the subjects are, however, frequently the most intellectually fruitful and turn out to be capable of extension.

Gehlen chooses as his point of departure the view represented most notably in classical philosophy by Fichte, that the essence of man is intentional *practice* and not an abstract reflective point of view of consciousness. In an early work he says,

> The analysis of the given concrete situation – the
> necessary question for the mature and thinking man:
> who am I and under what circumstances and conditions
> do I live – is the starting-point and this situation is the

[97] A collected edition of his writings is in course of appearing, Frankfurt, 1978– .

real concrete position in which I find myself, with these
contingent determinations, living together with these
others, under given, even rather artificial, conditions of
life, in a state and a people, with such a profession and
property and these skills, such a language and so forth.
And this analysis of the situation in which the thinker
finds himself yields the '*prima philosophia*', the initial
philosophical science which, for the sake of a name, we
intend to call philosophical *anthropology*. This reflection is
from the outset and in an unforced way historical, in
that the conditions of life in which I find myself have
developed already without my assistance; in that I find
my existence to be dependent upon and related to
countless historical conditions, the aggregate of which is
called culture, the question arises of the essence of man
as a social being, characterizable in such and such a way,
who can conduct his life only on the basis of a nature
which has been transformed in certain definite directions
and to whose essence as a human being definite facts
such as family, state, tradition, work, technique and so
on belong.[98]

The essential outlines of the anthropology which Gehlen's
main work, *Der Mensch, seine Natur und seine Stellung in der Welt*,[99]
was later to elaborate can here be recognized. Man is by nature an
agent. He is thus neither metaphysically nor biologically fully
determined: he determines his own essence in that he *makes* himself into what he is. This openness distinguishes him from in-
stinct-bound animals, so that he has to face both the possibility of
self-realization and the threat posed by the external world. The
external world continually presses in upon man as a challenge and
is experienced primarily as a 'burden'. Because of his undetermined existence, man has to defend himself against the danger of
being overwhelmed by irritation and attraction from the external
world. The sum of the achievements which man produces in his
practical activity, in order to secure his existence with regard to
this burden, is called *culture*. Gehlen thereby finds an answer in

[98] 'Der Idealismus und die Lehre vom menschlichen Handeln' (1935), in
Theorie der Willensfreiheit und frühe philosophische Schriften, Neuwied,
1965, p. 272.
[99] 1st edition, 1940; see also *Urmensch und Spätkultur*, Bonn, 1956.

cultural anthropology to questions which the philosophy of existence has raised, but turned into a plea for a revival of ontology, as in the case of Heidegger.

Culture creates, according to Gehlen, a second world of artificial objectivity in the form of *institutions*. Language, family-connexions,[100] social rules, customs, the formation of traditions, work, technique, represent in an anthropological perspective graduated institutions which 'stabilize' man's essentially undetermined nature. The nature of man makes the artificial products of culture necessary. In this way all the phenomenal forms of the human, social and historical world become intelligible from a single source. The anthropological foundation of culture relativizes, as a further consequence, the widespread over-valuation of history. However unremittingly history brings about changes, the essence of human beings changes little with it. The hopes of progress which anticipated an entirely new or completely different humanity in the future necessarily appear dubious.

The hope for change in the course of history, the toying with the possibility of producing radical alteration, come back in reality to a loss of substance and direction, which induces a mood of scepticism in those who are aware of it. From this conservative position, Gehlen has produced penetrating diagnoses of modern civilization. He has carried on a *critique of culture* in opposition to the popular Rousseauist version, with its laments about the loss of naturalness in culture. Instead, he has drawn attention to more complex cultural processes which convert the loss of tradition into aesthetic enjoyment and play an empty game with surrogates of the natural. His provocative slogan, 'Back to culture!', has been brilliantly opposed by Habermas in the name of progress and enlightenment.[101] To outsiders, of course, this may just seem like part of the typical *'querelles d'Allemands'*.

Gehlen's anthropology has been painstakingly developed in a specialized sociological direction in the work of *Niklas Luhmann*. Luhmann translates the idea of the burden imposed on man by the external world, or of the achievements of cultural stabilization which are thus produced, into the completely formalized modes

---

[100] Gehlen hailed as a welcome corroboration the structuralist insights of Lévi-Strauss' ethnology (*Les Structures élémentaires de la parenté*, Paris, 1949).

[101] 'Nachgeahmte Substantialität', in *Philosophisch-politische Profile*, Frankfurt, 1971.

of expression of cybernetic *systems-theory*. In this way he upholds an abstract fundamental model of the relation of a system to its environment. The relation is defined in such a way that the environment entails increased complexity for the system and the system stabilizes itself against this external pressure by bringing about a reduction of this complexity. The model of a system-environment relation which is not fixed but is constantly being actively re-established is connected in Luhmann with the categorial apparatus of Parsons' functionalist sociology. The simple depreciation of the pressing complexity or its reworking in terms of interpretation of meaning by an existing and self-maintaining system is particularly well suited to functionalist modes of thought.

Under the general title of *function* formal relations may be established between all possible data in such a way that the material differences between the terms can be disregarded. Since functions can be formulated in any respect one chooses, the points of relation become interchangeable. Luhmann is fascinated by the resulting limitless applicability of his model, which he tests in relation to social forms of organization of all kinds, bureaucracy and law, formation of consciousness and ideology, to economic and scientific institutions, to individual action and whole societies. The breathtaking flexibility of the application of the model of a reduction in complexity in the functional relation between system and environment tends occasionally towards vacuity, but in many fields leads to intelligent insights.[102] Luhmann has provided a stimulus to the whole spectrum of the social sciences.

It seemed therefore not unreasonable to expect that the sophisticated methods of functionalist systems-theory had finally furnished the key to all social phenomena. Classical sociology, from Weber to Parsons, had sought for such a key, until sociology began to break up into countless separate branches. The dream of a definitive global theory of the social brings Luhmann very close to making philosophical claims, in which Husserl's methodically rigorous and universal conception of phenomenology[103] seems in

---

[102] Some impression can be gained from the numerous topics dealt with in a collection of papers entitled *Soziologische Aufklärung*, Vols. I and II, Opladen, 1970– .

[103] See above, Ch. 1.

certain ways to be his model. In a vigorous debate with Habermas,[104] which has had widespread reverberations both in the social sciences and in philosophy, the dream has suffered a disturbing setback. Habermas' main attack follows the old line of differentiating a 'critical' from a 'traditional' theory.[105] Luhmann's all-embracing systems-theory appears as a new version of the old ideologies, which consistently promised information about the whole of reality and in so doing forgot their own limitations and entanglement with the status quo.

Habermas writes:

> The problems and solutions of theory are always also the problems and solutions of the society to which it objectively belongs . . . Behind the attempt to justify a reduction of the complexity of the world as the highest reference point of functionalism in the social sciences hides the unavowed commitment of the theory to ways of posing the questions which conform with the structure of domination, to defending the existing state of affairs in order to keep it in existence . . . Thus the theory is reserved for technocratic use. Revolutionary misuse is ruled out.[106]

Luhmann replies by drily characterizing the alternative model of the ideal dialogue, which Habermas had offered as an instance of a rationally directed critique of domination, as ineffective and remote from social reality:[107] 'I do not see how anything essential in the vital relations between men can be changed, or how men could form themselves, simply because one discusses the truth of the justification given for the importance of the ruling class or anyone else and arrives at a rational consensus.' The dispute between critical theory and systems-theory is still not over. It is no accident that the focus of the theory lies in the correct interpretation of *human action*. This fact makes a direct link with a complex of problems which has moved more and more into the foreground of the discussion of the philosophy of practice. To be sure, things here are in a completely fluid state, so that it is

---

104 Habermas and Luhmann, *Theorie der Gesellschaft*.
105 See above.
106 Habermas and Luhmann, *Theorie der Gesellschaft*, p. 170.
107 Ibid., p. 293.

impossible to refer to any assured and generally accepted knowledge.[108]

Action theory

Since Weber, sociology has been concerned with action as one of its most fundamental concepts, whereas philosophy only began to reflect on it later in the context of contemporary philosophy of practice. Now it is noteworthy how little attention was given for a long time to this fundamental category of ethics and politics. After Aristotle outlined at least the first beginnings of a theory of action, philosophy scarcely returned to the theme to any real extent.

Modern philosophy, from Hobbes through the empiricists and up to Kant, was content with an analogy with natural causality. It was held to be indubitable that action is a special kind of bodily movement, which is to be explained in the same way as processes in the objective world. A large part of so-called analytic action theory even up to the present day proceeds on this assumption,[109] which was kept immune from further questioning because other interpretations seemed inconceivable. However, the interpretation of action on the analogy of natural causality is self-evident only as long as the dominant paradigm of modern science suggests this way of thinking.

Classical sociology began in Weber with doubts about the unrestricted validity of the kinds of explanation given in the natural sciences. 'Interpretative sociology', based on a category of action as the most general form of determination of sociological objects, defines action as activity, the performance of which is meaningful and which is therefore to be meaningfully interpreted. The concept of meaning certainly forms a bulwark against any objectivist distortion of the structure of action, but is itself capable of being interpreted in a wide variety of ways. That is confirmed by the continuing discussion of meaningful action, from Schütz to Habermas and Luhmann.

It seems to me to be one of the errors of this discussion to shift

[108] See the collection, *Handlungstheorien interdisziplinär*, Vols. I–IV (ed. H. Lenk), Munich, 1979.

[109] One exception is R. Bernstein (*Praxis and Action*, New York 1971), who refers not only to continental sources but also to the pragmatist tradition.

the entire theoretical interest on to the *concept of meaning*. 'Meaning' can be interpreted phenomenologically, hermeneutically, linguistically or functionalistically without light being automatically shed on the genuine structure of action. The controversy between Habermas and Luhmann just referred to is itself a striking example of the way in which, though all the talk is about action theory, the dispute circles around the concept of meaning, which is interpreted in different ways. The fact that action theory has been overlaid by interpretations of meaning is shown in the tendency immediately to replace practice by meaning-related constructs such as the 'ideal dialogue' or the 'reduction of complexity'.[110] The unnoticed departure from the structure of practice under the banner of meaning, however, is ultimately no different from the analogy of action and natural causality, which is precisely what the recourse to interpretable meaning was intended to correct. In both cases misconceptions arise. How are they to be avoided?

There is a similar fault involved both in the concentration on meaning and in the analogy with natural causality. In both cases, namely, action is forced from the outset into the perspective of *external observation*. What is perceptible from the external standpoint of an observer who is not himself active appears as being the true essence of action. Thus one observes bodily movements and demands a causal explanation. Or else one goes beyond that and looks out for meaningful elements in the action, which can be understood in the framework of intersubjective communication. Causal explanation in a behaviourist manner and the interpretation of the meaning inherent in action are both determinations of practice which result from the standpoint of an observer. Because it seems so natural to us, this constant perspectival distortion does not attract any attention.

The genuine structure of action, on the other hand, must be determined from the activity itself, so to speak 'from the inside'. Hence, I propose to define actions as *accomplishments (Vollzug)*.[111] To define them in this way marks out the fact that they posit their

---

[110] Luhmann has made an ingenious attempt to substitute for the traditional concept of action his own systems-theoretical categories: *Zweckbegriff und Systemrationalität*, Tübingen, 1968.

[111] The following remarks are largely based on investigations which I have carried out elsewhere (*Handlung, Sprache und Vernunft; Grundbegriffe praktischer Philosophie*, Frankfurt, 1976).

existence themselves and also regulate it in the dimension of temporal extension. An accomplishment is the systematic realization of what an action is all about. It begins, is carried out and ends for no other reason than to realize this specific action. The accomplishment is the fulfilment of the very 'for-the-sake-of. . .' in any concrete activity. Linguistic philosophers have laid stress on the concept of 'performing' an action. We say, for example, that a ceremony is performed or an important political or legal act is carried out and mean by this that in the actualization it has been a matter of precisely this act and nothing besides. The 'performance' of an act, which is entirely familiar to us in such special ceremonial forms, gives us some insight into the genuine structure of practice in general. If we start asking about causes, reasons, willed decisions, value-positions, meaning-orientations, linguistic expressions and so forth, we are already going beyond the true structure of the practical act.

That practice in its inner nature is accomplishment was already quite correctly seen by Aristotle when he called it *energeia*. One does not have to be an Aristotelian to take up a further hint which results from this. If one refers to practice as accomplishment, one demarcates it from another kind of activity: *poiēsis* or *production*. The accomplishment is brought about in the realization of the act itself. The goal of production lies beyond the activity as such in the realization of something else. Practice, therefore, is structurally distinct from those processes which are directed towards the production of an object external to themselves. The object-determined activity may be aimed at the production of a concrete object, but also at bringing about a state of affairs, a change in the world etc. The result beyond the act as such guides thereby the manner and direction of the activity. Since the result can be objectively identified, guidance as to how to bring it about or to produce it is possible. Such guidance of object-determined activity in the widest sense we call *technique*.

What, however, is the situation in the case of practice, where no objectively identifiable criteria of a result to be produced exist to provide technical directives for the activity? The equivalents are the rules of practice, which guide the coherent realization of the act to be accomplished. The problem of rules for practice is the more difficult to solve because it is impossible, except for some boundary cases, to rely on any technical analogy. In fact we all follow these rules since human society has been at work on their development for a very long time. The rules for practice in the context of the subjective action of the individual are called *maxims*; the intersubjective rules which hold for collective action in groups or in society as a whole are called *norms*. Whereas for simple courses of action in given situations individual subjects have an immense number of more or less clearly defined maxims at their disposal, the socially accredited or even explicitly posited norms take care of the intersubjective agreement of maxims. Since the function of norms is the coordination of many individual actions in the social context, norms are based on maxims rather than abstractly replacing them. They must be spelled out in terms of maxims which are coordinate in all relevant cases for all agents. When everybody concerned follows the same maxim as his neighbour, norms have done their job.

The coordination of the individual actions of many agents is treated by every society as an elementary problem of organization. In historical reality, normative regulation develops on extremely different levels and in varying forms. There are established traditions, models which are further extended by education, social conventions, loose agreements among groups and positive laws of the state. All these forms should not be artificially reduced to a common denominator, for in them is expressed the concrete form of the normative regulation of the intersubjective complexity of specific actions.

The system of norms which is accepted at any given time is a mirror-image of the historical society and alters along with it. It must therefore be taken seriously in a historical perspective. Anyway, the most perfect and systematically constructed form of normative regulation is represented by the modern *legal systems* of highly developed societies. Sociologists of law such as Weber or sociologically interested jurists such as Hans Kelsen[112] have studied the rationality involved in the construction of such positive systems of norms. To see in it the only historically possible and effective realization of practical reason, however, is without question an over-simplification. The rationality inherent in a well-

---

[112] E.g. *General Theory of Law and the State* (translated by Anders Wedling), Cambridge, Mass., 1945; *Pure Theory of Law* (translated by Max Knight) Berkeley, Calif., 1967. On Kelsen, cf. H. L. A. Hart, *The Concept of Law*, Oxford, 1961.

structured legal system may satisfy the interest in theoretical clarity, while in reality it remains a matter for dispute what is to be called *reason* in the field of practice. Practical reason is something different from and more than the construction of a legal system. It will embrace the whole sphere of customs and usages, forms of life and institutions which have grown out of tradition. It will in this way extend right into the concrete accomplishment of the actions of individual agents. Since nothing here is defined by laws – legal specification is never able to cover all details and peculiarities of practical life – there is also no court to which the rationality of the action can be taken in any given case. Thus everyone is his own judge, or else the standards of decision are formed in the community of agents. Practical reason is always concrete reason and thus is in the last analysis inextricably interwoven with historical development. I believe that, on questions of this kind, the debate about a fully developed philosophy of practice which is currently taking place[113] can certainly still learn something from Aristotle or Hegel.

---

[113] In lieu of other examples, I may refer simply to the collection, *Materialien zur Normendiskussion* (ed. Oelmüller, Vols I–III, Paderborn, 1978/9; English translation forthcoming, New York), where Apel, Habermas, Lübbe and others argue about the rationality of norms, not without certain ideological overtones. A parallel interest in the concrete forms of practical reason can be seen amongst analytic philosophers, as shown perhaps by a selection under the title *Practical Reasoning* (ed. J. Raz), Oxford, 1978.

Concluding remarks

An essay normally has no definite end, since it is an enquiry which does not aim to produce assured results. How much more must a loosely connected series of essays content itself with an open-ended conclusion, when its real principle of unity is the presentation of complex debates in an epoch defined in purely temporal terms? To bring together different strands of a problem, approaches to questions and the viewpoints of different schools is to make use of a fiction which derives from the tradition of historiography. This is the fiction of the *unity of an epoch*. When looked at closely, no epoch is unified: each presents a varying number of phenomena depending on the interests of the enquirer and the focus of his vision. The multifarious phenomena which can be distinguished in any segment of history generally take on the distinctive aspect of a definite epoch only as a result of the unifying work of the historian. The fiction of the epoch is thus a useful instrument for creating order in history.

The idea of the epoch, however, becomes thoroughly questionable when it is applied not to the past but rather to the present. For every new present can for its part define itself as an epoch. The consciousness of an age to be expected tomorrow has as its only mark of distinction the distance from today, which will by then be in the past. Thus the boundaries between different epochs run together to infinity, so that the retrospectively helpful fiction of the unity of an epoch loses all meaning. The question whether what is understood as an epoch at present was really an epoch in the sense of a recognizable unity will admit of being settled only later. No one knows in advance what relativization will take place in our view of what is central at present, how ephemeral the dominant themes and how important the neglected figures will come to look at some future time. One thing, however, which it is already possible to know even now is that even the judgment of the future historian will not be final, because any historical judgment is open to yet later revision and the truth of a retrospective judgment can always be superseded in its turn.

These changing aspects could induce a total scepticism which would view everything without exception as relative. It would be just the counterpart to a narrow-minded dogmatism which is willing to take account of nothing beyond what is immediately before its eyes. The only defence against the extremes of scepticism and dogmatism is the conviction of the *unity of philosophy*. Certainly, this too is a useful fiction and anything but a completely realized historical fact. But it does permit us to select what is philosophically essential from the multiplicity of historical phenomena and thus promotes philosophical activity itself. The conviction of the unity of philosophy opens our eyes to what other epochs or other philosophical tendencies might possibly have to say to the philosopher. At the same time it makes impossible the unphilosophical conceit of considering what one happens to be working on oneself as philosophy in general, and for no other reason than that one is working on it oneself.

The unity of philosophy is thus a corrective to onesidedness and a stimulant to the business of philosophy. Anyone who is concerned about philosophy must, as it were, from the very beginning share this conviction. And he ought to the best of his ability to help to make sure that this fiction does not remain merely a fiction.

Index of names